Stage Management

Stage Management

Diane Norburn

THE CROWOOD PRESS

First published in 2018 by
The Crowood Press Ltd
Ramsbury, Marlborough
Wiltshire SN8 2HR

www.crowood.com

British Library Cataloguing-in-Publication Data
A catalogue record for this book is available from the British Library.

ISBN 978 1 78500 443 8

Frontispiece
A production of *Fiddler on the Roof*. Photo: John Haynes, Designer: Phillip Engleheart

Typeset and designed by D & N Publishing, Baydon, Wiltshire

Printed and bound in India by Replika Press Pvt Ltd

CONTENTS

ACKNOWLEDGEMENTS

I would like to thank the following people:

Everyone at LAMDA, particularly Joanna Read, Rodney Cottier, Rob Young, Rob Gale and the SMTT staff; the cast of *Sucker Punch* for their headshots and the Cs, E2s and directors for the production shots; Ian Brown and Mary Papadima. A special thank you to the stage management students past, present (and future). You make me a better stage manager and teach me something new every day. Your work has been invaluable to this book; Kate Jones, thank you for having my back.

Grange Park Opera: Wasfi Kani, Helen Sennett, everyone on *Oliver* and the best SM team, Laura Deards and Robert Perkins.

BBC TV: The BBC Proms team, Fran Kemp, Michael Ledger, Mei Ye Li and Val Fraser; Angela Young on CBeebies; Edward Gardner and the BBC Symphony Orchestra.

Designers: Roy Bell, Richard Bullwinkle, Nicky Bunch, Norman Coates, Dinah England, Philip Engleheart, Adrian Gee, Richard Kent, Ruari Murchison, Fi Russell, Dora Schweitzer, Nancy Surman and James Turner.

Midge Adams, Jamie Crawford, The Stag Theatre in Sevenoaks, Andrew Killian, Mountview, John Birger and Bill Kenwright.

Finally, thank you to my family and friends. Mum and Dad for your constant support and checking my grammar; David, Martin, Charlotte, Becky, Jake, Sarah, Andrew, Mila and Marnie and the Hs; Tim Oliver and Richard Crawley; Pauline, Mike and my friends at the Dukes; Brian Jones (Osborne), you led the way.

Photo credits: John Haynes and Richard Hubert Smith (*see also* individual captions).

ABBREVIATIONS

To avoid filling the text with long theatrical terms (over 200 instances of 'deputy stage manager', for example!), the following abbreviations are used in the text:

AD	assistant director
ASM	assistant stage manager
BECTU	Broadcasting, Entertainment, Communications and Theatre Union
CL	centre line
CM	company manager
CS	centre stage
CSM	company stage manager
DS	downstage
DSM	deputy stage manager
FM	floor manager
FOH	front of house
HOD	head of department
IOSH	Institution of Occupational Safety and Health
ITC	Independent Theatre Council
LD	lighting designer
LX	the lighting department
MD	musical director
MS	mid stage
OP	opposite prompt
OSL	offstage left
OSR	offstage right
PM	production manager
PPE	personal protection equipment
PS	prompt side
SM	stage manager
SND	sound department
SOLT	Society of London Theatre
TSM	technical stage manager
US	upstage

INTRODUCTION

Many people, even those who work in the theatre industry themselves, do not really know exactly what stage management teams do and what is involved in the job. Other than the props, furniture and set dressing, the work that the stage management department undertakes is behind the scenes and often goes unnoticed. The stage management team's work isn't obviously on show like other departments'. There is no set to show off, no lighting to be in awe of or sound to enjoy. Most people do not know that there is someone who is responsible for cueing the technical elements of the production and ensuring that everything happens at the correct time or that a member of the stage management team has planned the scene change. But the work we do in stage management is the glue that holds a production together. Stage management facilitates other people's creativity and solves problems, encouraging and assisting others to be the best they can be and, whilst the work we do may go unseen, that is the biggest compliment to receive as it means we have done a good job.

After a long and varied career in theatre stage management, film, TV and events, I now enjoy teaching stage management to a new generation. The opportunity to pass on my knowledge and experience to others who want to join this exciting profession is rewarding and humbling.

With over twenty-five years of experience, I believe I can say that I know the profession and what it takes to do the job successfully. Every day is different and that is the beauty of the job. I still love theatre and I work professionally whenever my teaching commitments allow. Once theatre is in your blood it never seems to leave you and the passion for the work will always be there.

WHY STAGE MANAGEMENT MATTERS

Stage management is integral to the theatre world. The department ensures that the production runs smoothly from day one in the rehearsal room to opening night and until the show closes. Stage management is the service industry of the business as it helps others to realize their ideas. Stage managers do this practically through the sourcing of props, furniture and set dressing as well as running any rehearsals and cueing the production, coordinating the technical elements and making sure they happen at the right time.

Stage management teams are also responsible for the organizational aspects of a production. They keep everyone updated with changes and amendments throughout the process, passing on relevant information and liaising with every department. They take notes from meetings and rehearsals, organize schedules and try to keep everything running to time. The team is responsible for problem solving, timekeeping and discipline and works closely with the acting company, looking after them and ensuring they are safe, healthy and happy.

OPPOSITE: A production of *School for Wives*. PHOTO: JOHN HAYNES. DESIGNER: PHILIP ENGLEHEART

SKILLS AND CHARACTERISTICS OF STAGE MANAGEMENT

Stage management draws on so many skills as the work is varied and always keeps you on your toes. You will need a mixture of common sense, some technical theatre knowledge and patience. However, the most important attributes to possess are excellent communication and organizational skills and a good sense of humour.

People skills are fundamental within stage management, as stage managers work closely with everyone on the production and it is crucial to be able to stay calm in a crisis. Being a good listener and being empathetic, approachable and caring will help when dealing with difficult situations but being confident, methodical and logical is especially important when you are running a tech and juggling numerous tasks. Flexibility and a willingness to adapt to ever-changing situations is vital, as nothing is ever set in stone and being self-reliant and self-motivated is imperative as you will need to be in control and prioritize your own workload, judging how long it takes to undertake and complete a task.

The trick with stage management is not to over-complicate a situation or a task. If you try to think clearly and use your common sense you will usually find the answer to a problem is relatively straightforward.

A CAREER IN STAGE MANAGEMENT

Expect to be challenged. Expect to be put under pressure and to be stretched both mentally and physically but, above all, expect the unexpected.

Every show you work on will be different. Even if it's the third production of *The Tempest* that you have worked on, the actors will probably all be different, the creative team may not be the same and the problems you face will be unique to that show. If you are working on a long-running show no day

will be exactly the same as the last. Maybe your lead actor will be unwell and an understudy will be going on for the first time, or maybe a new dresser has started and you need to keep an eye on where they are standing for a scene change. It could be as simple as it is raining outside and you've discovered a leak onstage.

Stage management is hard work – demanding but also satisfying and fulfilling. Stage managers work long hours as they are the first to arrive and the last to leave. They cope with constant changes, often at the last minute, and deal with problems and disasters that require them to stay calm and unflappable. Try to embrace the challenges and don't think of problems as a negative but take pleasure in solving them.

Always apply common sense, give 100 per cent commitment and above all else do the best you can and enjoy it. It's a great job to do and it often doesn't feel like work at all!

In this book, you will learn about the basics of theatre, the terminology that is used, the different ways to stage a show and the distinctive types of theatre productions. You will be given details about the production process and how a show is put together from day one of rehearsals to the last performance.

The duties of the stage management team will be examined in detail, with an extensive description of the responsibilities and tasks that are involved in putting on a production. You will find out about the hierarchy of the stage management team, how the jobs are divided up and who is expected to do what. Blocking and prompting will be explained and you will be given some ideas on how to run a rehearsal room and the best way of working with the director and actors.

You will see how to carry out a mark-up and receive advice on which questions you should ask the designer so that you can successfully find the right props and furniture for a show. You will discover how to prepare and plan for a scene change and how to recognize what items should be included in a risk assessment. Finally, you will learn how to run a show, the skills you need to master to cue a show, manage a wing and deal with un-expected situations that may arise.

READING THE BOOK

For whatever reason you are reading this book, whether you are an amateur stage manager wanting to learn more about the process, a student hoping to make stage management your career or you are simply reading it for pleasure, I hope you will find the information within it useful and easy to put into practice if you wish to do so. All the basic duties that you will be required to undertake have been outlined, and example paperwork has been included throughout so you can understand each element fully.

It is most important to understand that you can never know everything about stage management because it is a constantly evolving job. The basics are written here in this book and they will help you grasp the process and how to achieve the tasks you are set as a member of stage management. But each show is different, and you will constantly learn new things and find different ways of working with every new experience you have.

Welcome to the world of stage management.

1
THEATRE BASICS

Before looking at the detailed job roles and the work that the stage management team are expected to undertake, we need to discuss the basic terminology associated with the theatre world. These terms don't just relate to stage management but are used across the theatre industry.

THEATRE STAGING

The beauty of theatre is that no production is ever the same: the venues used are unlimited and the genres are numerous. Still, productions normally fall into one of the following staging types.

Proscenium arch Proscenium arch staging is probably the most common and the one that everyone will recognize. The stage is presented to the audience as if it were in a picture frame. The stage is raised and it usually has a curtain, known as tabs, at the front. There is often an apron, which is an extension that is at the front of the stage, beyond the proscenium.

End-on staging This is when the stage is at one end of the venue with the audience at the other. This is similar to proscenium arch staging but there is no picture frame at the front and the stage may not be raised.

Traverse staging Traverse staging is when the audience are positioned on two sides of the stage.

Thrust staging A thrust is when the audience are positioned around three sides of the stage. The stage extends into the audience.

OPPOSITE: A brand new theatre.

RIGHT: A proscenium arch stage.
DESIGNER: DINAH ENGLAND

ABOVE: A production in traverse. PHOTO: RICHARD HUBERT SMITH. DESIGNER: FI RUSSELL

Thrust staging. DESIGNER: RICHARD BULLWINKLE

In the round The stage in this type is in the centre of your venue and the audience are positioned all around the stage. You may often see this referred to as arena staging.

Black box or studio staging This is a flexible space and the seating can be moved according to the type of layout required by the designer, so that the production can be performed in any of the other types of staging, for example thrust or in the round.

Promenade This staging is the most flexible and involves the audience moving from area to area to watch the production, rather than staying in one place. This staging is often used for site-specific productions, for example in unusual buildings or outside.

A performance in the round. PHOTO: JOHN HAYNES. DESIGNER: DORA SCHWEITZER

A black box studio space.

STAGING TERMS

These terms are used when describing the areas of the stage. The important detail to remember is that they are taken from the standpoint of the person onstage when they are looking into the audience; this is often referred to as the actor's perspective.

The stage is divided into nine main areas, which are given specific names so that everyone is using the same terminology. The sound and lighting department often use alternative terms, however. They may refer to the stage as auditorium right and left, for example, because they operate the show from the auditorium.

First, the stage is split into thirds, from north to south and from east to west. If you are standing onstage the area to the right of you is known as stage right and the area to the left is stage left. The central portion is known as centre stage. When we are talking about the areas that are from north to south, we refer to the third nearer to the audience as downstage and the third furthest away from the audience as upstage; again, the central portion is centre stage. The reason that they are named like this is because English theatres in the past were built on a raked stage. When you walk on a raked stage you are literally walking down towards the audience or up towards backstage.

When written, the positions on stage are commonly abbreviated to their capital letters, for example DS for downstage, US for upstage and CS for centre stage.

When referring to the wings, there are two ways this is done. Following the above system of stage right and stage left, we can refer to areas

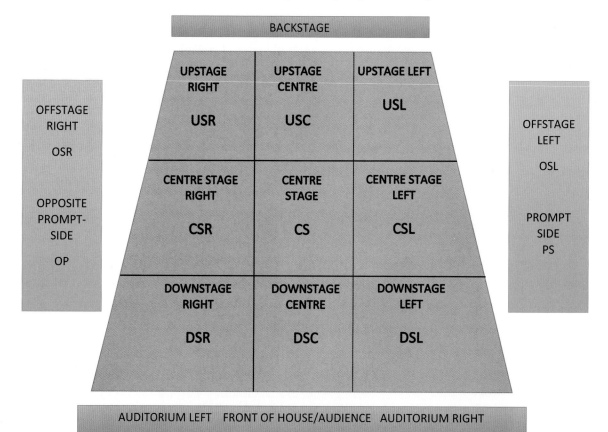

The areas of the stage.

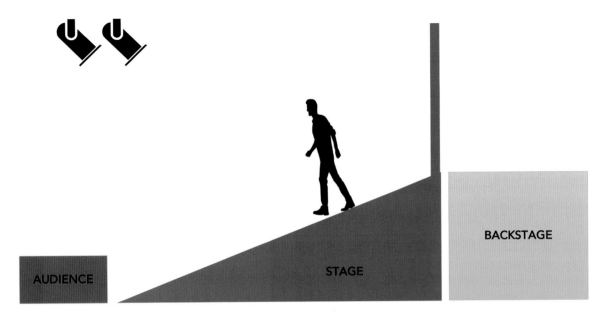

A side elevation of a raked stage.

as offstage right or left – OSR and OSL – and this is the simplest and most common method. The second way is to refer to the wings as prompt side (PS) or opposite prompt (OP). This terminology is still very much in use and you will often see big opera houses and classical musical venues refer to the wings in this way. The reason these names exist is, again, rooted in history. The prompt corner was in the wings where the prompter would sit and remind the actors of their lines. Prompt corner is traditionally on stage left, hence prompt side is the same as stage left. In modern times the prompter has now been replaced by the DSM, who usually still sits on stage left at prompt corner. However, if the stage left wing has limited space, prompt corner could be placed onstage right. In this instance prompt side does not change sides, however: prompt side is still SL and opposite prompt is still SR.

On a traverse stage or a theatre that is in the round the audience will be seated in a different configuration. You still need to divide the stage into different areas so you may choose to number the sections instead of using the usual terminology.

TRAVERSE STAGE

AUDIENCE		
1	2	3
4	5	6
AUDIENCE		

IN THE ROUND

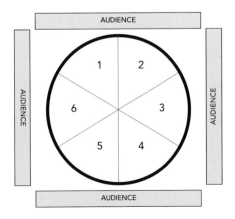

The areas of the stage when working in traverse or in the round.

BASTARD PROMPT

If the DSM and the prompt desk are situated on SR then the theatre is said to have a 'bastard prompt', because the prompt desk is not on prompt side. This is a term that never seems to be forgotten once you have heard it.

TYPES OF THEATRE COMPANY

Fringe Theatre

Small-scale productions are produced in fringe theatres. Often the plays are new writing, with up-and-coming playwrights, creatives, actors and technicians. In the UK, we seem to be following the American trend by calling these theatres 'off West End'. A lot of the venues are above pubs, such as the *Old Red Lion* or the *Finborough Arms* in London. There is also the famous Edinburgh Fringe Festival, which takes place over the whole of August. A lot of fringe productions employ staff on a profit-share, which means that they will only be paid if the show makes a profit. Whilst this is the downside, the work is exciting and it is rewarding to be one of the first people to put a production on. The stage manager will be working with just the actors during the run and usually operates sound and lights as well as undertaking stage management duties. Stage managers are usually employed on a show-by-show basis.

Repertory Theatre

Repertory theatre involves a number of productions that are produced by a resident theatre company for a season and performed on different nights, usually for a limited run. Often a number of shows are in rehearsal while others are performing and the next season is in the planning stage. When their own productions are not in performance a lot of the theatres will receive touring productions too. Most repertory theatres are based in the regions, such as the Dundee Rep or the Theatre by the Lake in Keswick. The National Theatre is the largest rep theatre in the UK. Stage managers must be highly organized as there could be two or more shows performing on alternate nights while rehearsals continue during the day for the next shows. Stage management teams will often be employed by the season.

Producing Houses

These are theatres that will produce their own shows but do not follow the rep system, for example the Young Vic and the Tron Theatre. They will rehearse and then perform a production and, while the current show is performing, the next one will be rehearsing. The actors work on individual shows but the SM team often work on all the shows. The theatres may also take touring productions and one-night shows or comedy acts when they are not producing their own work.

Touring or Receiving Houses

These are theatres that do not produce their own shows but will hire their venue out to producing companies. The theatre will have the bare minimum of permanent staff, often with only two departments backstage – lighting and construction. Casual staff will be hired in if the incoming company requires more personnel. Productions are wide-ranging, from one-nighters through to weekly, monthly or longer-term runs. Stage management teams are not hired by these type of theatres as they will be employed by the incoming productions.

These theatres fall into a few categories:

West End theatres The best-known type of receiving house. Producers can hire these theatres from a few months to many years.

No. 1 houses These are the larger-scale theatres around the country and you will find that big productions, such as musicals, will tour to them. They often play host to one-day performances, such as comedians, music events and bands too.

Mid-scale theatres These venues are smaller places that will be hired for one-night productions or weekly touring. A lot of plays will tour to these venues.

Producing Companies

The function of a producer and producing company is to bring together the best possible team to realize a particular script. They work independently from a specific theatre and will hire a venue for the production to play in. They must raise the finance, often finding backers or 'angels' and then hire the

creative team, actors and production personnel. A stage manager will be hired for a specific production and work for the producers from day one of rehearsals to the get-out.

Commercial and Subsidized Theatre

Theatre falls into two financial categories. Commercial theatre is made by producers and producing companies and is run entirely for profit. The commercial sector receives no grants and is a business, gaining the necessary finance from backers. Subsidized theatre does not usually make a profit on the productions and is chiefly supported by government grants and donated funds from other organizations, such as the Arts Council.

A production of the musical *Cabaret*. PHOTO: JOHN HAYNES. DESIGNER: PHILIP ENGLEHEART

THEATRE GENRES

Musicals

Musicals are always very popular and are found in all scales of theatre. Most people associate the West End of London with large musicals, with some, like *Les Misérables* and *Phantom of the Opera*, playing to audiences for many decades. Many of these musicals will have touring versions that will travel the country as well as internationally.

Plays

Plays are the staple of all types of theatres and can range from comedies, dramas and classic melo-dramas to new writing, Shakespeare and every-thing in between. A lot of theatres and companies will have their own ethos when choosing plays to produce – the RSC primarily perform the plays of William Shakespeare and his contemporaries, for example, while the Royal Court focus much of their work on new writing.

Children's Theatre or Theatre in Education (TIE)

This involves productions that are written for and aimed at children. They are often plays that are trying to educate and many have a moral mes-sage, such as anti-bullying or anti-drugs. There are various companies that are dedicated solely to this type of theatre, such as the Unicorn or Polka. Most large theatres operate an education department who will tour their own productions or a children-friendly version to schools and com-munity halls. These include the Belgrade Theatre, Coventry.

The stage manager will often be driving the van, running the get-ins and setting up the mini-mal scenery and technical elements. Everyone gets involved in setting up and the actors are ex-pected to help too. The SM can be hired on an individual production or on a full-time basis with a company.

Alternative or Community Theatre

These companies or theatres have been formed with a specific target audience in mind and their productions will often include members of the communities that they are trying to reach. Exam-ples include the Clean Break Theatre Company and the Chickenshed. Sometimes these compa-nies will tour to unusual venues, dependent on their target audience. For example, Clean Break Theatre Company may tour to women's prisons as their work is focused on women and crime. As with TIE, the stage management team will often be driving the van and leading the get-in, with the cast helping too.

Opera Companies

These companies will produce opera productions. They may be based in their own theatre, like the Royal Opera House or English National Opera at the Coliseum, or be touring companies, such as English Touring Opera. Many opera companies will perform their seasons during the summer months, such as Glyndebourne Festival Thea-tre or Grange Park Opera. Based in old stately homes with large gardens, the operas produced often have 90-minute intervals so that the audi-ences can dine in the restaurants or picnic in the grounds.

Ballet and Dance Companies

Ballet companies are usually independent of a the-atre and will take their productions into a venue. However, large companies, such as the Birming-ham Royal Ballet and The Royal Ballet, have prin-cipal venues, the Birmingham Hippodrome and Royal Opera House, respectively.

THE GREEN ROOM

The green room is a communal room backstage that is used by everyone on a production. It is where personnel usually go when they are on a break or to have their food as it is not good practice to eat in the dressing rooms. The name may have originated from the stage being called 'the green' or a London theatre in 1599 whose ante-room was painted green.

THEATRE HIERARCHY

The theatre hierarchy in the UK is very important and, while you won't find every individual job mentioned in each scale of theatre, the principles are the same throughout. It is best to refer to the related diagram for the exact order as the following list is organized by type of work rather than level, starting with theatre management and administration, followed by those who work directly on the production.

Theatre Management and Administration
THEATRE TRUST, BOARD OF DIRECTORS OR PRODUCER

These people sit at the top of the family tree. A theatre trust or board of directors will run the theatre, while a producer is involved with commercial theatre and will be the head of the production company. A producer is the instigator of a production, choosing the script, a creative team and the theatre in which to perform, while the board or trust of a theatre will run the theatre but will hire an artistic director to put the creative elements into practice. They will all, however, be responsible for the money for the project.

GENERAL MANAGER

The general manager is responsible for the overall running of the theatre or production company, making sure that all the costs stay within budget. This includes any building costs, staffing costs and show-related expenses. They report directly to the producers, board or trust and oversee any productions on their behalf.

ADMINISTRATOR

An administrator will control the finances and spending within a theatre and will be responsible for employee rights and pay. They will also distribute budgets to the various departments.

ACCOUNTANT

Working as a full-time employee of a theatre or company, the accountant will be responsible for all the financial matters relating to the theatre or production.

THEATRE MANAGER

The theatre manager is permanently employed and in charge of running the theatre building. They look after all aspects of front of house and in some theatres oversee backstage staffing and maintenance.

FRONT OF HOUSE MANAGER

The FOH manager is in charge of the theatre and they are responsible for the front of house requirements and anything audience related. This includes bars and restaurants, box office and FOH staff. They also oversee all health and safety aspects and ensure that the audience are looked after and safe.

PUBLICITY AND MARKETING MANAGER

Publicity and marketing is vital to raising the profile of a theatre or show and its success. The publicity and marketing teams will organize all the printing and distribution of the advertising materials and will organize any photo calls or press calls.

Production Staff
ARTISTIC DIRECTOR

The artistic director is employed by a theatre to plan the season of productions, whether

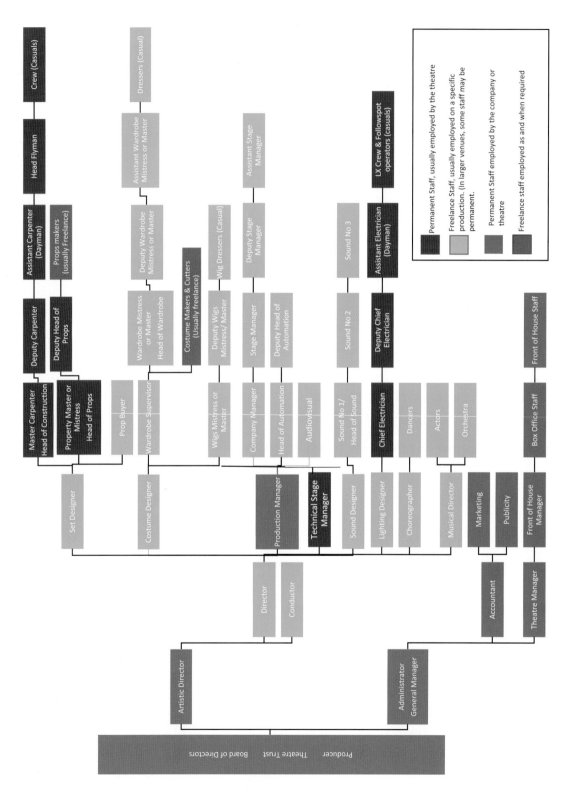

The theatre family tree.

The grid, which is at the top of the theatre above the stage.

DIRECTOR

The director is responsible for the creative concept of the production and its realization. They will choose the rest of the creative team and, with them, will create the style, look and feel of the production. They are responsible for directing the performers and working with the other production departments to lead them in the technical elements.

MUSICAL DIRECTOR/CONDUCTOR

The MD or conductor will be employed by the artistic director or producer and is responsible for the musical aspects of a production. They work closely with the director, choreographer and cast and will lead the orchestra. In an opera, a conductor will take on this role and will be on an equal footing with the director in seniority within the production.

CHOREOGRAPHER

Employed by the artistic director or producer, the choreographer is responsible for the dance

in-house shows or visiting shows, and to take on the creative aspects of the business. They work with the general manager and administrator in regard to budget allocation, publicity and marketing to raise sponsorship and raise the theatre's profile. They hire the creative teams for the productions, while also directing some productions themselves.

A box set. DESIGNER: RICHARD BULLWINKLE

aspects of a production. They work closely with the other creatives and 'direct' the cast and dancers in the movement that is required. They are often assisted by a dance captain, who is a member of the company.

Set Designer

The designer is responsible for the visual elements of the show, from the scenic elements to the costumes and props and furniture. They work closely with the director to create the vision of the production and will build a scale model of the set, and produce ground plans, working drawings and diagrams for the technical teams to work from. They will also provide costume designs if a separate costume designer is not employed, and will work closely with the stage management team in choosing suitable props, furniture and set dressing for the production.

Sound Designer

In consultation with the director, they will design the overall sound for a production. They will decide which equipment to use, where speakers should be positioned for the best sound and choose which pieces of music to use. They will oversee the installation of the sound rig, run the sound plot sessions and work up to opening night to achieve the best sound for the show.

Lighting Designer

The LD will produce the lighting design for a show after discussions with the director and often the designer too. They will draw up the lighting plan

A tension wire grid, which the technicians stand on to rig and focus the lights and speakers that are placed over the auditorium.

and choose which equipment to use. They will provide direction to the LX (lighting) department at the focus session, run the LX plot sessions and work during the technical rehearsal and dress rehearsals to light the production.

Production Manager

The production manager can be employed permanently by a theatre or company or could be hired to work on a single production. They will oversee all the technical requirements of a production and they are responsible for the overall health and safety. They will hire the technical staff and supervise them throughout the process. The production manager draws up the production schedule, chairs the production meetings and oversees all budgets and monetary issues. They will hire equipment, arrange transport and ensure the production is kept on time and within budget.

A Box Set and the Fourth Wall

A box set is made up of three walls of scenery with the downstage edge of the stage making up the fourth wall. A box set is commonly used to give the impression that the characters are in a room. You will often hear actors talk about the fourth wall. They have to imagine that they are in the room and that there is a wall between themselves and the audience.

TECHNICAL STAGE MANAGER

A TSM is employed in a receiving house and organizes and runs the backstage department. They will hire and timetable technical personnel, liaising with the technical staff from incoming companies to meet their requirements. They will also take responsibility for maintaining all the in-house equipment, the building itself and any health and safety issues.

HEADS OF DEPARTMENT

The heads of department will be employed by either the production manager or theatre manager in consultation with the creative teams, as they will usually have input into who they wish to work with. The HODs will take responsibility for the technical requirements of a production relating to their individual department.

WARDROBE SUPERVISOR

The wardrobe supervisor is hired to assist the designer in preparing the costumes for the production. They are employed by the production company and work during the production period up until opening night. They will employ costume makers to construct the garments and will help choose the wardrobe staff who will lead the team on the show.

WARDROBE MASTER OR MISTRESS

This is a key role and they are responsible for the wardrobe department for the entire run of the production. They lead the rest of the wardrobe team and ensure that the costumes are looked after. They will hire: the staff; their deputies, who will be permanently assigned to the production; and the dressers, who are employed on a casual basis.

WIGS MISTRESS OR MASTER

The head of the wigs department, they will be tasked with realizing any wigs that will be needed for the production and will hire any staff they need for the show, such as the wigs dressers.

MASTER CARPENTER

The master carpenter is employed as the head of the construction department. They are a permanent member of the theatre's staff and will oversee the building as well as hiring and leading the in-house team and casual crew. While they are not

A production of *Bury Fair* showing Restoration wigs and costumes. PHOTO: JOHN HAYNES. DESIGNER: RUARI MURCHISON

The fly floor, where the flymen work.

responsible for the incoming production's scenery, they will lead the get-in and get-out and help to maintain the set so it continues to run smoothly. If they are employed in a workshop they will oversee the building of the set, buying and costing the materials within budget and ensuring that health and safety rules are adhered to.

Head Flyman

The head flyman is hired by the theatre and will take responsibility for the fly floor. They ensure that all the scenery and related technical equipment is well maintained and that the casual staff employed on the show are trained and follow the production's requirements.

Head of Props

Not every theatre or company has a separate prop department and, if there isn't one, the work falls to the SM team. A dedicated prop department will source all the props, making, finding, designing and adapting them. Often a production company will hire a prop buyer to do the same job. If you do have a prop department on your production, the SM team will work closely to assist them.

Chief Electrician

The chief electrician is employed as head of the lighting department and is a permanent member of a theatre's backstage staff. They will look after the in-house staff, employ and supervise any casual crew, including follow-spot operators, and maintain the building and the equipment. As with the master carpenter, they are not employed by the incoming production, but will lead the fit-up and get-out, oversee all the rigging, focusing, plotting and rehearsals and will maintain the lighting rig throughout the production's run. They will also maintain the theatre building, all FOH lighting and will keep abreast of all health and safety requirements and updates.

The technical gallery or box, which is used by the technical operators during the show.

HEAD OF SOUND

The head of sound is often referred to as the sound No. 1. The HOD will usually operate the production at the sound desk. They will take care of all the sound requirements for the show and will oversee the rest of the sound team.

AUTOMATION

The head of automation will oversee the automation requirements of the production, chiefly operating and overseeing the machinery for the production. They will lead the rest of the automation team.

AUDIOVISUAL

This department will look after all the audiovisual elements of a production, such as projection and video. Sometimes a specialist company will be hired to set the system up and another member of the technical team will operate the show.

A production of *Her Naked Skin* using audiovisual screens. PHOTO: RICHARD HUBERT SMITH. DESIGNER: ROY BELL

TOP TIP

It is imperative that the stage management team meets up at least once a day in the rehearsal room so they can discuss the events of the day and any issues that have arisen.

ACTORS, DANCERS AND MUSICIANS

The actors and dancers will be hired on each show or season, and will be the face of the production. They will work closely with the director, choreographer and MD and will portray the characters within the show. The musicians will work with the MD or conductor and play with the rest of the orchestra from the pit to produce the live music for a production.

CASUAL STAFF

There will be a number of people employed on the run of a production on a casual contract. They are employed on a daily or weekly basis. On a long-running production, this could mean years of work, whereas in a touring venue you could be working one week, or even one day but not the next. Members of the crew, dressers, wig dressers and follow-spot operators are all casuals.

Stage Management Team

Last but not least is the stage management team, who are often employed by the company and not the theatre. However, in larger venues or repertory theatres you will find a permanent SM team or at least a team hired for a season. The stage management team is responsible for the smooth running of a show, organizing everything and communicating with all other departments and personnel. Later chapters will explain in detail what each role entails, but here is a brief summary to get you started.

PRODUCTION MANAGER

The role of production manager and where they sit within the theatre hierarchy has already been touched on above, but it is important to note that a lot of production managers start their careers in stage management and, as they tend to be the people that hire the SM team, they do sit at the top of the team.

A production of *The English Game*. PHOTO: JOHN HAYNES. DESIGNER: RICHARD BULLWINKLE

Stage management will work closely with the production manager, trying to stay within the budget they have allocated and assisting them in overseeing the health and safety issues involved with the production. Stage management are the timekeepers in the process and as the production manager compiles the production schedule, communication between them is vital. Any changes to the timetable need to be communicated to the PM and any schedule amendments that are consequently made need to be passed on to the rest of the company and crew via the DSM in rehearsal calls.

COMPANY MANAGER

The company manager leads the SM team. They tend to spend most of their time dealing with

paperwork, figures and any company issues that may arise. They liaise between the producers, theatre managers and the personnel who work on the show.

The company manager is responsible for the financial day-to-day running of the production, compiling the payroll for the acting company and stage management team and sending it to the producer's accountants. They will also authorize any overtime for the in-house staff and their casual teams. They work out, on a daily basis, the box office takings and the advance figures and include them on each performance's show report, which they send over to the producers.

They take responsibility for the administration and welfare of the acting company, organizing physiotherapy and, sometimes, doctor's appointments. They will take care of the general well-being of a company. A company manager will also be the liaison between the press department and the actors, often having to accompany the cast to radio and press interviews, especially when they are working on a tour. They will be responsible for handling the merchandise to FOH and making sure it is kept stocked.

This book will focus only on the three onstage roles of stage management. While the company manager role is an important one, it can be combined with the stage manager to make it a company stage manager position. A lot of the tasks outlined in Chapter 5 about the stage manager will be relevant to a company manager too.

STAGE MANAGER

The stage manager leads the team onstage and ensures all the information relating to the show is passed to each department. They are in charge of health and safety backstage and when the show is running it is 'their stage'. Nothing should happen without the SM knowing about it. They help the ASMs to collate props and furniture, manage the crew and organize any scene changes. They run the various rehearsals and keep a close eye on the time, making sure breaks are adhered to and that work gets done as quickly as possible.

DEPUTY STAGE MANAGER

The DSM attends rehearsals and works closely with the cast and director. They are in charge of the book, writing down blocking and issuing rehearsal notes, rehearsal calls and show reports. Once they get into the theatre, they sit at the prompt desk and call the show, cueing all aspects of the production, from scenery moves to lighting changes and actors' entrances.

ASSISTANT STAGE MANAGER

The ASM is in charge of props, furniture and set dressing. They will spend the rehearsal period sourcing the items. Once in the theatre, they will set up onstage and backstage and then run the wings during the production. They will assist the actors, help with scene changes and generally help everyone where possible.

BACKSTAGE CALLS

It is really important that you understand the backstage calls in whatever department you work, as timing is vital in theatre. The aim is always to start a show at the advertised time and that means getting the audience seated and the cast and crew ready. To help achieve this, the stage management team, specifically the DSM, is responsible for making tannoy announcements.

As far as backstage calls are concerned timings are always 5 minutes ahead of real time so that, hopefully, everyone will be ready and the show can

---

TOP TIP

It is becoming more common for cast to be involved in pre-show action as the audience enters the venue. A DSM does need to give the same time warnings to these cast members too, but there can only ever be one official half-an-hour call. If you need to give your pre-show cast members any calls this should be announced as the 'pre-show half-an-hour call' or the 'pre-show quarter-hour call' and so on.

Backstage pre-show calls

HALF AN HOUR CALL	QUARTER OF AN HOUR CALL	FIVE MINUTE CALL	BEGINNERS	CURTAIN UP
• MATINEE 1.25 • EVENING 6.55	• MATINEE 1.40 • EVENING 7.10	• MATINEE 1.50 • EVENING 7.20	• MATINEE 1.55 • EVENING 7.25	• MATINEE 2.00 • EVENING 7.30

The backstage pre-show calls and the times that they are called.

begin as soon as the audience are all seated. The half an hour call is made so that everyone knows there is half an hour left before the show starts, though in reality the half-hour call is made 35 minutes before curtain up. There is also a quarter of an hour call 20 minutes before the show starts and a 5-minute call 10 minutes before. Finally, the beginners' call is made 5 minutes before curtain up so that all those involved in the start of the show can make their way to the stage if they haven't already done so. The table here outlines the call system for two shows, one matinee at 2pm and one evening performance at 7.30.

TASK

Below is a list of jobs and responsibilities that the stage management team have. Take a look and see if you can work out who is responsible for what task: production manager, company manager, stage manager, deputy stage manager or assistant stage manager. Be careful, though, as some of the tasks might be undertaken by more than one member of the team.

Who:
Prompts the actors?
Helps with quick changes?
Is responsible for solving production problems?
Is usually the first technical person to be hired?
Is responsible for props and furniture?
Is the first to arrive and last to leave?
Works on scene changes?
Makes sure the correct breaks are taken?
Organizes physiotherapy for the acting company?
Runs the rehearsal room?
Organizes transport?
Dresses the set with the designer?
Ensures the set will fit into the theatre?
Works with the publicity department, organizing the actors to attend press and photo calls and assisting with their appearances on TV and radio?
Obtains the technical details, known as the rider, for the theatres, ground plans, fly plots, LX and sound equipment and so on?
Records the blocking?
Runs the technical rehearsal?
Has contacts with unions BECTU, Equity, UK Theatre and ITC?
Is responsible for health and safety?
Keeps a track of actors' hours?
Makes props?
Prepares and distributes production schedules?
Works in the prompt corner?
Ensures the stage and wings are set up correctly?
Writes thank-you letters for items borrowed?
Organizes timesheets?
Collates programme information?
Agrees and allocates budgets?
Makes front of house and backstage calls?

A view of a theatre backstage. GRANGE PARK OPERA

2
THE PRODUCTION PROCESS

Once the script has been confirmed, the planning has been completed and the staffing is in place, there are three basic phases to mounting a production: the rehearsal period, the production period and the run. This chapter will outline these stages so that you have a clear understanding of the process as a whole.

PRE-REHEARSALS

The work that happens before rehearsals begin is minimal in terms of stage management involvement, as SM teams are usually only employed from day one of rehearsals, although they may be hired on a daily rate to run the auditions, to prepare any equipment or to collate supplies prior to the first day, for example. It is nonetheless always beneficial to do some preparation for yourself before rehearsals begin. If nothing else you should read the script before you start.

The producer or artistic director will have chosen a script that they wish to produce. They will have raised any money that they need for the production, worked out the performance dates and hired a theatre. They will then decide upon the

---

TOP TIP

If you are required to run the auditions it is important to look after the creative team well and put the actors who are attending at their ease so they can perform to the best of their ability. You should have water ready for the auditionees and ensure you have any copies of the script or the score that they may need in case they have forgotten to bring theirs.

---

creative team, starting with the director and working from there.

The director will then need to have various meetings with the designer, working out what the set will look like, taking into account the theatre space and often visiting the theatre together to discuss the finer details. Once an idea has been settled on, the designer will need to go away and make a scale model of the set design. The first version is a draft so that it can be taken to the production manager to discuss the feasibility of the set and, very importantly, whether the ideas can be translated practically and within the budget. The first scale model is known as the 'white card model' as the designer will not worry about the specific colours and they will make it out of white card.

There will probably be more meetings between the production manager and designer, as the PM will need to work out some basic costings as well as ensure that the ideas that have been submitted by the designer are workable. Alongside this, the producer and director will need to start casting the production and the production manager will need to start hiring the technical staff. Once this is complete the contracts and scripts will be sent out.

The designer, at this point, is making a more detailed model box of the production as the design will now have been signed off by the PM. The model box will be made to scale. In the UK, the scale is usually 1:25, which means that the model and everything in it is twenty-five times smaller than it is in real life. The set and scenery will now be painted the correct colours and the props and furniture are also made to scale.

The designer will also have to prepare various working drawings and, again, these are to scale. They will produce a ground plan that is

A white card model box of *Stars in the Morning Sky*. DESIGNER: RICHARD BULLWINKLE

A completed model box for *When the Rain Stops Falling*. DESIGNER: ROY BELL

SCALE

In the UK, metric measurements – centimetres and metres – are used, which is why the working scale is usually 1:25. The USA and Canada use imperial measurements – inches and feet – so the scale is 1:24.

a scale drawing of the stage with the set within it. It is a vital document as each department will use it to plan their own logistics. For example, the LX department will work out where to rig lights, sound will need to plan the position of their speakers and the PM will need to decide on which bar to hang any flying pieces. Stage management will use the ground plan to provide a mark-up for the cast and director to work on. This is a plan of the set, which is placed onto the rehearsal room floor.

The designer will also prepare other diagrams and paperwork. The construction department will need working drawings of the scenery so they

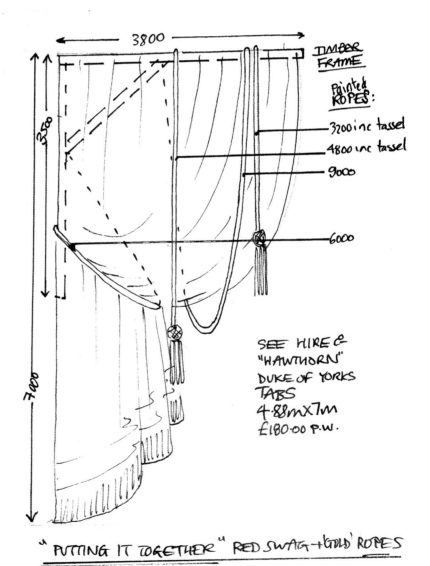

A working drawing of a curtain. DESIGNER: PHILIP ENGLEHEART

can build it; the wardrobe department will want designs of the costumes; and stage management may want designs of specific props that may need to be made. Often a designer will also prepare a prop and furniture list. However, stage management should not rely on this and should always prepare their own lists too.

The production manager will need to arrange and book a rehearsal room and then pass all the information for it onto the stage manager. Calls will then be made to ensure everyone knows where rehearsals are, when they start and who will need to be present.

THE REHEARSAL PERIOD

Depending on the scale, budget and complexity of the production, rehearsals can be only a few weeks or can run for months. On existing productions, cast change rehearsals are often only a few weeks. This is because the show is already up and running and the rehearsals are solely for the new cast members to learn their roles or, as often referred to in musicals, their tracks. These rehearsals will take place around the performances, as any current cast members will be continuing to perform. This does enable the new cast members to watch the production as an audience member, however, and they may also get the opportunity to go backstage and follow, or shadow, the cast members they are replacing. This is a quick and easy way for new cast members to learn a show as it allows them to see the mechanics of a production and become familiar with the technical elements too.

On new productions the rehearsal periods will inevitably be longer. Everyone will be using the rehearsal period to plan and work through the script and to make decisions about how to achieve the director's and designer's vision. There will need to be time to build the set, make or hire the costumes, source props and furniture and for the actors to rehearse with the director. Technically complex shows may rehearse for three months in

a rehearsal room then a further month or more in the theatre. While this is a rarity, it can happen on big commercial productions.

First Day of Rehearsals

The first day of rehearsals is exciting if not a little nerve-racking. It is the chance for everyone involved in the rehearsal and creative process to be in the same room, to meet each other and to see what the director and designer have decided the production will look like and their thoughts on it. This meeting does not usually include any in-house or casual staff as they don't start working on the production until it moves into the theatre.

MEET AND GREET

The meet and greet is when everyone sits in the rehearsal room and introduces themselves; this is usually as simple as your name and job title.

MODEL BOX SHOWING

The designer will then show the model box. This is an opportunity for everyone to see what the set will look like and to understand what each piece of scenery does, how everything works together and how it will work within the theatre. They will explain when the play is being set and where in the world the action is taking place. It is the chance to ask initial questions and for everyone to have a clear understanding of the vision of the designer and director. The model box showing is not limited just to the model itself as the director may talk about the play and the designer will probably show the costume designs.

READ-THROUGH

After the model box showing is completed, there will probably be a read-through. This is when the cast read their lines and sing the musical numbers for the first time. It may be quite rough as it will undoubtedly be the first time most of them have read their lines audibly or sung the songs, but it is a useful method for everyone to hear the piece

A designer showing the model box to the cast and production staff on the first day of rehearsals.

out loud so that they can visualize the production. It is very different reading a script to hearing it spoken by the actors. We all imagine different things when we read. You may well have read a book then, on seeing the film version, felt disappointed as you had very different ideas. When you hear a read-through it gives everyone a clearer picture of the production as the characters will come alive.

The read-through also serves to give everyone an initial timing of the production and enables them to make any notes on what they are hearing. The director will often interject with their ideas and what is happening with the set during each of the scenes.

Mark-Up

The stage management team needs to provide a mark-up in the rehearsal room before the cast get up and start blocking the show. It is usually one of the first things the stage management team does, often before the meet and greet happens, although obviously this is dependent on the SM having the ground plan from the designer by that point. The mark-up is vital in the rehearsal room as it enables the cast to move practically around the space, to see how much room they have and where specific set pieces are. It helps the director to plan the staging and is useful for other departments physically to see the space that is involved.

Facilitating the Rehearsal Room

The rehearsal room is looked after by the stage management team, primarily the DSM, who is in rehearsals with the director and acting company. The team is on hand to facilitate any requests the director, acting company or creative team may have. This may include setting up keyboards for the musical director, putting up reference material, costume drawings and set pictures for the cast and adding additional scenic elements to the mark-up. In a recent production I worked on, there were planks of wood that were lifted and set vertically on the floor at certain points during the play. It was imperative that the actors were aware of them and where they would be, so constructing stand-ins and putting them into rehearsals helped the transition to the theatre run smoothly and helped the actors work out their blocking.

Aside from rehearsal requests, the team will also be doing any menial tasks, such as cleaning and tidying, ensuring the catering supplies are restocked, that there is enough toilet roll and so on, and that the kitchen, if there is one, is kept hygienic.

It is important that the SM team remains flexible during this period as it is a highly intensive creative period and things are constantly changing. One day they may be asked to get furniture into rehearsals and then, the next day, the same furniture needs to be removed and strengthened so the actors can stand on it. The team will be dealing with constant requests and demands while still trying to do their own work, but should try to remain calm and organized and keep on top of things.

As rehearsals progress more time should be spent in the rehearsal room. It is really important to watch the rehearsals, see what each scene looks like and how the props and furniture are being used. Each member of the team needs to know the show well so they are able to execute their roles

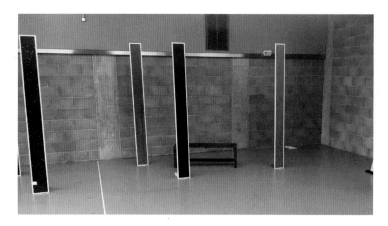

Scenic elements of the set need to be replicated in the rehearsal room so the actors can get used to their position.

once they are in the theatre. It is obvious when a team has not seen enough of the rehearsals.

Production Meetings

During the rehearsal period, there will be regular production meetings. These usually occur once a week and allow all the technical staff on the production to be in the same room to discuss any technical problems or issues or to raise any questions. The acting company does not attend these.

Production meetings are called by the production manager, who will chair them. This is not an opportunity to go into specific departmental details that won't affect anyone else, but it is a forum to discuss items that may affect one or more departments.

The PM will issue the production schedule and discuss any changes that have been made since the last distributed version and they will bring up any high-risk items for discussion, such as naked flames or smoking. They will also discuss any set changes that have been made, in reference to the ground plan, so each department can be informed. The PM will also encourage decisions to be made and raise any issues that are becoming contentious.

The PM will ask each department if they wish to say anything. It is usual for them to start with the creatives, then move around the table. The stage manager should talk on behalf of the SM team and should only raise items that will affect

other departments. For example, crew in costume will concern the designer and costume department and if you are using any practical lighting or sound props this will involve the lighting and sound teams. The DSM should try to sit next to the director so they can remind them of anything they wanted to ask. While it is best for the SM to raise any questions the SM team has, this does not mean to say that the ASMs or DSM should sit in silence. If a question is raised that they can, or need to, answer, they should do so as their input to the production is as valuable as everyone else's.

Once the rehearsal period is over, the stage management team should clear the rehearsal room, pack up the production's belongings and move with them into the theatre.

A production meeting in progress.

THE PRODUCTION PERIOD

This stage in the process is when the production moves into the theatre. It runs from the get-in to opening night. The production manager will issue a production schedule, which clearly outlines what activity is happening when. It should be followed religiously; if there are any delays or problems, the PM will have to re-schedule it and send out a new version. As with a lot of the paperwork that the SM team send out, it is always 'subject to change and alteration'.

Get-In

This is the time when all the technical equipment and scenery is taken into the theatre. As you would expect, this involves a lot of manual handling and lifting as the items are often large, awkward and heavy. A lot of theatres have a separate door through which to do the get-in. This entrance will have direct access to the stage and the scene dock, so is called the dock door. As stages are often not at street level, you may find that there is a winch or lift that has to be used too.

The production manager will have arranged transportation to the venue and will have fixed the schedule. It may be that all the departments do their get-in alongside each other, or they may be staggered. Stage management will often be the last department to do their get-in as rehearsals are usually still going on while the other departments are working in the theatre to fit the show up. As most of the SM team's belongings and show requirements are needed in rehearsals they cannot be moved until just before the cast go into the theatre.

LX and Sound Rig and the Fit-Up

This is the process of erecting the set, rigging the technical equipment, bringing in the costumes and getting the stage ready for the rehearsals that will happen onstage. This has to be scheduled well, as, for the most part, departments will need space and time to themselves to set up rather than working around each other. Stage management are usually the only department not to have any dedicated time to themselves to get ready but will work around everyone else.

The lighting department will need to rig the lanterns and the sound department will need to rig their speakers on the bars before the set goes up, as the bars they rig them on are typically flown in to a suitable working height at stage level. This is so each of the departments can safely rig heavy equipment quickly and removes the need for ladders or access equipment at this point.

Depending on the size of production, the fit-up can be a day or two or take a few weeks. Where possible, the set will have been constructed completely off site, so that once it is in the theatre it just needs to be put back together.

Sound Balance

This is the dedicated time that the sound department have to work in the space and it is when they make sure the rig is working correctly, that the speakers sound good where they are positioned and that they are correctly balanced in terms of volume and quality of sound. The theatre obviously needs to be completely quiet for the sound department to achieve this.

If you are working on a production with live music the sound balance is when the musicians are in the theatre for the first time. There will be a seating call for them so they can make sure they have enough space for their instruments and to play comfortably. The sound department will then check that each instrument sounds its best, is balanced and that each player is happy.

Any time that the sound department need silence onstage will be referred to as quiet time. This means no one can work on the set, use power tools or make noise. You will often find that the only people who work onstage during this time are the set painters.

PRODUCTION SCHEDULE			A Midsummer Night's Dream
DATE	TIME	DETAIL	PERSONNEL
Tues 21st August	10.00	LX and Sound Rig	LX, Sound
	13.00	Lunch	
	14.00	LX and Sound Rig	
	18.00	Dinner	
	19.00	LX and Sound Rig	
	22.00	Call to end	
Wed 22nd August	09.00	Unload truck and Fit-up	Construction, LX, Sound
	13.00	Lunch	
	14.00	Fit-up continues	
	17.00	Dinner	
	18.00	Fit-up continues	
	22.00	Call to end	
Thurs 23rd August	09.00	LX Focus	Construction, LX
	13.00	Lunch	
	14.00	LX Focus	
	18.00	Dinner	
	19.00	Sound balance (Quiet Time)	Sound, Scenic Artist
		Paint call	
	22.00	Call to end	
Fri 24th August	09.00	LX Dark time	Director, Lighting Designer, LX, SM, Construction
	10.00	LX Plot	
	13.00	Lunch	
	14.00	LX Plot	
		Wardrobe Van arrives (Construction to help unload)	
	17.00	Dinner	
	18.00	LX Plot	
	22.00	Call to end	
Sat 25th August	09.00	Sound plot	Director, Sound Designer, SM,
	13.00	Lunch	
	14.00	Sound plot	
	18.00	Dinner	Full Company, Creative Team, SM, Construction
	19.00	Scene change rehearsal	
	22.00	Call to end	
Sun 26th Aug		No Call	
Mon 27th August	09:00	Cast into costume	Full Company, Creative Team, Technical Teams
	10.55	Half hour call	
	11.30	Technical Rehearsal	
	13.00	Lunch	
	14.30	Technical Rehearsal	
	18.00	Dinner	
	19.30	Technical Rehearsal	
	22.00	Call to end	
Tues 28th August	09.00	Cast into costume	Full Company, Creative Team, Technical Teams
	09.55	Half hour call	
	10:30	Technical Rehearsal	
	13.00	Lunch	
	14.30	Technical Rehearsal	

	18.00	Dinner	
	19.30	Technical Rehearsal	
	22.00	Call to end	
Wed 29th August	09:00	Work on stage	Full Company, Creative Team, Technical Teams
	12.25	Lunch	
	13.25	Actors warm up and fight call	
	13.55	The Half	
	14.30	Dress 1 (Photographer in attendance)	
	17.55	Dinner	
	18.55	The Half	
	19.30	Dress 2	
	22.00	Call to end Work on stage	
Thurs 30th August	09:30	Work onstage	Full Company, Creative Team, Technical Teams
	12.55	Lunch	
	13.25	Actors warm up and fight call	
	13.55	The Half	
	14.30	Dress 3	
	17.55	Dinner	
	18.55	The Half	
	19.30	Performance 1	
	22.00	Call to end	

ALL CALLS AND TIMES ARE SUBJECT TO CHANGE AND ALTERATION

Stephen Taylor 1ST AUGUST 2017 V1

SITZPROBE

A Sitzprobe might take place in the theatre once the orchestra have had their sound balance. This is the first time the cast come together with the musicians and they will sing through the musical numbers. It is run by the musical director and, if it is done in the theatre, the sound department will have a chance to balance the actors' levels with the musicians. The actors will usually have microphones for this.

PAINT CALL

A paint call might also happen at this point. This is when the scenic artist can come into the theatre and paint anything on the set that they need to. This can be just a touch up if something has been damaged during its journey to the theatre, or it

OPPOSITE AND TOP: A production schedule.

RIGHT: A dock door, which is used for bringing the scenery in and out of the theatre.

All departments working together during a fit-up.

The lighting department have to bring the bars down to stage level to rig them.

A sitzprobe taking place. This is the first time the cast sing through the musical numbers with the musicians.

could be that the floor needs to be painted once the set is in place.

LX Focus

This is the time given over to the lighting department, so they can focus each light according to the lighting designer's wishes. Stage management and crew may need to be on hand to position any scenery and stage management will help set up the furniture for each scene, as they will know the show better than anyone else. It is a good idea to ask the lighting designer in advance of the focus what they would like to be there, as they don't always want the correct furniture, which can then be in rehearsals for the cast to use. When LX are working onstage and they need to light the stage, this is known as dark time.

Stage management will move into the theatre just before the scene-change rehearsals or the plot sessions. They will do their get-in, bringing all the props and furniture into the space and then setting-up the wings. This often happens during the lighting department's focus sessions, so have a torch to hand so the set-up can be done in limited light.

At this point check that a quick-change area has been arranged, which is equipped with a mirror, a clothes rail and, where possible, is carpeted. The wings may also need carpeting, depending on the cast's footwear, as their footsteps can sometimes be very loud backstage.

Take the time to check that fire exits are kept clear, that there is enough space for everyone to move around safely and that any obstructions are clearly marked. We mark obstructions with white gaffa so that they can be visible in the dimmed lighting backstage. This includes the edges of risers on stairs, or treads as they are referred to in theatre, entrances on curtains, any technical equipment at head or foot level and any sightlines that may be crucial.

Sightlines are imaginary lines that are used to work out what can be seen from the extremities of the auditorium. They are vital when setting props and furniture backstage as you do not wish an audience to see them until they are meant to. If you can see the audience when you are standing in the wings, they will be able to see you.

Scene Change Rehearsal

If you are lucky to have time in the schedule you may have been allocated a separate scene change rehearsal. This rehearsal is done in working lights and it is attended by the cast, director, designer, SM team and any crew needed to work on the scene changes.

It is an opportunity to work through the scene changes without the complication of the technical aspects of the production, and is really beneficial for saving time in the technical rehearsal. By running through the scene changes before the technical rehearsal, tricky moments can be worked through and problems ironed out.

Even if there are no scene changes, this is still a good opportunity to get the cast onto stage for the first time and become familiar with the scenery and the practicalities of it as well as becoming acquainted with the theatre space itself. This will include their journeys to and from their dressing rooms and the space they will inhabit during the production. The next time they will be onstage is during the tech, when they will have a million and one other things to think about, such as trying to find their light, getting used to being in their costumes and remembering their lines.

LX and Sound Plots

The LX and sound plots are the sessions when each department, working with the director and DSM, start to put cues in the book, ready for the technical rehearsal. These will not be the final cues as they will almost definitely change during the tech, but they are a starting point. The plots are attended by the individual technical departments, stage management teams and crew. The acting company do not attend.

The lighting designer will use their plot time to go through each cue point with the director and build the lighting states. The DSM will mark the cue points in the book and the rest of the stage management team will be onstage moving any piece of furniture, directing any scenic changes and standing in for the actors. This process, known as walking the lights, is so the lighting designer and director can see what the lighting state looks like with someone in it.

The sound plot is for the sound designer to play any cues for the director and to decide on any sound levels. The DSM is usually the only member of the stage management team who is directly needed for the sound plot as they will need to write the cues in the book. Having said this, the SM team should make use of the time for their own work as the stage will typically be empty. They can quietly set up the wings and complete any items that may need to be finished.

The production desk will be set up. This is a work station that is set up in the centre of the auditorium for the creatives to sit at during the production period.

The lighting board is usually moved to the desk for the production week and the DSM will join the creatives here during the plot sessions.

> **TOP TIP**
>
> If a single member of the SM team is working it is a good idea for the rest of the team to be using the time too. This fosters a good teamwork ethic: in the immortal words of the three musketeers, 'all for one and one for all'.

The director, DSM and lighting designer sitting at the production desk during the lighting plot.

Technical Rehearsal

The technical rehearsal is the time when everyone employed on the production comes together to work through the play from start to finish, refining all the technical elements, the blocking and every aspect of the production. It should, primarily, be about the practicalities of the show, such as the lighting, sound, scenery and costume. It will also include the actors' entrances and exits, how they work within the set and the mechanics of it. The actors will also need to work with any specific props so they can get used to how they function and they will practise with the timings of any sound or lighting cues that may affect them in the performance. The director will want to take the opportunity to work with the cast, especially if the technical teams are resolving a problem. They will be using every minute that is available to them.

Ordinarily the play is worked through in its entirety in a methodical way. This ensures that all the departments and the acting company are content with the results and that the creative team are satisfied that their vision is being met. It can be, by its nature, a very slow process and you will find that people often get distracted and lose focus. It is up to the stage management team to keep on top of the rehearsal and ensure that everyone is ready to restart when necessary and prepared for what is coming up.

For the stage management team, it is a very hectic time and arguably the best session in the whole process. It is the first time the SM team will be doing their cues and working through the show properly.

The stage manager will be running the rehearsal, usually standing on the front of the stage, directing and leading it. They will be liaising between the director and DSM and informing everyone where in the production they will be working from, what sequence is being done and what needs to be reset, in terms of scenery, furniture and costumes. An SM needs to be aware of every eventuality. For example, an actor may be having a problem with their costume or a piece of scenery may not be working as it should. It is also important to know if a scene needs to be performed in full for an actor to practise a quick change.

The DSM will be under a great deal of pressure, cueing for the first time, keeping on top of any changes and stopping when something has not gone according to plan. They will be liaising with everyone technically on cans (portable headsets) and operating cue lights for everyone to take their cues. The DSM runs the show at this point and nothing should happen without their say-so and their cue.

The SM, DSM and director should create a triangle of communication so that the information can flow between them. The director and DSM can often not see each other during a tech and therefore the stage manager is used as the go-between, relaying information between them.

The ASMs, meanwhile, will be running the wings, making sure that the cast are happy with everything, that they have their props and are ready for the next section of the tech. They will be supporting the SM, solving any problems if they can and, where possible, taking the initiative themselves rather that interrupting the SM. They will be standing onstage when the action is stopped, so they can listen to any changes and be there for the SM if they need them. Thinking ahead is vital. Props need to be prepared for the next scene and the ASMs need to be proactive in resetting the stage with the props and

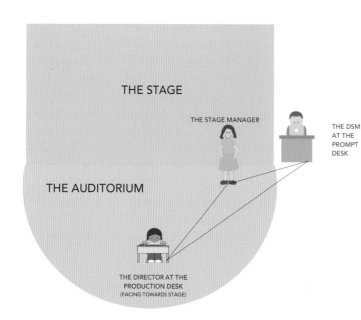

THE STAGE

THE STAGE MANAGER

THE DSM
AT THE
PROMPT
DESK

THE AUDITORIUM

THE DIRECTOR AT THE
PRODUCTION DESK
(FACING TOWARDS STAGE)

The triangle of communication between the director, SM and DSM during the tech.

BOTTOM: The cast and stage management listening to the director during the technical rehearsal of *Bury Fair*. DESIGNER: RUARI MURCHISON

furniture so everything is in the correct place when the action is taken back to a previous point.

Portable headsets are usually worn by the stage management team during this session to help with the smooth running of the tech. This is so that they can talk to each other when needed and pass on information. The stage manager, however, still needs to relay everything out loud as not everyone has headsets. The director will get restless and anxious if they do not know what is happening and this can make for a very tense technical rehearsal, which is no fun for anyone.

In certain circumstances, when you are running out of time, the director may decide to do a cue-to-cue. This is when you work from one technical cue to another and skip the dialogue so that you can move through the production quicker. This does not just mean the technical departments' cues, but should also include any of the actors' actions, such as entrances, quick changes or sequences that are technically demanding, such as fights.

Dress Rehearsal

Once the technical rehearsal is completed, the next process is the dress rehearsal. If you are lucky you will have more than one. This is when the show is performed, hopefully without stopping and with all the elements of the production completed and as the audience will see them. It will be the first time that everyone will be able to run their cues, perform their show and see how everything works together. They are still working rehearsals, though – for example, the lighting designer will be adapting their lighting states and changing cues with the board operator and DSM as the action is happening.

The creative team will be watching and taking notes on anything that doesn't work or any changes they wish to make. After each dress rehearsal, the creative teams will give out their notes verbally. This feedback is often given in two sessions, one to the technical teams and one to the acting company. The DSM attends both. Each person or department will be given the opportunity to speak so they can mention any errors that were made and any aspects of the show that didn't work. It gives everyone the chance to voice concerns or raise changes that need to be made for the next dress rehearsal or performance.

The director will give the actors any notes in their session. While these will mostly be creative notes to do with their individual performance, it is vital that the DSM is present in case there are any technical issues that are brought up that affect the acting company. For example, an actor may not have stood in the correct place to be lit and the DSM can relay that to them, or an actor may have not been able to hear a sound cue so the DSM will note this and pass it onto the sound department. As in rehearsals, the DSM is the link between the acting company, creatives and technical teams and this continues throughout the process.

THE RUN

Once the final dress rehearsal has taken place it will be time to perform the production in front of an audience. Everyone will be doing their job in full. The SM will be running the stage, keeping everything running smoothly as per the director's wishes. The DSM will be cueing the show, calling front of house and backstage announcements and keeping everything to time. The ASMs will be running the wings, helping with scene changes and making sure that the props and furniture are set and looked after.

Previews

Depending on the scale of the show, there may be preview performances. These are in front of an audience and are a precursor to opening night. The audience will probably have paid a reduced rate

DRY TECH

A dry tech is a technical rehearsal without the cast. It is a time for the technical departments to work through all the technical elements of a production without the actors being present. You may sometimes hear the technical teams refer to an 'actors' tech'. This is not necessarily a positive phrase as it means that the technical time is being used more for the actors and their work, which can lead to frustration for the technical teams.

A performance of *The Children's Hour*. DESIGNER: RICHARD BULLWINKLE

for their tickets and be aware that the production is still a work in progress.

Opening Night

Often known as press night, this is classed as the first official performance of the completed show. It will be attended by the press and it is this performance that is reviewed. The producers will be present, along with the creative team and invited guests. They can often be red carpet affairs, as this is the opportunity for the producers to make everyone aware of the show's opening and to try to attract publicity. This is usually followed by the first night party or drinks, when the producers get to thank everyone who has been a part of the show, the backers, the production company, theatre staff, technical teams, the actors and everyone else who was involved.

Once the show has opened there is rarely time to relax. Not only will you be making sure that the show runs smoothly but understudy rehearsals will need to take place, cast changes may occur and there will probably be regular maintenance to attend to. The stage management team become the eyes and ears of the management and will continue to keep up the standards that have been set by the creative team. A get-out will happen after the final show, ensuring the theatre is completely clear.

TASK

Choose a play to work from so you can practise each element of stage management as you read through this book. Each chapter will offer some ideas at the end, which will relate to the elements just discussed.

STAGE MANAGEMENT TOOLS

As a stage manager, you should have a decent tool kit with you at all times. This doesn't mean just the kind of tools you will find in a DIY store, although these are imperative to have, but other items too. As with boy scouts, a good member of stage management is always prepared and over the years items will be added to kits as new requests crop up on every show. For example, I always carry around spare hearing aid batteries ever since I worked with an actor who asked if I happened to have one. I may never need them again but I have them if I'm asked. Below is a list of the very basic kit you should invest in.

Vital SM Tools
- Stopwatch
- Personal watch
- Torch – either a head torch or a Maglite, which is smaller and more directional. If you attach a lace onto it and cover the end in LX tape, you can hold it in your mouth without damaging your teeth if you need both hands to do a task

Mark-Up Tools
- Scale ruler – this should be metric as we mostly work to 1:25, sometimes 1:50
- Chalk
- Numerous rolls of different-coloured PVC tape (known as LX tape)
- A cloth tape measure
- Chalk line

Stationery
- Notepads
- Plain A4 paper
- Numerous pens and pencils – 2B pencils are good for DSMs, especially if you write hard on the page
- Lever-arch file (a DSM may need more than one)
- Scissors
- Hole punch
- Hole re-enforcers
- Highlighter pens
- Sticky notes
- Stapler and staples
- Pencil sharpener
- Glue
- Superglue
- Sticky tape
- Ruler – a flexible one helps you put cues in the book neatly
- Marker pens
- Sticky tac
- Elastic bands
- Paper clips
- String

First Aid Kit
- Plasters (hypo-allergenic)
- Safety pins of various sizes
- Antiseptic wet wipes

Miscellaneous Items
- Sewing kit
- Needles
- Fabric scissors
- Shoelaces
- Pocket knife
- Scalpel
- Suntan lotion for outdoor productions
- Umbrella for outdoor productions
- Matches
- Lighter
- Screwdrivers – Phillips and flat-head
- Hammer
- Hot glue gun and sticks
- Batteries
- Phone chargers
- USB cables
- Glow tape
- Gaffa tape
- Basic DIY tools for prop makes and maintenance

3

THE ASSISTANT
STAGE MANAGER

Put in the simplest terms, the assistant stage manager, commonly shortened to ASM, is responsible for props, furniture and set dressing. From the beginning of the process, they supply the rehearsal room with the items that are needed to assist the actors and director in their work. This includes sourcing the actual items required for the production and then the movement of them backstage and onstage. Alongside this, the ASM supports the rest of the SM team and the production as a whole. This can mean anything from running errands for the director who can't leave the rehearsal room, to making tea for the lead actor who has been in the rehearsal room all morning without a break. While the ASM is the lowest ranking member of the team and is often called upon to do menial tasks, the job is vital to the production and it takes energy, stamina and resourcefulness as well as a creative leaning and a strong attention to detail to fulfil the role.

PRE-REHEARSALS

This may sound obvious, but the first thing to do as an ASM is read the script. From this reading, make a provisional prop and furniture list. It is important to list everything that may be needed so it can be discussed with the designer. A good ASM will put a lot of time and thought into this first list, thinking about the questions that will need to be asked to

OPPOSITE: The truck set with the props and set dressing ready for a performance of *Oliver* by Grange Park Opera. DESIGNER: RICHARD KENT

obtain the right item for the production in terms of look and detail. With regular updating, the same list should see you through the whole process from rehearsal to the show and then the final source sheet.

Provisional Prop and Furniture Lists

Props and furniture may be mentioned in the stage directions or in the character's words. While some items will be obvious, think 'around' an item. The list should include everything needed for the production that will be the ASM's responsibility to find. For example, if the stage directions mention that a character has an umbrella and that they have just come inside to shelter from a storm, you would deduce that an umbrella needs to be sourced. But what else might be required and added to the list? For the audience to believe the action, the umbrella would need to be wet, or look wet. To achieve this a water trigger sprayer could be added to the prop list so water can be sprayed over the umbrella (and the actors) just before it is used, or it may require something more permanent. This could be achieved by placing small blobs of glue from a hot glue gun on the umbrella, so add a glue gun and glue sticks to the prop list.

Notes then need to be added. These should include any information gained from the script, any assumptions that can be made and any further ideas or questions that may need to raised. In terms of the umbrella, add which character uses it but there may not be any other details. To help find the correct umbrella, further questions need to

PYGMALION
ACT ONE

Covent Garden at 11.15 p.m. Torrents of heavy summer rain. Cab whistles blowing frantically in all directions. Pedestrians running for shelter into the market and under the portico of St. Paul's Church, where there are already several people, among them a lady and her daughter in evening dress. They are all peering out gloomily at the rain, except one man with his back turned to the rest, who seems wholly preoccupied with a notebook in which he is writing busily. The church clock strikes the first quarter.

THE DAUGHTER *[in the space between the central pillars, close to the one on her left]* I'm getting chilled to the bone. What can Freddy be doing all this time? He's been gone twenty minutes.

THE MOTHER *[on her daughter's right]* Not so long. But he ought to have got us a cab by this.

A BYSTANDER *[on the lady's right]* He won't get no cab not until half-past eleven, missus, when they come back after dropping their theatre fares.

THE MOTHER. But we must have a cab. We can't stand here until half-past eleven. It's too bad.

THE BYSTANDER. Well, it ain't my fault, missus.

THE DAUGHTER. If Freddy had a bit of gumption, he would have got one at the theatre door.

THE MOTHER. What could he have done, poor boy?

THE DAUGHTER. Other people got cabs. Why couldn't he?

Freddy rushes in out of the rain from the Southampton Street side, and comes between them closing a dripping umbrella. He is a young man of twenty, in evening dress, very wet around the ankles.

THE DAUGHTER. Well, haven't you got a cab?

FREDDY. There's not one to be had for love or money.

THE MOTHER. Oh, Freddy, there must be one. You can't have tried.

THE DAUGHTER. It's too tiresome. Do you expect us to go and get one ourselves?

FREDDY. I tell you they're all engaged. The rain was so sudden: nobody was prepared; and everybody had to take a cab. I've been to Charing Cross one way and nearly to Ludgate Circus the other; and they were all engaged.

THE MOTHER. Did you try Trafalgar Square?

FREDDY. There wasn't one at Trafalgar Square.

THE DAUGHTER. Did you try?

FREDDY. I tried as far as Charing Cross Station. Did you expect me to walk to Hammersmith?

THE DAUGHTER. You haven't tried at all.

THE MOTHER. You really are very helpless, Freddy. Go again; and don't come back until you have found a cab.

FREDDY. I shall simply get soaked for nothing.

THE DAUGHTER. And what about us? Are we to stay here all night in this draught, with next to nothing on. You selfish pig--

FREDDY. Oh, very well: I'll go, I'll go. *[He opens his umbrella and dashes off Strandwards, but comes into collision with a flower girl, who is hurrying in for shelter, knocking her basket out of her hands. A blinding flash of lightning, followed instantly by a rattling peal of thunder, orchestrates the incident]*

THE FLOWER GIRL. Nah then, Freddy: look wh' y' gowin, deah.

FREDDY. Sorry *[he rushes off]*. THE FLOWER GIRL *[picking up her scattered flowers and replacing them in the basket]* There's menners f' yer! Te-oo banches o voylets trod into the mad. *[She sits down on the plinth of the column, sorting her flowers, on the lady's right. She is not at all an attractive person. She is perhaps eighteen, perhaps twenty, hardly older. She wears a little sailor hat of black straw that has long been exposed to the dust and soot of London and has seldom if ever been brushed. Her hair needs washing rather badly: its mousy color can hardly be natural. She wears a shoddy black coat that reaches nearly to her knees and is shaped to her waist. She has a brown skirt with a coarse apron. Her boots are much the worse for wear. She is no doubt as clean as she can afford to be; but compared to the ladies she is very dirty. Her features are no worse than theirs; but their condition leaves something to be desired; and she needs the services of a dentist].*

THE MOTHER. How do you know that my son's name is Freddy, pray?

THE FLOWER GIRL. Ow, eez ye-ooa san, is e? Wal, fewd dan y' de-ooty bawmz a mather should, eed now bettern to spawl a pore gel's flahrzn than ran awy atbaht pyin. Will ye-oo py me f'them? *[Here, with apologies, this desperate attempt to represent her dialect without a phonetic alphabet must be abandoned as unintelligible outside London.]*

THE DAUGHTER. Do nothing of the sort, mother. The idea!

THE MOTHER. Please allow me, Clara. Have you any pennies?

THE DAUGHTER. No. I've nothing smaller than sixpence.

THE FLOWER GIRL *[hopefully]* I can give you change for a tanner, kind lady.

THE MOTHER *[to Clara]* Give it to me. *[Clara parts reluctantly]*. Now *[to the girl]* This is for your flowers.

THE FLOWER GIRL. Thank you kindly, lady.

THE DAUGHTER. Make her give you the change. These things are only a penny a bunch.

THE MOTHER. Do hold your tongue, Clara. [To the girl]. You can keep the change.

THE FLOWER GIRL. Oh, thank you, lady.

A page of script from *Pygmalion*.

OPPOSITE: A provisional prop and furniture list taken from the page of script.

PYGMALION
PROVISIONAL PROP AND FURNITURE LIST

PERIOD; LONDON EARLY 1900'S

Act	Sc	Pg	Prop/Furniture	Character	Setting	Notes	Source	Cost	Photo	Done
1	1	1	Umbrellas	Various		"Torrents of rain" How many? Colours? Who has them, ladies or men? Size? Are they wet, or do they need to look wet?				
1	1	1	Water sprayer			To spray rain if needed – Freddy's umbrella is dripping and his trousers are "very wet around the ankles"				
1	1	1	Glue sticks			For glue gun to make rain droplets on umbrellas				
1	1	1	Bags	Various	Personal	Handbags and bags for the pedestrians? Colour? size? How many? Is this SM or Wardrobe?				
1	1	1	Theatre Programmes?			It is 11.15pm so maybe some of the pedestrians have been to the theatre.				
1	1	1	Notebook	Man	Personal	"writing busily" in notebook. How big is it? Pocket sized or larger? Does it need to fit in his pocket? What material is it bound in, leather? Colour, Black? Is it new or old? Lined & colour of paper? White or vellum				
1	1	1	Writing implement	Man	Personal	Is it a pen or pencil he's writing with?				
1	1	1	Umbrella	Freddy		"dripping". Man's umbrella. Colour? Size?				
1	1	1	Basket	Flower Girl		Full of flowers. How big? Shape, circular, square, oval? Does it have a handle? Is it wicker? Colour? Dirty? How old is it? Her costume is dirty, old and worn.				
1	1	1	Flowers	Flower Girl		In the basket. How many are there? Violets are mentioned. How are they tied? Ribbon or string? Artificial or real?				
1	1	1	Flower ties.	Flower Girl		Flowers tied up with ribbon or string?				
1	1	1	Money - Sixpence	Clara	Personal	In her a purse? In her bag? Sixpence as she says- "Nothing smaller than a sixpence"				
1	1	1	Purse	Clara	Personal	In her bag. What size? Does it have a zip or clasp? Material? Colour? How much money is in it?				

P Clark , ASM, Pygmalion pygmalion@ email.co.uk 06545 663 664

V1 12/5/2017

be asked. Think about the character: let's say he's a businessman who's just finished work, in which case it's probably a man's umbrella. But what colour is it? Is it a walking or a folding type? What if the character says that he borrowed it from his wife – the umbrella would then be very different.

REHEARSALS

On the first day, the ASM will assist the rest of the stage management team with the mark-up and then help to set up the rehearsal room for the meet and greet, model box showing and read-through. You may be asked to make tea and coffee and get any items that the director needs, such as tennis balls for getting-to-know-you games or something to play a DVD or music on.

During the model-box showing and read-through it is important to take detailed notes, as this will assist in refining the provisional prop and furniture lists. This will help to tailor the list to the specific production that is being worked on. The director and designer will have already decided where they are setting the play, in what period of time and the look and concept they wish to portray. For example,

when reading a play by Shakespeare it's easy enough to write all the props down that are mentioned, but it's only once you have seen the model box that you can start being more specific. I have worked on a number of productions of *A Midsummer Night's Dream*, all set in different periods and locations, including a hotel in the 1920s, various locations in the 1950s, Ancient Greece and one in the future. In each of these productions the prop may have been the same type but the specifics altered dramatically. A cup is a cup, but it will probably look very different in each production or time period.

Make detailed notes and take photos of the model box so the provisional lists can be updated in preparation for the meeting with the designer. You will look very silly if you ask the designer what colour sofa he would like on the set when he has already stated in his model box showing that everything on the set is royal blue.

First Meeting with the Designer

Have an initial meeting with the designer as soon as possible in the process, after allowing enough time to first do some research on the period and

LAMDA's 2013 production of *A Midsummer Night's Dream*. DESIGNER: PHILIP ENGLEHEART. PHOTO: RICHARD HUBERT SMITH

LAMDA's 2016 production of *A Midsummer Night's Dream*. PHOTO: RICHARD HUBERT SMITH. DESIGNER: JAMES TAYLOR

obtain picture evidence of examples. You will then have a definite idea of the items you are looking for and the specifics. Go through each item from the beginning of the script to the end.

Rehearsal Props and Furniture

Rehearsal props and furniture items are invaluable and it is imperative to get items into rehearsals as soon as possible. Aim to have a stand-in for each item on the provisional list before the end of your first week of rehearsals. The actors will need to start using the items, working out what they need them to do and how to use them. There is no need to put the actual prop in and it doesn't matter if it's not close to the real item, so long as the cast can use it in a similar way. For example, you may not have a walking stick that they can use, so a walking umbrella will work just as well. Do ensure that the DSM knows what each item is supposed to be. Write a removable label on the item so it is obvious.

Keep up to date with the rehearsal props too. As soon as a new prop is requested get something into rehearsals for it, otherwise the actor and director may forget that they requested it and decide they do not need it. This, frustratingly, often happens with an item that you have spent ages looking for or it's the prop you lovingly made and are most proud of – getting a stand-in into rehearsals immediately reduces the risk of your efforts being wasted.

TOP TIP

Pictures, photos and visual aids are vital tools for an assistant stage manager and should be used throughout the process. It is better to show your designer and director a picture of an item that you think is right rather than trying to explain how something should look by words alone. Using visual images means that everyone involved can see whether it is the right item and will not need to try to imagine what is being described.

Using Rehearsal Notes and Calls

The deputy stage manager should issue rehearsal notes after every rehearsal. These are any comments that have been noted from the rehearsal room, including requests that the director or actors have made and any other changes that everyone on the production needs to be aware of. Notes should be divided into departmental headings. The ASM will need to read the stage management notes, but it is important to read

every note, not just the SM ones. As a member of the stage management team you will be expected to know all aspects of the show and another department's notes may affect you and your job. For example, if the costume department gets a note about a character being very poor and their clothes being dishevelled this could be relevant to a prop that character will have.

Get into the habit of reading rehearsal notes on a daily basis (if the show is rehearsing daily). It should be the first thing you do. This will ensure that if something has been added or decided against it can be acted on quickly. You may have planned to go and buy an armchair and if you haven't seen the note to say the armchair is now a stool, you would be wasting valuable time and possibly money. Action everything mentioned as quickly as possible, edit the prop and furniture lists regularly and keep on top of rehearsal props and requirements when they are listed.

Calls also come out on a daily basis. Read them to ensure that all the props are in the rehearsal room for that day's scenes. If a scene is being rehearsed, the more you ensure rehearsal items are available to the director and cast, the easier your job will become. Find out if a prop is required and also how the item is to be handled. It is important to remember that, in the theatre, items aren't always used for the purpose they are made for.

TOP: Rehearsal props set up for a rehearsal.

A rehearsal room set up with props and furniture.

Production Meetings

These are meetings that are attended by the technical teams and the creatives. Actors are not present. It is an opportunity for the key production personnel to be in one room and to discuss any important information that everyone should know about. It is a chance to raise questions, get answers and for decisions to be made. From a stage management point of view the meetings should never become a glorified prop meeting. After all, the lighting designer isn't bothered about the twenty-four-piece dinner service that you have been asked to find, what colour it is or what size the dinner plate is. That information, while vital to the designer and SM team, is not relevant to other departments. The points that should be raised are those that affect other departments. For example, a practical light that you are sourcing will affect the lighting department, who need to make it work, the construction department who may need to fix it to the set and the designer and director, who need to choose what it will look like.

Use the production meeting to raise questions on items that the creatives are being indecisive about or have differing opinions about. By raising these issues in the meeting, the parties involved can talk to each other rather than you becoming the go-between. It is also a good forum in which to raise questions that you need an answer for and that you may need others to witness. If costume have agreed to supply all the bags for a production, for example, you might like them to confirm this at the meeting when there are others present to hear it.

Understand How a Prop Works

It is important to fully understand how a prop is expected to perform in a production and its specific usage. As previously mentioned, a prop isn't always used the way it was intended, so often it will need to be adapted to fulfil the creative expectations. An umbrella may be used in a variety of ways. It may actually be an umbrella, but what if it is used as an oar for a boat, or part of a dance routine and needs to have confetti coming out of it when opened. Get this information from the rehearsal notes, from conversation with the DSM and the actors involved and by visiting rehearsals as much as possible and watching the action.

Chairs being used as a design feature. Everyday items are often used in an unusual way. DESIGNER: PHILIP ENGLEHEART

Setting up the Rehearsal Room and Learning the Prop Setting

An ASM will not be based in the rehearsal room the entire time. Hopefully the stage management office will be in a room adjoining but this is not always the case. Attend rehearsals on a daily basis, once if not twice to help the rest of the team set up the room ready for the rehearsal and to help clear up at the end of the day. You may be lucky enough to have a dedicated room for your rehearsals but, more often than not, the room will be a shared space that often holds other regular events, such as taekwondo evening classes or private hires for birthday parties.

If the room is shared, the SM team's organization and packing skills will be employed on a regular basis. While this can be a trial at times, the advantage is that the ASM will have extensive opportunities to learn the prop set-up and the show. Even if the room is not shared, the ASM still needs to know the set-up so they can take responsibility for this when they get into the theatre. Try to keep the setting exactly the same in the theatre as it has been in rehearsals to help the actors find their items easily when they are in the theatre.

Take the opportunity to get to know the cast and director, ask any questions about the props or furniture and get the answers immediately. Stay and watch some of the rehearsals once you have set up and go early in the evening to see some more. In this way, you will begin to piece together the show.

Working on Rehearsal Runs and Compiling Cue Lists

When the director schedules a run in the rehearsal room, go and watch it. Sometimes this happens very late in the process so keep an eye on the rehearsal calls for earlier sequences that may be run. If a scene is being run that is particularly prop heavy, go and watch it to see how the actors use the props. See how they treat the props and, if they are heavy-handed or use the objects in a very physical way, you may need to actor-proof your props to make them last longer.

Use the DSM's setting list to set up for the runs, then start to update it to make them your own. Ensure the right props are in the rehearsal room for the actors to use and pay close attention to props that may be missing or may not be working as they were intended to.

Don't just sit and watch the runs as if you were an audience member. While it is good to enjoy what the actors are doing, remember why you are there. It's a good idea to watch it from the side that you will be working on, if you have been assigned a specific wing to run. You can then start piecing together cues that you may need to undertake in the show. It will also allow you the opportunity to foresee any issues that may arise. For example, one of the actors may exit carrying a tray loaded with crockery then have a quick change and re-enter minutes later carrying a suitcase. You then know that you will need to be waiting in the wings for the actor to take the tray off them, help with the quick change then hand them the suitcase. The ASM's job is to assist the actors backstage and by thinking ahead you will be able plan any cues you will have.

Props and Furniture Actuals

The main aim for the ASM during the rehearsal period is sourcing the actual props and furniture that

---

TOP TIP

To-do lists are incredibly useful for all the team, but especially handy for ASMs. At first you may just have a list of items to source, but once you have found the item you will have to collect it and then you may need to adapt it. Once you have completed the item you will need to show it to the director and designer for their approval. By using separate sheets with different headings such as 'to buy', 'to make', 'to source', 'to collect' and 'to approve', you can ensure that every element of your work is checked off and you don't miss anything.

will be used during the production. Any avenue of sourcing is open – hiring, buying, borrowing or making. Imagine you are a detective and think around a prop. The most obvious solution is not always the best, cheapest or easiest one. Your first instinct may be to go to a hire company for the 1950s sofa you need, but check your local second-hand furniture stores or local paper as there may be something suitable there. It may need re-upholstering to help achieve the desired look, but it will be the cheapest option and it also means the item can be added to your stock. You may even be lucky enough to find your local second-hand furniture store is willing to lend it, which would be even better.

When you are sourcing items, prioritize your time effectively. You may have a scene change rehearsal first, in which case the furniture will be first on your hit list. Think about what actuals would be beneficial to get into rehearsals. As long as the rehearsal item is the right size and does what it is meant to, then it is not a priority to get the actual item into rehearsals. There will be items that are imperative to get to the actors as quickly as possible so they can rehearse with them and get used to how they work. This will help speed the process up when you are in the theatre. It gives the actors and director the chance to work with an item, experiment with it and see if it is fit for purpose and does exactly what they want it to do. The ASM will also be able to see it in action too and amend and adjust it if it needs it.

Furniture and scenic elements that were sourced by the ASMs for *The Sea*. DESIGNER: NANCY SURMAN

Props that were sourced for a production of *The Sea*. DESIGNER: NANCY SURMAN

Thanks, Adverts and Complimentary Tickets

Find out from the producers if there are any resources that are available to you to help when

trying to borrow items. If you are able to offer an advertisement, thanks in the programme or any complimentary tickets, these can act as a carrot to whoever you are talking to and can help you negotiate a better outcome.

If you phoned up a furniture company local to where the production was being put on in order to borrow an armchair, the company might be

> **TOP TIP**
>
> Use a light spray of hairspray to dull a shiny surface. A large mirror, for example, could cause a reflection from the stage lighting and affect the audience's view by shining directly into their eyes.

The SM team sourced the furniture, props and picture frames for a production of *The Sea*. DESIGNER: NANCY SURMAN

more agreeable if you could offer an advert in the programme. They may feel that it was a good exchange as it would be free advertising for them and they may gain business from an audience member. Two complimentary tickets for a show would be another good incentive: it doesn't matter what type of production it is – amateur, professional or school – the offer of a night out to the theatre is often appealing. If you happen to have a well-known actor in your company you will find this a great help when trying to borrow items or get discounts. Name dropping at this point is advantageous. A free ticket to see Judi Dench onstage in a sold-out production will work wonders for your propping.

THE PRODUCTION PERIOD

Clear the Rehearsal Room

Once the final rehearsal in the rehearsal room is over, you need to help pack up in readiness to transport the props and furniture to the theatre. Ensure that everything has been packed and included. The best way of doing this is to have a checklist of items. Maybe use the setting list or have boxes pre-marked. It's the easiest thing to forget an item, especially a personal prop that an actor has used for the whole rehearsal period. Always check the toilets and kitchen for missing props.

Make a collection of items that need to be returned to the stores – that is props and furniture that were used for rehearsals only. Rather than taking them to the theatre it's best to get them back to where they belong. There is no point in cluttering the wings with surplus props.

Before the mark-up is removed, double-check that any furniture positions that have been made in the rehearsal room are transferred to the ground plan. They will be needed as soon as you get to the theatre to mark the furniture in readiness for the scene change rehearsal and plot sessions.

Get-In

The first day at the theatre the team will be unpacking the items, equipment and tools: this period is known as the get-in and fit-up. Usually, by the time stage management are called, the set, lighting and sound rigs will be up and the team will be working around the other departments to set up the wings, prop tables, onstage settings and set dressing.

As you will see in later chapters, it is often a jigsaw puzzle backstage and you need to ensure that the furniture is placed in the most convenient place, leaving enough room for the safe movement of personnel, set and show requirements and the fire exits are clear.

Use the time to set up the prop tables, clearly marking the items so they can be easily found and are accessible. Take the opportunity to finish any makes and generally make sure everything is completed.

A well laid-out prop table.

Scene Change Rehearsal

The scene change rehearsal is the first time the cast will have been onstage. It is a great opportunity for them to become familiar with the set and for the stage management team, crew, designer and director to work through any scene changes without all the other technical teams present. It helps iron out any issues that may arise and can often help the technical rehearsal run smoothly. Furniture should be prioritized in this rehearsal and it is imperative to have the actual items present so the finer details can be worked through, such as how many people it takes to carry a table offstage and if it will fit through the entrances and exits. Hopefully this will be a formality, as you will have planned well and thought through the logistics of transporting items when you were propping.

This rehearsal is usually done in working light and with no sound. The ASM will follow their cue sheet, running the wings and generally assisting the stage manager, who, at this time, will be running the rehearsal from the stage. Try to keep an eye on the crew as they will not know the show and may need assistance.

Plotting Sessions

There are two main plotting sessions – lighting and sound – and the ASM should be available for both of these.

LIGHTING PLOT

This is when the LX designer, director and set designer go through each scene and build the lighting state slowly, putting cues in the book with the DSM and making sure they have a starting point for the technical rehearsal. The ASM will be moving furniture and props and helping with scene changes. They will also be expected to 'walk the lights'. This means being onstage and standing in for the actors so that the creative team can check that the actors will be lit and that the feel of the production is achieved.

For an ASM this can feel like a long and non-productive day as a lot of the time they will be standing or sitting still. It always comes at the wrong time in the process as it is the time when props need finalizing and getting ready for the tech. However, it should not be a wasted session for stage management as they can work on props while still walking. Are there any non-messy jobs that still need to be completed, paper props that need finishing or any sewing or knitting that can be done?

TOP TIP

When you walk the lights for an LX plot you should look downstage so that your face can clearly be seen. The DSM will tell you where to be positioned so that the actors' blocking can be replicated. You will be asked to move around the set. Try to keep looking into the auditorium when you are walking around so that the director and lighting designer can still see your face.

The stage management team working during the plot. The SM and ASMs are onstage while the DSM is at the production desk.

BELOW: Two ASMs working on props during a plot session.

Sound Plot

While not usually directly required for this session, the ASM should attend on the basis that if one of the team is working (in this case the DSM – *see* Chapter 4), the others should be too. It is a good opportunity to finish the prop setting, prop makes and any messy, quiet jobs. While the stage will be in use for the sound plot, it is done in working light so the ASM can dress the set, adding detail such as curtains and ornaments, paint props or flameproof items. Remember to check with the sound department that this is OK, though, as it is their session and they should not be disturbed.

If there are any practical sound items, such as a working radio, this is a good time to hand it over to the sound department so they can check it is working. The ASM may also be required to read in for an actor so that sound levels can be checked or sound effects such as reverb can be worked through.

The Technical Rehearsal

The technical rehearsal is the time when every detail of the show is worked through. It is a notoriously slow process but within the stage management team there is rarely time to relax or take stock. Make sure everything is set up as it will be for the shows. Props tables need to be set, drinks and food made and actual items used and working accurately. Take the time to make sure the actors know how their props work as this will ensure the tech runs as smoothly as possible. This is the last time the actors will be able to get used to a prop before the dress rehearsal.

During the technical rehearsal, the ASM will follow their cue sheet, running the wings and helping with scene changes and quick changes. Ensure everyone knows what is happening and that you are prepared for anything that is coming up. It is important to remember that the crew, dressers and any casual staff will not have been involved in the rehearsals and will therefore not be familiar with the show, its order or requirements. You will have to be the eyes and ears of the team, as the DSM is working from the prompt corner and the stage manager is running the rehearsal from onstage.

The ASM needs to keep listening, both backstage and onstage. Listen out for any conversations the actors or technical teams may be having about upcoming issues and, if possible, try to resolve them before they become a problem. When the action stops onstage, come out onto the stage to hear what the director is saying, whether it's a change in prop setting or a cueing change for a piece of scenery. Be visible to the stage manager so they can delegate to you, whether it is to remark furniture, find a prop that is needed onstage or to find an actor who needs to be onstage. It is also important to document any changes that happen, whether it is the setting of props on a prop table, actors entering in different places or scene change requirements.

DURING THE RUN

Once the technical rehearsal is complete there will be dress rehearsals, previews and the shows. The ASM will need to work the wings as they have on previous rehearsals and, once again, follow their cue sheet, help with scene changes and quick changes and do their best to keep the show as polished and identical to the opening night as possible. Props can be reset for the next day afterwards. Keep them well maintained so that they are always in good working order.

Cue Sheets

Compile a cue sheet, which is a comprehensive and detailed list of all the things to be done during the show, whether it is helping with a quick change, setting a prop, being part of the scene change or paging a door for a cast member to enter quickly. It is used as a reminder to what cues there are but also will be used if someone else needs to take over and perform your cues for you. The more straightforward the cue sheet is, the easier it will be for someone else to follow.

Setting List

Produce a setting list that records where every item is set, whether it is onstage or offstage or in a dressing room, so that everything can be set identically for every performance. It must include every little detail, such as how much sugar is in a sugar bowl, or the exact setting of a tray. As with the cue sheet, it should be easy to follow so that someone else can set the show up correctly.

Scene Changes

An ASM will be involved in scene changes, whether moving furniture or setting and clearing props. Work with the crew and assist them in their job, overseeing them to make sure the changes run smoothly. The ASM will be responsible for the finer setting details, the exact positions for props and furniture, leaving the larger set items to the crew.

Quick Changes

The ASM supports the costume department with quick changes. This may include 'torching' the change so both the actor and the dresser can see to tie a shoelace or to fasten any buttons, or handing an actor a prop or giving them some water. In certain circumstances, in a small production, the ASM may be the only one available to help with a change.

Stage management and crew working on a scene change.

Book Cover

The ASM may have been engaged as an ASM/book cover. This will mean that if the DSM is unwell or off for any reason they will get the opportunity to call the show and undertake the DSM role.

Appearances

Another role that may fall to the ASM is to undertake a small walk-on role or an appearance onstage. This happens less often than it used to, but you should be aware that you may be asked. Obviously if you have signed a contract that states you will appear onstage you must fulfil that, but if you are asked at a later date and you

> **TOP TIP**
>
> It is important not to rush into moving up in the stage management hierarchy before really experiencing the ASM job fully. Take the opportunity to learn on the job and from others in the team. Watch how those above you approach their roles, as once you become a deputy stage manager, you won't often have the opportunity to work with another DSM again and the same goes for being a stage manager – usually there is only one DSM and SM on a production.

do not feel comfortable then you should not feel obligated.

POST PRODUCTION

The Get-Out

Start to clear your props during the final performance – the quicker you pack the items, the sooner other departments, such as lighting and construction, can get on with their jobs. Obviously, the items onstage cannot be cleared until the show is finished, but a good ASM can have the majority of the backstage props packed up by the time the curtain comes down. Naturally, this is dependent on how many cues they have during the show. Packing quickly is a really useful skill to have mastered, especially when you are working on a tour, as the sooner you leave the theatre after the last performance the sooner you can be on your way to either the next venue or to your home for a much-needed day off with your friends and family.

Prop Source Lists

Source lists are important and should be handed to the stage manager to be included in the book

Props being prepared for packing during a get-out.

as a record of the production. The source list is a detailed record of each item, where it was acquired from, whether it was bought, hired or borrowed, how much it cost, its size, colour and any specific details. If there is a specific contact person, include their phone number, the website or their email details and include a photo of the item. All of this information is vital if the producers want to remount the production at a later date or if they sell the show to another company. In the West End, for example, shows are often sold to another production company, who will then take it on tour.

Returns

If the production is completely finished, return all the props and furniture that have been borrowed or hired and ask the stage manager where the rest of the items will go. Sometimes items that have been bought specifically for the show are put into storage, but they can be sold or just thrown away.

Programmes and Thank-You Letters

It is important to do thank-you letters to all those companies that have helped with any props or furniture items. While you may never need the item you borrowed from them again, they may be able to help you with another item for a future production. Don't forget, due to the freelance nature of the job, your contacts are vital to you. You will be helping your career and yourself, as an individual, if you take the time to nurture and thank those who have helped you do your job effectively. If you also offered an advert or a thank you in the programme you should send a copy of this with your letter too.

Being an assistant stage manager is a rewarding role. There is a fair amount of creativity within the job, from prop and furniture sourcing to making items, and you will get to interact with everyone on the stage. You are an integral part of the production.

TASK

Try writing a prop and furniture list for your chosen production. List the details of what you are looking for, the questions you will need to ask your designer and director before you start sourcing and any other information you can glean from the script. Don't forget to include any items that aren't mentioned but may be needed, and do some research on each item too.

PROPS AND FURNITURE SOURCE SHEET

ANOTHER COUNTRY

Summer, 1932, An English Public School

SC	PG	FURNITURE/PROP	NOTES	SETTING	SOURCE	COST	PHOTO
1	7	5 Chairs	Wooden	2 around table 2 SL wing 1 SR wing	National Theatre Prop store Kennington Park Business London SW9 6DE 020 7820 1358	£12.40 each for 5 weeks	
1	7	Noticeboard	900 wide x 700 deep Typed Rules (See script page 19 for rule 16B), Club details, Society Timetable, Library details Cream paper Some typed (check font) some hand written in blue. With Pins	CS panel	Board Construction Green material – A1 Fabrics, Shepherd's Bush Papers – Make Drawing Pins from stock	£8.00 for Board £5.99 for Green Felt	
1	7	Binoculars	For looking out of window (glasses) With strap	Bennett DS Window Seat	Borrowed. Mr Arnold Arnold Antiques 27 Hammersmith Road W14 3ST 020 87421234	£0	
3	30	Beds x5 Mattress' come with beds	Black, made up of three parts 1980x800 Velcro straps sewn onto mattress to attach to beds	In a row, Backstage	Trading Post 1 Beresford Avenue Wembley Middlesex HA0 1NU 0208 903 3727	£106 each for 5 weeks	
4	43	Lamp	'Carefully shaded for reading' Small light with brown cable, will be plugged into wall	Offstage side of table	Ebay.co.uk Modern 15-Classic-Bankers-Table-Desk-Office-Light-Lamp-in-Brass-Green-	£23.49	

* SOURCE, RESEARCH, HIRE, BUY, BORROW, MAKE AND MAINTAINS PROPS AND FURNITURE.
* REHEARSAL AND ACTUAL ITEMS

THE ASSISTANT STAGE MANAGER

* SUPPORTS THE REST OF THE TEAM, MEETING UP AT LEAST ONCE A DAY

IN REHEARSALS

* HELPS WITH THE MARK UP
* ATTENDS THE READ THROUGH, MODEL BOX SHOWING AND MEET AND GREET AND TAKES NOTES
* ATTENDS AND RUNS THE PROP AND FURNITURE MEETINGS
* KEEPS UP TO DATE WITH REHEARSAL NOTES
* SETS UP THE REHEARSAL ROOM, LEARNING THE PROP AND FURNITURE SETTING
* KEEPS THE PROP AND FURNITURE SETTING LIST UPDATED
* UNDERSTANDS HOW THE PROP WORKS
* WORKS ON THE RUNS
* STANDS IN FOR AN ACTOR
* WATCHES AS MUCH OF THE REHEARSALS AS YOU CAN
* KEEP A LIST OF THANKS FOR THE PROGRAMME
* ARRANGE COMPLIMENTARY TICKETS FOR ANYONE WHO HAS HELPED WITH PROP BORROWING
* RUNS ERRANDS

POST PRODUCTION

* WORKS DURING THE GET OUT, PACKS THE PROPS AND CLEARS THE STAGE QUICKLY
* RETURNS PROPS AND FURNITURE
* COMPILES A PROP AND FURNITURE SOURCE LIST
* THANK YOU LETTERS
* SENDS THE PROGRAMME TO ANYONE THAT HAS LENT PROPS OR HELPED

PRODUCTION PERIOD

* CLEAR THE REHEARSAL ROOM, PACK THE PROPS AND FURNITURE AND USE A CHECKLIST
* HELPS TRANSFER THE FURNITURE MARKS TO THE GROUNDPLAN
* RETURN REHEARSAL PROPS
* DOCUMENTS ALL PROPS AND FURNITURE SETTINGS AND MAKES DETAILED PLANS
* USES THE SETTING LISTS AND KEEPS THEM UPDATED
* WALK THE LIGHTS
* KEEP LISTENING AND ALWAYS BE AWARE OF CHANGES
* CHECK THE CREW, DRESSERS AND ACTORS ARE READY AND WHERE THEY SHOULD BE
* RE-SET THE STAGE DURING THE TECH

THE RUN

* RUNS A WING, AND LOOKS AFTER THE PROPS AND FURNITURE
* PERFORMS A SHOUT CHECK
* COVERS THE BOOK
* WORKS ON SCENE CHANGES
* HELPS WITH QUICK CHANGES
* APPEARS IN A PRODUCTION
* ATTENDS AND WORKS ON UNDERSTUDY CALLS

The ASM's job roles.

OPPOSITE: A prop source sheet for *Another Country*.

4
THE DEPUTY STAGE MANAGER

The deputy stage manager, DSM, is the eyes and ears of the production and therefore the hub of the show. They are responsible for compiling the prompt copy, which holds all the production's information. They work in the rehearsal room with the director and the actors and they relay information between the director, the other creatives and the technical team. In the theatre, they cue the production and ensure everyone is kept informed of what is happening at all times. There is a lot of paperwork involved in this role.

A good DSM will enjoy working closely with directors and actors and have a good working knowledge of the other technical departments, so they can understand what everyone else's requirements are. To be a successful DSM you need to be excellent at multi-tasking, staying calm, patient and unflappable.

PRE-REHEARSALS

Before rehearsals begin it is really important to do some preparatory work as, once rehearsals start, there will be a lot of paperwork to compile and send out and the DSM's focus will be in the rehearsal room.

Create the Prompt Copy, the Bible or the Book

The prompt copy, bible or book is the document that the DSM uses from day one to the end of the production. It is a vital up-to-date copy of the script, which contains the actors' moves, set changes, technical cues, costume information and every detail pertaining to running the show. It is a comprehensive record of the production and everything should be noted down in it. It is indeed the 'bible' of the show and is the property of the producers.

To prepare, obtain a copy of the script printed on A4 paper, single-sided. If you are doing a musical it is best to include the piano score for the musical numbers rather than relying on just the script, as it will be easier to pinpoint the cue points on a score. If you are working on an opera or ballet you will usually need to work from the score alone. Then make up the page that is going to be placed opposite the script. It should have three columns: one for blocking, one for cues and one for the notes about the cues. A book is made up differently depending on whether you are right-or left-handed – *see* Chapter 8.

Scenic Breakdown

The scenic breakdown is an important document that will be used throughout the process. This document is a comprehensive page-by-page breakdown of which character appears on each page of the script. It will help you when preparing the rehearsal calls and working out any quick changes and the timings of them. It is a working document that can be amended at any time. If the director decides a character will appear at a different point it can be added to the document.

OPPOSITE: The view from a prompt desk onto the stage.
DESIGNER: NANCY SURMAN

UNCLE VANYA
ACT TWO

The dining room of Serebrakoff's house. It is night. The tapping of the watchman's rattle is heard in the garden. Serebrakoff is dozing in an arm-chair by an open window and Helena is sitting beside him, also half asleep.

Serebrakoff: (Rousing himself) Who is here? Is it you Sonia?

Helena: It is I.

Serebrakoff: Oh, it is you, Nelly. This pain is intolerable.

Helena: Your shawl has slipped down. (She wraps his legs in the shawl) Let me shut the window.

Serebrakoff: No, leave it open; I am suffocating. I dreamt just now that my left leg belonged to someone else, and it hurt so that I woke up. I don't believe this is gout, it is more like rheumatism. What time is it?

Helena: Half past twelve. (A pause)

Serebrakoff: I want you to look for Batushka's works in the library to-morrow. I think we have him.

Helena: What is that?

Serebrakoff: Look for Batushka to-morrow morning; we used to have him, I remember. Why do I find it so hard to breathe?

Helena: You are tired; this is the second night you have had no sleep.

Serebrakoff: They say that Turgenieff got angina of the heart from gout. I am afraid I am getting angina too. Oh, damn this horrible, accursed old age! Ever since I have been old I have been hateful to myself, and I am sure, hateful to you all as well.

Helena: You speak as if we were to blame for your being old.

Serebrakoff: I am more hateful to you than any one.

Helena gets up and walks away from him, sitting down at a distance.

Serebrakoff: You are quite right, of course. I am not an idiot; I can understand you. You are young and healthy and beautiful, and longing for life, and I am an old dotard, almost a dead man already. Don't I know it? Of course I see that it is foolish for me to live so long, but wait! I shall soon set you all free. My life cannot drag on much longer.

FOH CLEARANCE

LXQ 34 } GO
SND G 12 }

VISUAL
AS LXQ 34 IS COMPLETE
USL G/L } GO
DSR Q/L }

VISUAL
AS HELENA SITS ON SOFA
LXQ 35 GO

VISUAL
AS HELENA SWITCHES LAMP ON
LXQ 36 GO

Blackout & Houselights out 5 secs
FOH music out 3 secs

Serebrakoff enters
Helena enters

LX state up 6 secs

SB NT USL
H NT DSR

① H ↑ → + SB

② H → + USR TBL

③ H → + SB

④ H → + USR desk

⑤ H puts lamp on

Lamp on snap

⑥ H ↓ SL CH.

REBECCA
ACTORS SCENIC BREAKDOWN

Character	Act 1 Scene 1																		
	5	6	7	8	9	10	11	12	13	14	15	16	17	18	19	20	21	22	23
Frith	▓	▓			▓	▓	▓										▓	▓	
Mrs Danvers					▓	▓		▓						▓	▓	▓			
Beatrice Lacey	▓	▓	▓	▓				▓	▓	▓	▓								
Giles Lacey	▓	▓	▓	▓				▓	▓		▓	▓	▓	▓					
Frank Crawley			▓	▓				▓	▓	▓	▓	▓	▓	▓					
Robert					▓	▓	▓	▓											
First Maid					▓	▓													
Second Maid					▓														
Maxim De Winter						▓	▓	▓	▓	▓	▓		▓	▓		▓	▓	▓	▓
Mrs De Winter						▓	▓	▓	▓	▓	▓						▓	▓	▓
Jack Favell																			
Second Footman																			
Mr Coleman Fortescue																			
Mrs Coleman Fortescue																			
Colonel Julyan																			
William Tabb																			

Character	Act 1 Scene 2															
	23	24	25	26	27	28	29	30	31	32	33	34	35	36	37	38
Frith	▓	▓						▓	▓							
Mrs Danvers										▓	▓		▓	▓	▓	▓
Beatrice Lacey																
Giles Lacey																
Frank Crawley				▓	▓	▓	▓									
Robert		▓														
First Maid	▓															
Second Maid	▓			▓												
Maxim De Winter							▓	▓	▓	▓	▓	▓				
Mrs De Winter	▓	▓	▓	▓	▓	▓	▓	▓	▓	▓	▓	▓	▓	▓	▓	▓
Jack Favell				▓												
Second Footman																
Mr Coleman Fortescue																
Mrs Coleman Fortescue																
Colonel Julyan																
William Tabb																

D Smyth
DSM. Rebecca
smythd@email.co.uk   06754 532 413

V1 26th April 2017

An actors' scenic breakdown that shows when actors appear in the play page by page.

OPPOSITE: A page of a book that the DSM works from.

Rehearsal Risk Assessment

It is really important to compile a rehearsal risk assessment before rehearsals start, as accidents can happen at any time. Think about the risks that could occur and provide control measures to limit these risks. The DSM assesses the rehearsal period only. Unfortunately, it is a reality today that we could, as individuals, be liable for injuries and accident, so this is a vital document to protect yourself as well as everyone else.

Prepare a generic risk assessment for every show, including factors such as vocal or muscle strain if the actors aren't warmed up properly, illness if an actor has to eat during the course of the production or the possibility of injury if they are required to stand on a piece of furniture. Pay attention to everyday risks, such as an actor burning themselves on a hot kettle in the rehearsal room or the procedures required in the event of an emergency evacuation. Once these risks have been listed, think about the specific items that are relevant to the production, such as if a fight is mentioned, or if the script mentions a character climbing a ladder.

At this point, you probably won't know what the set looks like or what other requirements the director will have in the rehearsal room. There may be pieces of set in rehearsals, especially if the set has different levels or there might be moving furniture. These risks can be added to the risk assessment as they arise. As with most of the paperwork produced, the risk assessment is a working document that is amended throughout the process.

Scene Synopsis

The scene synopsis is a basic précis of the story of the piece. It is best to divide it into acts and scenes, depending on how the playwright has broken it down. Try to remember the Ws when writing this: **when** the action takes place, for example the period or year; **where** the action takes place, for example the geographical location and

A rehearsal room showing different levels and obstacles – a good example of why a risk assessment must be compiled.

if it's in, say, a character's bedroom or a school; **who** is in the scene; and finally, **what** happens. It is important to be brief as it may be used at a later date for the programme. You will not want your audiences to know exactly what happens before they see the show.

Provisional Prop and Furniture List

Whilst it is the ASM's job to prepare this list, it is useful for the DSM to produce one too. Working in rehearsals, the DSM will need to set up each scene and ensure the actors are using the correct rehearsal props. They will also need to add to this list when items are added throughout the rehearsal period.

Sound, LX and Costume Lists

It's useful to break down the items that are listed in the script to give you an idea of what requirements are originally listed. Again, you will add to these as rehearsals progress, but it helps everyone to have the same starting point. Costume quick change lists are especially useful from the start of the process so any timing problems can be flagged up early on.

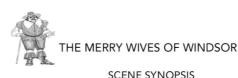

THE MERRY WIVES OF WINDSOR

SCENE SYNOPSIS

Act One
Scene 1

Shallow, Slender, Sir Hugh Evans, Page, Falstaff, Bardolph, Pistol, Nym and Anne Page - Pages House in Windsor.
Falstaff talks with Slender and the local parson. Slender mentions he wants to marry and Evans suggests Anne Page. Evans insists that Page and the Host of the Tavern form a committee to settle the disputes. Shallow and Evans say the marriage to Anne has been proposed.

Scene 2
Sir Hugh Evans and Simple -Page's House Windsor.
Evans sends Simple, Slender's servant, to Dr Caius' house with a letter for his housekeeper. Mistress Quickly tries to encourage Anne Page to marry Slender.

Scene 3
Falstaff, Host, Bardolph, Pistol and Nym - A Room at the Garter Inn.
Falstaff plans to seduce Mistress Ford and Mistress Page. He has written letters to them. Pistol and Nym decide to tell Ford and Page of Falstaff's intentions.

Scene 4
Mistress Quickly, Simple, Rugby, Doctor Caius and Fenton - A room in Doctor Caius' House.
Mistress Quickly tells Simple that she will assist in Slender's proposal. Dr Caius arrives and Quickly hides Simple in the cupboard. Dr Caius finds Simple who tells him why he is there. The doctor is angry because he wishes to marry Anne Page himself. Caius writes a letter challenging Evans to a duel.

Act Two
Scene 1
Mistress Page, Mistress Ford, Ford, Pistol, Nym, Page, Mistress Quickly, Shallow and Host - Page's House.
Mistress Page and Mistress Ford read Falstaff's letter. The two women plot revenge and employ Mistress Quickly as their messenger to Falstaff. The women's husbands find out about Falstaff's plans. Ford bribes the Host to introduce him to Falstaff as "Brook".

Scene 2
Falstaff, Pistol, Robin, Mistress Quickly, Bardolph and Ford - A room at the Garter Inn.
Quickly delivers messages from the wives to Falstaff. Mistress Page wants a meeting but Mistress Ford makes an appointment for that morning. Quickly leaves, and Ford, disguised as 'Brook', arrives. 'Brook' gives Falstaff a gift of money and confesses that he has fallen in love with Ford's wife. He then asks Falstaff to seduce her, Falstaff accepts.

Scene 3

Doctor Caius, Rugby, Host, Shallow, Slender and Page –A field near Windsor.

As Dr Caius waits for Evans to start the duel, the Host, Shallow, Slender, and Page appear. All but Slender leaves who pines over Anne Page.

Mary Grant.
DSM
Merry Wives. MW@email.co.uk 06543 332 442

A scene synopsis, which is a précis of the play.

 SUCKER PUNCH

Cast Headshots

Milly Roberts
Becky

Jonathan Ajayi
Leon

Noah Anderson
Ray

James Clarke
Tommy

Elliot Edusah
Troy

Harry McMullen
Charlie

Beki Mpala
Squid

Norman Fox, DSM
Suckerpunch
SP@email.co.uk 06754 532 413

Cast Contact List and Cast Photo Sheet

Get the cast's contact details from the producers or the production manager. It is often the responsibility of the DSM to compile a cast contact list and issue it. It should include phone numbers and email addresses and, if relevant, agent addresses. You often find that well-known actors will only include their agent's details as they will not want all and sundry to be able to contact them directly. It is important, however, that the stage management team have their personal phone numbers in case of emergencies. Their postal addresses may also be useful in case you need to post scripts or contracts.

The cast contact list should also include the contact details of stage management, the creative teams, any vocal or movement coaches and possibly the wardrobe and wigs department. Always check with the creative team, especially the director, whether they are happy to have their phone number on the sheet. Directors often do not want to be contacted directly by the actors as they have spent all day working with them and may not want to receive calls at the end of the day.

Produce a cast photo sheet. This is a really useful document for all personnel to have so they can

Hayfever

CAST CONTACT LIST

NAME	ROLE	PHONE NUMBER	EMAIL ADDRESS
CAST			
Samantha David	Myra Arundel	06876 525 416	Sdavid@email.co.uk
Janine Green	Sorel Bliss	06986 526 872	jgreen@email.co.uk
Martina Holland	Jackie Coryton	06521 642 123	martinehol@email.co.uk
Claire Randall	Clara	06987 625 765	randallc@email.co.uk
Helen White	Judith Bliss	06754 413 324	Helenw@email.co.uk
John Hardcastle	Richard Greatham	06543 567 789	Johnh@email.co.uk
Robert Norman	David Bliss	06422 112654	robnor@email.co.uk
William Roberts	Sandy Tyrell	06423 111 222	wroberts@email.co.uk
Jack Tucker	Simon Bliss	06453 444 222	jackt@email.co.uk
CREATIVES			
Carol Phillips	Director	06543 657 987	carolph@email.co.uk
Frank Salmon	Designer	06098 075 647	franksal@email.co.uk
Claudia Samuels	Assistant Director	06712 530 650	clauds@email.co.uk
Janet Monks	Vocal Coach	06927 654 812	janmo@email.co.uk
Maggie Prince	Movement Coach	06965 052 752	mags@email.co.uk
Terri Unwin	Wardrobe Supervisor	06678 765 452	terri@email.co.uk
Greg Hunter	Fight Director	06524 126 970	greghunt@email.co.uk
STAGE MANAGEMENT			
Ben Bean	Company Manager	06534 489 007	bean@email.co.uk
Roger Humphries	Stage Manager	06543 123 456	humph@email.co.uk
Sarah Todd	Deputy Stage Manager	06879 987 654	todd@email.co.uk
Oliver Wilson	Assistant Stage Manager	06098 978 908	wilson@email.co.uk
Jenny Jones	Assistant Stage Manager	06425 750 918	jjones@email.co.uk

Sarah Todd
Deputy Stage Manager
06754 532 413   hayfever@email.co.uk

OPPOSITE: A cast photo sheet showing the actors' headshots and the characters they are playing.

RIGHT: A cast contact sheet with the contact details of the cast.

TOP TIP

Ensure you include the phrase 'subject to change and alteration' on any document that specifies a time. In the theatre industry timing is important but, due to the nature of the work, it is not always possible to keep exactly to a schedule. If you use this phrase you will ensure that no one can get disgruntled when they were called for a certain time but rehearsal didn't start until an hour later. It is also a good idea to send out all the paperwork as a PDF as well as a word document. The majority of people now own smartphones and PDFs can be read much more easily on them.

get to know the cast really quickly. Get the actors' headshots from the producers, as they will have received them for the programme.

You will need to contact actors before rehearsals start so they know what the call for the first day is. However, it's best not to issue the contact sheet until you have checked the actor's details in person with them on the first day.

Rehearsal Call for First Day

The stage manager will contact the director to find out what the first day requirements are, what time the actors are called and who else will be needed. It is the DSM's responsibility to issue a rehearsal call for the first day and to include a map to ensure that everyone knows where the rehearsal room is – not just the cast, but the technical and creative teams as well.

REHEARSALS

First Day of Rehearsals

On the first day, the DSM will help the rest of the team set-up the rehearsal room, putting out enough chairs for the company, creatives and the technical teams. They will also help organize tea and coffee facilities, set up a table for themselves and the director and a table for the designer to show the model box.

Mark-Up

The DSM may need to help the rest of the team with the mark-up. This is done as soon as possible and often happens on the first day before the meet and greet. The DSM should always know the mark-up well as they will be the one in rehearsals working with it. Have a copy of the ground plan in rehearsals so it can be referred to if any questions are asked about the size of the set or specific measurements. Be clear about how the set works, which way doors open, how set pieces appear onstage, if they are pushed or automated and how they function. The DSM can then answer any questions that arise in the rehearsals and also, very importantly, pre-empt any changes that may need to be made in advance of working in the theatre.

Meet and Greet, Read-Through and Model Box Showing

The DSM will ensure everyone is present before the session starts. Once the meet and greet has taken place, the designer will talk through the model box and the ideas and concepts behind the scenic elements of the production. It is important that the DSM takes comprehensive notes as they will need to set up the rehearsal room every day for all the different scenes and settings of the play and pass the correct information on to the cast and directors. The DSM will also need to be familiar with all the specific details so they know what to add to notes. They will also need to inform the director of any conflicting issues or differences – for example, knowing which way a door or a trapdoor is hinged may affect the way the actors work in rehearsals and may require the blocking to be altered accordingly.

The DSM should issue model box notes with the first day's rehearsal notes so that everyone has the details and, if anyone was missing, they are aware of what was discussed. The DSM should also take as many photos as possible to help jog memories in the rehearsal room and to confirm details if they are asked to do so at any time.

Once the designer has talked through the model box, the cast will be asked to read through the play. It is imperative that the DSM times this to help the producers to estimate the running time of the production. This information can then be published in any marketing information and will enable the front of house management to plan ahead. It will also flag up any issues, such as if the orchestra will go into overtime. Where possible, the DSM should collate the times of each individual unit, scene or act as this will be useful to other technical departments, such as sound, who will need to know how long to make the sound cue that plays under a specific scene.

Rehearsal Calls

Rehearsals calls are the daily schedule of what is going to take place in the rehearsal room. Primarily these are for the actors, director and the creatives that are running rehearsals. However, they are issued to everyone on the production as they may wish to attend rehearsals. For example, the sound and lighting designers will need to see what has been blocked so they can work out their plans, or wardrobe may want to measure the cast. Other departments may want to ask the director questions and will need to see when breaks are scheduled so they can arrange meetings. The information included in the call is what is being

A rehearsal taking place.
GRANGE PARK OPERA

rehearsed, where the rehearsal is taking place, the call times and any other relevant information. Each call includes the date and is numbered to avoid confusion. Calls need to be issued as soon as rehearsals have finished, if not before, so that everyone has enough notice for the next day.

It depends on the individual producers, companies or venues as to how the calls are issued but this can happen in a variety of ways. Professionally the call is posted on a noticeboard at the stage door or in the rehearsal room. It is also a best practice to send the call out daily or weekly to each individual's email account. If the calls are issued in these two ways this should be sufficient for all cast members to see them. You may also be provided with a voicemail account so the cast can phone and hear a recorded message of the call.

Rehearsal calls can come in many varieties, such as music calls, dance calls, voice calls, fight calls and so on. The list is endless as productions come in so many forms. Each call should be on a separate sheet to, hopefully, avoid confusion. For example, if you were working on a musical you may have many rehearsals running concurrently: a rehearsal call with the director, a music call with the MD and a dance call with the choreographer. In this instance, you would issue three separate calls. If this does happen, in a musical the director's rehearsal will take precedence over the other calls. If the director wishes to rehearse with one cast member but the MD also wishes to rehearse with the same cast member, the director's call takes priority. This is different in other forms of theatre:

for example, in opera the director and conductor hold the same status and, therefore, have equal claims on cast members and their rehearsals.

Most of the time there will be no issues in organizing calls as the creative teams will work around each other's requirements as, after all, everyone is working towards the same goal. The problem for the DSM and the most time-consuming element is ensuring that there is no overlap and that the cast have enough time within their individual calls for travel time and breaks. The actors' scenic breakdown that has been compiled is a vital document when working out which actors are needed. The director may specify that they wish to rehearse from page numbers rather than scene numbers. Often just reading the script is not enough to see who is needed: you may have a cast member who does not speak for four pages but is imperative to the scene. A scenic breakdown shows who is onstage at any one time.

Whichever type of rehearsal call is being written, you will see from the example that the formatting is exactly the same. The information is easy to follow and clear for the reader to digest. Importantly the date and venue is listed first, then the time of the specific call, what is being rehearsed and which actors are required for that scene. You can also see the phrase 'to join'. This saves space as you only need to list those actors who are not in the previous scene rather than repeating all the actors that are required.

In all of our paperwork, when we refer to cast members rather than characters, the cast are referred to as Miss and Mr. Even if your actress is married and legally a Mrs, she will still be known as Miss. We also list ladies first, then gentlemen and alphabetically by surname. It may seem like an old-fashioned way of working, but it does means that you don't have to worry about cast billing, who is the 'star' and who you list first. At the time of writing, gender neutrality has become increasingly under discussion. Whether this will change how we address the cast or the audience is unclear at the moment, but, at present, the old-fashioned approach is still the norm. It is just one of the things we do in theatre and it is respectful and traditional.

THE MILL ON THE FLOSS

REHEARSAL CALL 10

Date: 26ᵗʰ May 2017
Venue: Holy Trinity Church Hall, TS12 3BX

TIME	TO REHEARSE		CALLED
10.00am	Act 1 Scene 17. Philip returns.		Miss Hayden Miss Taylor Miss Wills Mr Brook Mr Terry
10.45am	Act 1 Scene 13. The Auction House.	To Join	Miss Harris Mr Stuart
12.00am	Act 1 Scene 16. Romeo and Juliet	To Join	Miss Arthur Mr Brown
1.00pm	LUNCH		
2.00pm	Run Act 1		Full Company
4.30pm	Act 2 Scene 1. The debt is paid.		Miss Harris Miss Hayden Mr Brook Mr Brown
5.15pm	Act 2 Scene 2. The Whipping	To Join	Miss Taylor Mr Terry
6.00pm	CALL TO END		

ALL CALLS ARE SUBJECT TO CHANGE AND ALTERATION

K Fisher, DSM
kfisher@email.co.uk   06754 532 413

25/05/2017

A rehearsal call with details of what is happening in the next rehearsal.

Rehearsal Notes

Rehearsal notes are written on a daily basis after a rehearsal has finished and issued to the creative and technical teams and the producers, but not the cast. The notes must be sent out before 10am the following day so they can be read before the start of the next rehearsal; most DSMs tend to issue them at the end of the day while everything is still fresh in their minds. It is a comprehensive document outlining any notes, requests or changes that have been made that day. The notes are written in departmental headings so they are easy to read.

The DSM should note everything that is mentioned by any of the creatives or cast. This includes items that may only be a possibility, could be changed at a later date or have been noted previously. It is good practice to talk to the director at the end of the rehearsal to confirm which notes are to be included and that you have understood them correctly. If this doesn't happen for some reason and you are in doubt as to whether something should be noted, err on the side of caution. A note can always be amended at a later date if it is not correct, but it could be disastrous if you chose to ignore something. You could find yourself in an awkward position if the director asks where an item is and no one is aware of it because you did not inform them.

There are many items that are not clearly one specific department's domain. For example, if the director would like a light fitting on the wall, which heading would you put the note under? Your first instinct would be to note it under lighting, which is absolutely correct, but while the lighting department will make the light work, they may not have the fitting in their stock, so it will be the stage management team's responsibility to source it. It doesn't stop there, though, as the designer will need to know it has been requested as it is their set design and they will have an input into the style and look of the light. Once it's been sourced and made to work it will need then to be added to the set, which is a construction job. In short, some items may need to be added to the lists for two departments or more. In this case they are repeated, referring to the lead department's note, as you can see in the rehearsal note shown. If the item affects more than two departments it is often best to put it under a general heading, which is there for notes that everyone should read.

It is important to follow up on rehearsal notes and never to assume that something is being taken care of just because it was written down. If a specific piece of music has been requested and the scene is being rehearsed the next day, ask the stage manager to chase it up with sound. After all, the director will ask you where it is and it is preferable that you pre-empt them. Let them know you have it or explain why it isn't available. It shows the director that you are on top of all the notes and thinking ahead, and that they can trust and rely on you.

Prompting

Professionally we do not use a separate prompter, as prompting is the DSM's responsibility and is a vital element of the role. Prompting is providing an actor with their next few words when they have

TOP TIPS

When prompting it is a good idea to follow the script with your finger so you have a reference point as to where you are in the page, and regularly look up from the script so you can see the actors' faces. This will help you deduce if an actor has dried or is pausing in the action. Mark any pause that is made on the script so you don't feed an actor a line at the wrong time. There is nothing more embarrassing than prompting an actor only to be told that they were acting.

Hopefully your actors will call for 'line' or say 'please' when they forget their lines. Others may click their fingers or, on very rare occasions, swear. Whilst it is very frustrating for actors to forget their lines, neither of these last two are very polite or conducive to a good working relationship and it is worth asking the actor, privately, to call for a line instead.

Cat's eye
<u>Rehearsal Notes 12</u>

Date: Tuesday 7th March 2017

<u>General</u>
1   Mr Edwards was 10 minutes late due to public transport delays.
2   The director would like the interval to be between Act 1 Scene 6 and Act 2 Scene 1.

<u>Design</u>
1   Please see SM note 4

<u>Production Management</u>
1   See SM note 2.
2   See Construction note 1

<u>Stage Management</u>
1   The Director would like sweets for Scene 12. There needs to be at least 12 small brown paper bags and they should be full, the sweets should be wrapped as they may be thrown around in the action.
2   The trap door will be left open during Act 1 scene 2 after Sammy has entered. It will be closed as he exits in the same scene.
3   Is the fight coach available for a session with Miss Cook on Friday?
4   The Director mentioned that she would like a standard lamp in the living room set. This will be switched on by Sally during the scene.
5   A tray with a plate of sandwiches, 3 cups and saucers and a pot of tea will be needed for Act 2 Scene 10. This will be consumed. It is brought on by Mrs Dalglish and will be set on the USL table.

<u>Sound</u>
1   The director has asked that the pre-show music is a selection of classical pieces by Beethoven. Please could the Sound Designer get some into rehearsals for the director to listen to.

<u>Lighting</u>
1   Please see SM note 4
2. Act 2 Scene 6 will be at sunset. The director would like to be able to see the sunset through the window.

<u>Construction:</u>
1   The trapdoor needs to have a handle underneath so that it can open it easily. However, the trap door will remain open for some time during the scene so should not be a trip hazard. (see SM note 2 for details)

<u>Wardrobe</u>
No notes

<u>Script Changes</u>
1. Act 1 Scene 3 The line "Thomas help me up, I need to get some water" is cut.

S Watts
DSM
Cat@email.com   06754 532 413

A rehearsal note outlining any details or changes that occurred in that day's rehearsal.

A DSM working in the rehearsal room.

forgotten their lines. The DSM must be on the ball and follow the script at all times because they will look a total fool if they are asked for a prompt and are unable to come back quickly with the line.

Make certain that all the cuts, inserts and line changes are marked accurately and clearly in the script. If there are large sections that have been changed, it is easier to type, print and glue them onto the page. If possible, obtain an electronic version of the script so you can amend the script as you go, print it when you need to and issue it to other departments as needed. It is also a good idea to keep a copy of the old script so you can reference it. This is especially useful if you are working on new writing and the writer later decides the old version works best.

Always prompt in a clear, strong and audible voice but do be sensitive to the scene that is being played. Don't bellow across the room if someone has dried during a love scene. Be louder, however, if you are rehearsing a musical with a large company.

Before starting rehearsals find out from the director how faithfully they want to adhere to the script. Some will want the cast to be word perfect, others won't mind if the odd word is misplaced.

However, be mindful that wrong words can change a sentence or, in a Shakespearean production for example, can alter the metre of the text.

At the beginning of the rehearsal period the actors will be reading from the script, so this will enable the DSM to concentrate on the blocking and other elements of the job. Once the cast start to work without their scripts, known as coming 'off book', they will need more prompting and this must take priority. Towards the end of rehearsals, the company will be more secure with their lines and the DSM can once again concentrate on the blocking.

Never interrupt the rehearsal to correct a line. The best thing is to note the line error and inform the actor at a suitable moment. Try to correct them early enough so they don't learn a line wrong. Once you are rehearsing the complete show, note every error and talk to the actors personally. Actors in America are often issued with a document listing any errors, but this is not common practice in the UK and may not be well received. Talk to the actors and inform them of any mistakes.

Be aware that if an actor is missing from rehearsals, or unable to speak, the DSM will be required to read in. As with the prompting, be clear and audible and don't make a fuss about it.

It is rare for an actor to call for a line during a performance. If they lose their way, they will usually muddle through and get back on track themselves. Actors are taught to ad lib and to help each other. However, if you are asked for a line mid-performance, you must obviously try to aid your actor.

Blocking

Blocking is the actor's movement onstage and, as a DSM, we notate these moves so that we know at any time where each actor is. We also make notes of furniture positions, props that are carried by the actors and anything relating to the specifics of the production. In the prompt script, there is a separate column relating to the blocking.

There are many reasons why we keep a record of this information. The actors or director may forget what they did previously, an understudy may need to be rehearsed in, or there may be a cast change. It is an invaluable resource for the LX plot, when the actors are not present and the DSM is responsible for telling the lighting designer where actors are positioned. They will also be directing the ASMs to stand in for the actors and setting the stage with the furniture.

The way blocking is written is a form of short-hand as it would be almost impossible to note these moves with a large cast in longhand. While there are various nuances that individual DSMs may have in their notation, the same basic premise is followed and it is possible for most experienced DSMs to to read each other's blocking. As with all other stage management paperwork, it is important that it is understood and can be followed by anyone else.

Breaks

The DSM needs to keep an eye on breaks and ensure that the cast are given the appropriate lunch and dinner breaks, as well as tea breaks, and that the schedule in the rehearsal room is kept to. Overtime can be accrued if breaks are not adhered to and, unless this has been accounted for in the budget, the production manager will not thank you if breaks are infringed. It is always a good idea to pre-warn the director that they have 10 minutes left before the cast are due a break so they can finish what they are currently doing. Choose a suitable time to let them know – interrupting them in the flow of a rehearsal is not good practice.

The director and DSM during rehearsals in the rehearsal room.

Rehearsal Room

Usually, as the DSM is in the rehearsal room on their own with the cast and directors, they are responsible for the room, keeping it ordered and organized. Think of the rehearsal room as 'your room' when you're working as a DSM as nothing should happen in there without you knowing about it.

The DSM in Rehearsals

Working as a DSM in rehearsals is not the desk job that many people think it is. A lot of the time you will, of course, be sitting working on the prompt copy, but you also need to be active and proactive, getting up to change furniture positions, reset props and generally preparing for the scene ahead. While actors often help, it is the DSM's job to ensure nothing is forgotten. It can get frenetic when you are working on runs of the play at the end of the rehearsal period, as you will be following the script, prompting, checking blocking and timing the scenes as well as jumping up to move props, furniture and sometimes set pieces. You also need to be prepared to make sound effects should the action need it. For example, if a phone rings, you will vocally make the sound. It can feel awkward at first, especially if it is an unusual sound, but it is quicker and less hassle for you to make it yourself rather than play a sound effect in.

Try to work from, and refer to, the prop list, so the props are ready, and ensure that the right items are being used for the right scenes. This will help the director, actors and ASMs to work out if props are actually needed or if anything else should be added. Note any setting details about them on a setting list, which will eventually be handed over to the ASMs.

As the director mentions lighting changes, sound effects or any other technical element, write it in rehearsal notes but also document it in the prompt script. This is so that the DSM can remind the director in the various plot sessions or the tech. It will also help to write provisional cue sheets for the other departments, provide wardrobe with provisional quick change lists and the stage manager with set changes so they can plan the scene changes and master cue sheets. The DSM also needs to supply the stage manager with a list of where they would prefer the cue lights to be and a list of who need headsets.

Attend any meetings with the director and minute them. This will ensure that everyone is kept abreast of what has been discussed, as it may affect another department. If the lighting designer and director have had a meeting where they discussed a lightning effect, it would be imperative that the sound designer knew about this as they will probably need to supply a thunder sound effect. If they see this written in the minutes they will be able to pre-empt the request. You will also attend the production meeting and are often asked to take the minutes for them. It's best to try to sit next to the director at a production meeting so that you can remind them of anything they wanted to raise or answer any questions they may have.

As you can see, the deputy stage manager has a varied, complicated and time-consuming job in rehearsals. Try to think of yourself as a telephone receiver, as any information that you receive is immediately passed onto the relevant department. There should be no detail that only you are party to. Share the knowledge and ensure it is a completely open and honest process.

THE PRODUCTION PERIOD

Once rehearsals are finished and the rehearsal room is clear it is time to move into the theatre and start the process of physically putting all the elements together. It is important to work closely with the rest of the team and help them too. While the DSM has their own very important job to do, please don't forget that they know the show best and must involve themselves in prop setting and the finer details that the ASMs may not know as well.

A DSM and lighting designer in a plotting session.

Plotting

There will usually be a lighting plot and a sound plot, and these will often be the first sessions the DSM will attend in the perfomance venue. The DSM will work with the individual designers and the director to set the cues in the book in readiness for the technical rehearsal.

Let's say the first session is the lighting plot. The DSM sits at the production desk with the director, lighting designer and, probably, the lighting programmer. The stage will be set up for the opening of the show and the LD will build the lighting state. The DSM will be directing the ASMs, letting them know where they need to stand and what they need to move. Once the cues are built, add them to the book. It is advisable to ask the director whether there will be any other cues that are called at the same time. As the plots are done in layers, this will help to see the sequence of cueing and will save time for future plots and the tech. Once a state has been built, the DSM will help to change any set or furniture items, working with stage management and crew to ensure the lighting designer has the correct staging to work with.

Take the opportunity, when working on the plots, to place any standbys in the book, half a page before the cue, and any calls that will need to be made.

Calls in the Book

The DSM is also responsible for all the front of house and backstage calls that are made throughout the performance itself. Backstage calls, known as courtesy calls, are made to the actors and are usually placed two pages before the actor's entrance. They are to let the actor know they are due onstage. Again, observe the convention of calling the actors alphabetically by surname and list women first (Miss first, then Mr, A–Z). They are known as courtesy calls as the actors need to take responsibility for their timings on themselves and shouldn't rely on the calls. If there is a problem onstage and the DSM's attention is needed elsewhere the actors still need to enter at the right time and should not blame the lack of a call for them missing their entrance. In really busy shows, to save time, instead of calling individual actors, make a general call for the scenes that are coming up.

The DSM will make calls for the technical teams as well as the various front of house calls that ask the audiences to take their seats, and give them timings to curtain up and the end of the interval.

Scene Change Rehearsal

There may be a separate scene change rehearsal before the tech. This is when the actors, director, designer, crew and stage management work through the play in the working light without the other technical departments. However, sound may attend if there is music that the scene changes are dependent upon. This session allows the actors to become familiar with the set, the venue and their individual timings and journeys. It is also a great opportunity for everyone to have time to acquaint themselves with the specific set details and how everything works together, without the time pressure of the tech.

The Technical Rehearsal

The technical rehearsal is the first time the DSM will get to practise the show from the prompt desk. It is a slow process, where each sequence is worked through slowly and, often, copious times, to ensure the sequence works. As a DSM, it is a highly pressured time as you will be at the hub of the rehearsal, talking to every department, making changes in the book and ensuring that everyone is up to date with the changes before moving on to the next part. Time is always precious and you will often feel compelled to move on once a sequence is successful. It is very important that the DSM feels comfortable with what has been cued as the next time they will get to practise it will be in the dress rehearsal. Ensure that any changes are clearly written in the book so they are understandable.

The prompt corner, where the DSM works during a show. GRANGE PARK OPERA

Dress Rehearsals

The dress rehearsals are full rehearsals of the show in its entirety. They are a chance for everyone to practise the show as a complete entity and to see what works, what doesn't and if anything needs adjustments. It will be the first time the DSM will get to call the whole show and it can be a nerve-racking, yet exhilarating, process. The aim is for the show not to stop even if something goes wrong, and everyone will need to focus and concentrate. The DSM will need to think on their feet if things do go wrong and – the hardest thing of all – try to forget if they've cued something wrong so it doesn't affect the rest of the show. Note everything that wasn't correct so that it can be discussed in notes with the director and other departments.

Note Sessions

Note sessions happen primarily after dress rehearsals, but can be called by the director at any time. These are sessions where the departments come together to discuss things that have gone wrong and to amend, adjust and talk through changes.

DURING THE RUN

Calling the Production

Once the final dress rehearsal is complete, the next time the DSM sits down at the prompt desk will be to call the show itself in front of the first paying audience. The aim, at this point, is to maintain the show,

A DSM cueing at a prompt desk that is front of house rather than at prompt corner.

The prompt copy, monitors and cue lights that the DSM works with during a production.

so that every performance is faithful to the original intentions of the director and the other creatives.

Show Reports

The DSM will also be responsible for keeping notes on the times of the shows and any errors that occur so that a show report can be written. These are issued after every performance and dress rehearsal and they include details on any observations that are made and, importantly, any resolutions that have been made in respect of the error. For example, if the heel of an actor's shoe breaks and this causes them to fall over, the resolution would be that wardrobe have been informed and that they will mend or replace the shoe.

It often depends on the scale of theatre as to who actually writes and issues the show report but it is good practice for the SM and DSM to write it together. You will find, in larger productions, that it

is then forwarded to the company manager, who adds the ticket sales onto it and then issues it.

The Prompt Desk

The DSM works from the prompt desk. This is a piece of equipment with all the technical items that are needed to run the show. The DSM will use cue lights and headsets to cue the show and microphones for the backstage and front of house calls. You will also have monitors to see various views of the stage and the musical director, if it is a musical.

POST PRODUCTION

Updating the Book

Once the production has closed the DSM will need to make certain that all the show information is in one place within the book. This is the bible of the show, so it should be a comprehensive document of everything, from every department. This includes photos from the costume department, any saved discs with effects from the sound department, plans and working drawings from construction, setting lists and source sheets from stage management, plans and kit lists from lighting. Cue sheets need to be included from all departments.

The Get-Out

The DSM will also be employed to help the rest of the team with the get-out, packing props and furniture, removing set dressing and any returns that need to be made.

At any time, the DSM may need to deputize for the stage manager, as they are the next in line in seniority.

TASK

Try to write a scenic breakdown for act one of your chosen script. List all the characters and note which page they appear on. Once you have done this, why not attempt to write a rehearsal call. Choose a few sequences, add times and work out which cast members you would need.

IN REHEARSALS

* ATTENDS THE READ THROUGH, MODEL BOX MEETING AND MEET AND GREET. TAKES NOTES AND MINUTES IT.
* COMPILES PROVISIONAL CUE SHEETS FROM REHEARSALS
* ENSURES BREAKS ARE ADHERED TO
* SETS UP AND RUNS THE REHEARSAL ROOM
* WRITES AND ISSUES REHEARSAL CALLS AND NOTES
* WRITES THE BLOCKING AND PROMPTS THE ACTORS
*HELPS WITH THE MARK UP
* WRITES A SCENE SYNOPSIS, SCENIC BREAKDOWN AND REHEARSAL RISK ASSESSMENT
* ATTENDS THE PRODUCTION MEETINGS AND OTHER MEETINGS WITH THE DIRECTOR AND MINUTES THEM
* IS AWARE HOW THE SET WORKS
* COMPLIES THE CAST CONTACT LIST
* MARKS CUES IN THE BOOK AS THE DIRECTOR MENTIONS THEM
* COMMS AND CUE LIGHT LIST
TIMES THE READTHROUGH AND RUNS ETC
* CREATES THE PROMPT COPY, THE BIBLE OR THE BOOK
* KEEPS UP TO DATE WITH THE REHEARSAL NOTES AND FOLLOWS UP ON THEM
* MAKES SOUND EFFECTS IN THE REHEARSAL ROOM, DOORBELLS, TELEPHONES ETC

PRODUCTION PERIOD

* ATTENDS THE PLOTTING SESSION PUTTING CUES IN THE BOOK AND ADVISING OF BLOCKING
* WRITES FRONT OF HOUSE AND BACKSTAGE CALLS IN THE BOOK
*WRITES COURTESY CALLS IN THE BOOK
*MAKES TANNOY CALLS
* HELPS WITH PROP AND FURNITURE SETTING
* CUES THE TECH AND DRESSES FROM THE PROMPT DESK AND NOTES EVERYTHING CLEARLY
* COMPILES DRESS REPORTS AND NOTES
ATTENDS TECHNICAL AND ACTORS NOTES

POST PRODUCTION

* ENSURES THE BOOK IS UP TO DATE
* HELPS WITH THE GET OUT, CLEARNG THE THEATRE AND THE DRESSING ROOMS

* MEETS UP WITH THE TEAM AT LEAST ONCE A DAY
* WORKS CLOSELY WITH THE DIRECTOR AND ACTORS

THE DEPUTY STAGE MANAGER

* COMMUICATES WITH THE TECHNICAL TEAMS AND CREATIVES ENSURING EVEYONE IS KEPT UP TO DATE

THE RUN

* CALLS THE PRODUCTION
* ATTENDS, RUNS AND WORKS ON UNDERSTUDY CALLS.
* WRITES THE SHOW REPORTS

The DSM's job roles.

5

THE STAGE MANAGER

The stage manager is the senior member of the team onstage and is directly responsible for the rest of the stage management department and all the duties that they are expected to fulfil. Even if a company manager is employed, the stage manager will still be in charge of all the onstage requirements. They will oversee the production, ensuring all duties are covered, either undertaking them personally or delegating to the rest of the team. The paperwork involved is extensive, as they maintain the stage management budget, write risk assessments and monitor health and safety. They liaise with all the other departments, ensuring that everyone is kept informed of any production requirements or situations that arise.

You need to be highly organized and possess excellent communication skills to work as a stage manager. You must be able to remain calm and patient in trying circumstances, and a good sense of humour is a trait that will come into play regularly. If you like being in control and juggling numerous tasks at once, you will enjoy the role of stage manager.

PRE-REHEARSALS

Just like the rest of the team, the SM should read the script and make their own provisional prop and furniture list. This is important, as the SM will be working out a provisional budget, costing the props and furniture that are required and assisting the ASMs with sourcing. The stage manager also

OPPOSITE: The stage manager working onstage during a technical rehearsal.

needs to be an authority on the production almost from the start of the process, as everyone will expect questions to be answered and for the SM to foresee any problems that may occur.

Making Contact
CONTACT THE PRODUCTION MANAGER

Before rehearsals start the SM will need to contact the production manager, first and foremost, to see who the SM team are, if this is not already known. They must also find out from the PM where the rehearsal room is and, if possible, visit it. Contact the owner or caretaker of the space and find out about any requirements, rules or other bookings that will affect rehearsals. It is commonplace to rehearse in church or community halls and the SM team will often be issued with a key for the door as the venues aren't always staffed. Find out from the PM what hours the room has been booked for and whether evening and weekend rehearsals and after-rehearsal meetings can take place. Are there any groups, such as scouts or brownies, judo classes or choir practice, that use the space in the evenings or any functions booked for weekends? All of these could mean you have to completely clear the room on a regular basis.

Check to see if there is somewhere you can safely store items. Expensive props, computers or keyboards are best locked away when you are not in the building. Ascertain if a mark-up can be put down, as a few places do not like the floor to be marked with tape. A way round this is to invest in some dance flooring, put the mark-up on it and then roll it out every day. Toilet roll, bin bags, hand towels, tea cloths, tea, coffee, sugar, milk, cups and a kettle may not be supplied, in which case they need to be bought. Obtain a ground plan from the PM, so that the mark-up can be done. If it is a complicated set it is a good idea to do some preparatory work on it beforehand.

Either the PM or the producers will provide the contact details of the cast and technical teams so that contact lists can be made and everyone can be invited to the first day's rehearsal. You will also need copies of the script in case someone forgets theirs and any other scores or music that may be required.

CONTACT THE DIRECTOR

It is always best to call the director personally and to make the initial introductions on behalf of the whole SM team as the last thing they will want is for the whole team to call individually. Find out what the director wants to do on the first day, if they need anything special in rehearsal, such as a speaker to play music, and if there is anything the team can do for them before the first day.

CONTACT THE REST OF THE SM TEAM

The SM will then need to talk to the rest of the team, passing on any relevant information and giving them a call time for the first day. The DSM will need to know what the director has planned so they can issue a rehearsal call to the cast and the ASMs may need to buy items for the rehearsal room.

Technical Contact List

The SM can start to compile the technical contact list. This should include everyone's names, job title, phone number and email address. Do check that the information is correct before issuing as this will save you time and a lot of reissuing. Unlike the actors' paperwork, this is not done in alphabetical order but in order of importance, usually with the creative team first then each department starting with HOD. It is best to include the producers and theatre management in the list too. The technical contact list is not issued to the cast.

Information Pack

It is a good idea to compile an information pack, both for the rehearsal room and the theatre. This is only for stage management to use and is a quick-stop reference to anything that you may be asked about. The company may not know the area that they are rehearsing in and the SM team may be asked questions about the services and local area, such as local doctors or dentists, or where the nearest cash point or post office is. Travel information is useful, so find out about the local tubes and buses and where the nearest mainline train is. It is always good to know where the local emergency services are too, such as police stations and hospitals. Physiotherapists are especially handy to list, especially if the production is a musical or dance show.

When touring, you will find a lot of the local information is kept at the theatre in the company manager's office. However, it is a good idea to find out about travel information before getting to the venue as the company will need to know how to get to the venue and the best routes. It is a good idea to get the theatre's digs lists. This is a list of accommodations in the surrounding area. Often hotels and B&Bs will be included, but the most useful numbers are for short-let flats or rooms. Often you will find that local people advertise their

TOP TIP

If you are touring, plan in advance and book your own accommodation in plenty of time. Regulars to touring will have favourite places to stay, and the best digs, usually more self-contained and at a better price, will get booked well in advance. Remember as well that some towns and cities have more than one theatre so the accommodation may be listed in more than one theatre.

POSH

Technical Contact List

Name	Role	E-mail	Mobile
Andrew Harrison	Director	aharris@email.co.uk	06765 424 131
Fiona Read	Designer	read@email.co.uk	06875 635 817
Glenda Timms	Lighting Designer	glntimm@email.co.uk	06980 987 654
Jake Tidd	Vocal Coach	jtd@email.co.uk	06753 514 322
James Redfern	Fight Director	jimRed@email.co.uk	06754 525 342
Robert Grey	Production Manager	robgrey@email.co.uk	06909 009 880
Jeff Walters	Company Manager	Waltersj@email.co.uk	06757 665 665
Donna Stern	Stage Manager	dstern@email.co.uk	06441 533 610
Joan King	Deputy Stage Manager	joanking@email.co.uk	06556 776 888
Stephen Preston	Assistant Stage Manager	prest@email.co.uk	06911 221 662
Helen Oldman	Assistant Stage Manager	oldman@email.co.uk	06765 332 424
Matthew Boxer	Chief Electrician	boxerm@email.co.uk	06726 556 665
Stuart Palmer	Deputy Chief Electrician	stupalmer@email.co.uk	06755 456 678 06980 909 090
Sean Smith	Production Sound Engineer	ssmith@email.co.uk	06431 121 387
Sarah Redman	Sound Assistant	Sarsred@email.co.uk	06573 277 611
Alex Asquith	Production Carpenter	alasq@email.co.uk	06745 890 990
Rosie Mann	Costume Supervisor	rosiem@email.co.uk	06787 787 878
Eileen Dodds	Wardrobe Supervisor	eileendodds@email.co.uk	06009 009 887
Becky Manners	Deputy Wardrobe Supervisor	becksman@email.co.uk	06773 334 554
Charlotte Earl	Hair and Make-up Supervisor	charearl@email.co.uk	0673 554 667

J King, DSM
joanking@email.co.uk   06556 776 888

V1 20/9/2017

A technical contact sheet, which includes the creative and technical teams' contact details.

spare rooms for short-term rent. Each individual is responsible for booking their own accommodation.

Allergy Forms

Allergy forms are vital and should be written in advance of rehearsals so they can be distributed to the company to fill in on the first day. The information is important as you may need to administer first aid, deal with an emergency or accompany someone to hospital. It is vital to know if anyone has allergies. The SM team may need to provide particular food or drink for a production or the wardrobe department may need to use an alternative washing powder.

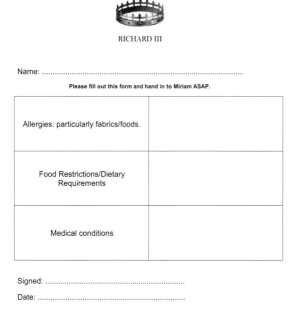

RICHARD III

Name: ....

Please fill out this form and hand in to Miriam ASAP.

Allergies: particularly fabrics/foods.	
Food Restrictions/Dietary Requirements	
Medical conditions	

Signed: ....

Date: ....

All information within this form will be kept confidential.

Miriam Alison
Stage Manager – *Richard III*
06099 980 769 maryal@email.co.uk

An allergy form is completed so that the SM team are aware of any health issues.

REHEARSALS

Preparing the Room

As mentioned previously, the SM team will need to arrive at the rehearsal room early on the first day and set up the room. There needs to be enough seats, usually arranged in a circle, for everyone to sit down – company, creatives and technical teams. Ensure that the model box is positioned in full view of everyone. Take an anglepoise light and extension lead to the rehearsal room on the first day in case the model box need some extra lighting to enable everyone to see it clearly.

Mark-Up

The SM will lead the mark-up and it is best to do it as early as possible in the rehearsal period and first thing in the morning before anyone arrives in the rehearsal room. Try to prepare and measure the ground plan before arriving on the first day as this will save time. Don't forget to bring the tools needed, the ground plan itself, scale ruler, cloth tape, chalk line, various different-coloured LX tapes to mark the floor and scissors or a knife to cut the tape.

Refreshments

Like the other members of the team, the SM must greet everyone as they arrive and help provide refreshments. It's good to have a reason to talk to everyone and to introduce yourself.

Meet and Greet, Model Box Showing and Read-Through

First, check that everyone has arrived, ask them to take a seat and then start the introductions. The SM will lead this. You may be nervous about doing this but it does not need to be lengthy. Say

A stage manager leading a meet and greet on the first day of rehearsals.

hello and welcome, then ask everyone to introduce themselves and say what their role is. The SM should start.

It is always a good idea to have asked the director how they want this session to work. Once the introductions are over, the director often likes to talk to everyone, to explain their ideas for the production and to introduce the play. Others may want the designer to start by showing the model box. Finally, the read-through will take place. Like all other members of the SM team, the SM will need to take notes, especially taking note of any health and safety requirements and elements that they may need to take responsibility for.

Once the first day is over, the SM will need to attend rehearsals on a daily basis, developing a relationship with the director and getting to know the cast. They will need to facilitate any requests that the director, company and DSM may make and, where possible, meet with the rest of the SM team at least once a day.

Rehearsal Notes

The SM must read rehearsal notes on a daily basis and keep up to date with any problems, changes or requirements that crop up.

The DSM is in rehearsals so the SM becomes the messenger between the director and the rest of the production team. This means that they must understand any notes that have been issued and must follow them up. If, for example, the director has asked for a window in the set instead of the door, the SM will first need to ensure that the designer has read this and that it is possible. They will then confirm this with the construction department. Once this change has been actioned they will then get in touch with the DSM, who will pass the good news on to the director. This chain of events is even more important if something has been requested that is not possible.

The SM will also need to relay any issues that have been raised by other departments back to the director, for example requests that cannot be met and need to be changed.

Production Period and Performance Risk Assessments

One of the biggest responsibilities of the stage manager is compiling the risk assessments and the related paperwork, such as flame, smoking and weapon plots. The DSM compiles the risk assessment for the rehearsal room, but the SM is responsible for writing risk assessments for the period in the theatre. This will include any rehearsals as well as the performances. It is likely that the SM will write two, one up to the final dress rehearsal and one from opening night onwards. This is because the risks and the people affected will change once an audience is in the theatre. More detailed documents will also be needed to outline any high-risk items and how these will be made safe. These will include any naked flames, weapons or smoking.

Petty Cash and Budgets

As the head of the stage management team, the SM is responsible for maintaining the stage management budget and looking after any petty cash that has been received. Once there has been an initial prop meeting, the team will have a clearer

Actors rehearsing a fight. The stage manager needs to compile a risk assessment for any items or activities that may cause injury, like a fight.

TOP TIPS

Update the budget every time a cost is confirmed or something has been bought. By doing this the budget will always remain correct and you will always know how much has been spent and how much money is remaining.

Never spend your own money: always use petty cash. While it is rare, productions can be cancelled or stopped for various reasons and you do not want to be in a position where you personally lose money when you aren't reimbursed.

idea of what props will be needed and the SM can submit a provisional budget to the production manager. The items should be listed individually and should include a costing, which should be an educated guess of the final price.

If, for example, a candlestick holder is on the prop list, candles and matches may also be required, and they would be listed and costed separately. You would then need to do some research, and this is where the internet is invaluable. Go onto websites and cost the items. Is the candlestick a period one? Can a modern copy be found or would it need to come from a prop hire company? Then cost the candles by working out the total amount needed. How long will they be burning

for? How many are used per show and how many shows do you have? The same is then done for the matches. If you list the three items separately, as the ASM should in the prop list, it reduces the risk of an item and its costing being omitted.

Petty cash will be handed out by the PM. This is physical cash to spend. It is not extra money on top of the budget, but a float to buy any items you need. It is vitally important to keep receipts for everything you spend, otherwise you will be liable for any shortfall. Keep a track of any petty cash that is issued to the rest of team by using petty cash vouchers, often referred to as whities. These can be bought in stationers. Get them signed and keep them with the cash.

When planning a provisional budget, do not forget to include any additional costs that may be incurred. Tools and equipment to make props, such as paint or glue, are often forgotten, as are transport or postage costs. Props need to be collected and returned and items will need to be transferred from the rehearsal room to the theatre or venue. Transport is expensive, so always include these costs unless the PM says otherwise. They may have costed transport in a separate budget, or there may be a van at your disposal or, even better, the rehearsal room is in the same building or complex as the performance venue.

PRODUCTION: The Sea
GROSS BUDGET: £600.00

DEPARTMENT: Stage Management   02.06.17

Date	Supplier	Order number	ITEM	BORROW	BUY	MAKE	HIRES	TRANS	VAT	NET
					Gross		Figures			
12/05/2017	AMAZON		Seaweed			£3.75				£3.75
	Furniture shop		Stool	£0.00						
	Homebase		Lanterns x 2	£0.00						
15/05/2017	Ebay		Haberdashery Counter		£200.00				£40.00	£160.00
	Prop store		Wicker Table	£0.00						
	Prop store		Wicker Chairs x2	£0.00						
	Prop store		Wooden Till	£0.00						
21/05/2017	Donna's dresses		x5 display dummys		£30.00				£6.00	£24.00
	Prop store		Shop door bell	£0.00						
	Frank Smith		Canvas bank bag			£0.00				
	Ebay		Umbrellas		£22.60				£4.52	£18.08
	Simon Taylor		Bike	£0.00						
	Prop store		Cup	£0.00						
	Make		Paintings			£10.00			£2.00	£8.00
	Framers		Picture frames	£0.00						
	St Lukes school		Upright Piano	£0.00						
	Prop store		Ash			£0.00				
	St Lukes school		Piano Cover	£0.00						
	Prop store		Tea Flask	£0.00		£0.00				
	National Theatre		National Furniture Hire				£207.00		£41.40	£165.60
	Shepherds Bush market		Blue Velvet		£121.00				£0.00	£121.00
	Rowing club		Punting Pole	£0.00						
	Tube -free		Newspaper	£0.00						
	Prop store		Sheet Music			£0.00				
		pm 1089	Transport					£14.85		
		pm 1200	Transport					£10.97		
		pm 1211	Transport					£21.95		
		pm 1213		£0.00	£373.60	£13.75	£207.00	£47.77	£46.00	£187.75

GROSS TOTAL £642.12
Remaining £42.12
£642.12

ABOVE: A completed budget showing the final costs for a production.

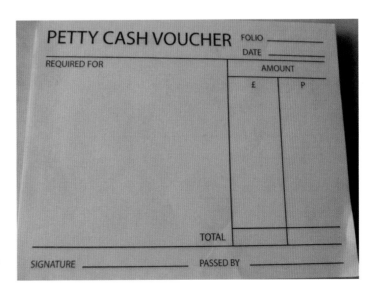

PETTY CASH VOUCHER FOLIO _____
DATE _____

REQUIRED FOR | AMOUNT
£ | P

TOTAL

SIGNATURE _____   PASSED BY _____

A petty cash voucher used to keep a record of petty cash expenses.

Transport

The stage manager is responsible for arranging any transport, either to pick up and return props or to get items between rehearsal rooms and your venue. You may need to book it yourself or give the PM the details. Always ensure you have all the relevant information, such as the full address, including the postcode, and any contact names and phone numbers. While this may sound obvious you would be surprised how often these things are forgotten. Think about what size of vehicle will be needed. Sometimes it's better to hire a larger van straight away rather than finding everything won't fit in a smaller one and having to order further transport.

Helping the ASM with Prop and Furniture Sourcing

The SM has a lot of paperwork that must take priority, but once this is done, they need to help with the props and furniture. It is a good idea to take on the more technical props, if there are any. Items such as weapons are a good thing for the SM to take responsibility for, as there will be a lot

of paperwork included and they are a high-risk item.

Arranging Meetings and Calls

The DSM will be busy in rehearsals, so it's the stage manager's responsibility to arrange any additional support staff that the director may need for the production. If there are fights in a production, a fight director will need to attend rehearsals and choreograph the sequences. The director will request other appointments to be made, such as meetings with the lighting or sound designers, or the wardrobe supervisor.

Production Meetings

The SM will attend the production meetings with the rest of the team and ask any questions on behalf of the department. Remember that it shouldn't become a glorified prop meeting; instead, raise points that will affect other departments, such as practical lamps or stage management in costume. Production meetings are also a good time to confirm any high-risk items, such as weapons, naked

A van waiting at the dock door ready for the get-out.

flames or smoking and to discuss items that the director and designer are giving conflicting or unclear answers on. In this way, other people will witness the answers and can back you up at a later date, if necessary.

Comms and Cue Lights

The sound department provide the cue lights and the means to communicate when running the show. This is usually done with either wired or wireless headsets. In theatre these are referred to as 'cans'. The specific requirements need to be issued to the sound department so they can accommodate them. It is a good idea to go through the requirements with the DSM as they know where the cue lights are best placed and who will need a set of cans. Don't forget that cue lights will be needed so the actors can be cued for their entrances and the crew can be cued for scene changes. The lighting designer will need cans for the tech and dress rehearsals.

Compiling Programme Information

Throughout the rehearsal period the SM needs to collate any information that may be needed in the programme. This includes cast and creatives biographies and their headshots. The director may

AN INSPECTOR CALLS

COMMS AND CUE LIGHT LIST

COMMS		CUE LIGHTS	
SL Wing		On the Backwall	
SR Wing		USL Door	
Flyman		USC Door	
Sound Operator		USR Door	
LX Operator			
2 x Follow spot Operators		SL Door	
AV Operator		SR Door	
3 x wireless comms for SM Team		Second level	
		SL Door	
Tech & Dresses		SR Door	
LX Designer			
Sound Designer		USL	
		USR	

Will Clough
SM. An Inspector Calls
inspector@email.co.uk 06778 556 557

A comms and cue light list that is given to the sound department so they can set the system up for the show.

also wish to include some information on the play or some background material for the audience to read. The brief synopsis that the DSM should have written may also be added. Ask the creatives and technical teams if they have any thanks they wish to include and don't forget the thanks for the props that the SM team have borrowed.

Fly Plots, Cue Sheets and Scene Change Plans

Before getting into the theatre and starting to work, the SM will need to compile initial paperwork for the show personnel to follow. It is imperative to remember that the crew are hired on a casual basis and will not have seen any of the rehearsals. They may have no idea about the production, the requirements or their involvement in the show. The cue sheets, therefore, must be easy to follow and straightforward. They should be foolproof. All paperwork must be clear and simple so that anyone could pick it up and follow the instructions.

Plan the scene changes, allocating personnel to each job. This needs to be done as soon as

TOP TIP

The director may ask for a headset during the tech so that they can talk to the DSM. This should be avoided. The director may feel that is saves time but it also puts added pressure onto a DSM. Having a director on cans may affect the relationship between the technical departments listening and how the DSM relays information and ultimately cues the show. The director may ask for a microphone instead, also known as a 'god mic'. This is a better option as then everyone can hear the director's comments.

> **TOP TIP**
>
> Make sure that the cue sheets are distributed to the crew, dressers and any other personnel in advance of a rehearsal. This is so they can read them beforehand and have an understanding of what they will be asked to do. Don't forget that they will not have been involved in any of the rehearsals, so giving them their cue sheets in advance allows them to become familiar with the show.

possible, as the production manager will need to be consulted so they know how many people need to be employed on the show. While the director often uses cast for scene changes onstage, the SM will still need to write it all down and have a clear idea of who is doing what.

Company Schedule

The production schedule is issued by the production manager and this is given to the creatives and the technical teams. The cast are not included. Once you have this, it is a good idea to compile a company schedule for the cast. Use the production schedule as a template but take off any technical sessions that are irrelevant to them, such as plot sessions, focus sessions and rig days. This will ensure that the cast get plenty of notice about any days they will be needed in the theatre and what evenings and weekends they will be called for.

Dressing Room Lists and Signing-In Sheets

Signing-in sheets and dressing room lists must be compiled. Signing-in sheets are left at the stage door as they are a clear indication of who is in the building at any one time in case of emergencies.

Dressing room lists can be a minefield. Plan well ahead and spend time thinking about the cast and who gets on with who. During the run of the production your life will be made much easier if the allocations are right. One mistake can mean constant moans from actors about the habits of other cast members and this makes for an unhappy company.

Think about who is placed nearer the stage, how many people are in each dressing room and what the show requirements are. Think about the practicalities, such as costumes or footwear or if there is nudity. Does anyone have to get wet or dirty or do they have numerous quick changes? Even if an actor is onstage for a lot of the show it would be prudent to place any of these people nearer to the stage. The closer their room is to the stage the better.

Dressing rooms should always be single sex, but if you find you are having to ask cast members to share limited space then a simple curtain or screen is the obvious choice to erect. Everyone's dignity must be respected.

Lead cast members are usually placed nearer the stage in their own individual dressing room. Pay particular attention to the hierarchy of the actors when deciding which room they are placed in. There is often a dressing room that is regarded as the 'number one' dressing room, because it is decorated to a higher standard, has better facilities, such as an en suite, or may simply be the one that it is the closest to the stage. It will serve you well to make sure that your lead actor gets that room. This can be tricky if you are unable to determine who the lead is. There may be two people of equal billing, or maybe the 'star' name has undertaken a smaller role. If this happens, be diplomatic. It may seem old-fashioned, but it's often a good idea to put a female lead in there instead of the male lead, especially if the actress is older.

Chorus and ensemble are usually placed furthest away as these rooms will have multiple occupancy. Try to put cast members who get on together in the same room. Following these simple guidelines should make for a happy company.

TERRA NOVA
COMPANY SCHEDULE

Date	Time	Details	Notes
Wed 24th Nov	09.00	Rehearsals as called	
	18.00	Dinner	
	19.00	**Scene change rehearsal**	
	21.45	Call to end	
Thurs 23rd Nov	09:00	Cast into costume	
	09:55	Half hour call	
	10:30	**Technical Rehearsal**	
	13.00	Lunch	
	14.30	**Technical Rehearsal continues**	
	18.00	Dinner	
	19.30	**Technical Rehearsal continues**	
	21.45	Call to end	
Fri 24th Nov	09:00	Cast into costume	
	09:55	Half hour call	
	10:30	**Technical Rehearsal**	
	13.00	Lunch	
	14.30	**Technical Rehearsal continues**	
	18.00	Dinner	
	19.30	**Technical Rehearsal continues**	
	21.45	Call to end	
Sat 25th Nov	09:00	Cast into costume	
	09:55	Half hour call	
	10:30	**Technical Rehearsal,**	
	13.00	Lunch	
	14.30	**Technical Rehearsal continues**	
	18.00	Dinner	
	19.30	**Technical Rehearsal continues**	
	21.45	Call to end	
Sun 26thNov		No Call	
Mon 27th Nov	09.00	Rehearsals as called	
	17:15	Dinner	
	18:15	Warm-up	
	18:40	Fight Call	
	18.55	The Half	
	19.30	**Dress 1**	
	21.45	Call to end	Photographer present
Tues 28th Nov	09.00	Rehearsals as called	
	12.15	Lunch	
	13.15	Warm-up onstage	
	13:40	Fight Call	
	13.55	The Half	
	14.30	**Dress 2**	
	17.15	Dinner	
	18:15	Warm-up onstage	
	18:45	Fight Call	
	18.55	The Half	
	19.30	**Performance 1**	

ALL CALLS ARE SUBJECT TO CHANGE AND ALTERATION
Craig Scott
SM Terra Nova
terra@email.co.uk 06879 435 623   V2 12/11/2017

A company schedule is issued to the cast so they know when they will be needed in the theatre.

A typical dressing room.

Timesheets

Timesheets are vital throughout the process and they need to be filled in every week. You may be on a buy-out contract, which means you do not get paid overtime, but it's still important that you and the company know the hours you are working. The stage manager will collate the team's timesheets and pass them onto the CM, who will work out the wages. Get into the habit of filling your timesheet in on a daily basis to ensure you are keeping an accurate record. When you are working long hours, it is easy to forget the exact hours you work.

Name: **Tabitha Arnold**   **Week Ending: 12.09. 16**
Production: Fiddler on the Roof

Day		Hours Worked			Total	Total Hours Worked
	am	9.30	to	13.00	3.50	
Monday	pm	14.00	to	18.00	4.00	
	eve		to			7.50

Day		Hours Worked			Total	Total Hours Worked	
	am	10.00	to	13.00	3.00		Scene Change
Tuesday	pm	14.00	to	17.30	3.50		Rehearsal
	eve	18.30	to	21.30	3.00	9.50	

Day		Hours Worked			Total	Total Hours Worked	
	am	9.00	to	13.00	4.00		Tech
Wednesday	pm	14.00	to	18.30	4.50		
	eve	19.30	to	22.00	2.50	11.00	

Day		Hours Worked			Total	Total Hours Worked	
	am	9.00	to	13.00	4.00		Tech
Thursday	pm	14.00	to	17.00	3.00		
	eve	18.00	to	22.00	4.00	11.00	

Day		Hours Worked			Total	Total Hours Worked	
	am	9.00	to	13.00	4.00		Tech
Friday	pm	14.00	to	17.30	3.50		
	eve	18.30	to	22.00	3.50	11.00	

Day		Hours Worked			Total	Total Hours Worked	
	am	9.00	to	13.00	4.00		Dress 1 & 2
Saturday	pm	14.00	to	17.30	3.50		
	eve	18.30	to	21.00	2.50	10.00	

Total Hours:	60.00

A timesheet showing the hours that the SM has worked during the production process.

Use 24 hr clock for hours worked
When adding up;   .25 = 15mins, .5=30mins, .75=45mins

THE PRODUCTION PERIOD

Clearing the Rehearsal Room

Before leaving the rehearsal room and moving into the theatre, transfer any marks that have been made on the floor onto the ground plan. Then, as soon as you get into the theatre put the marks down on the set. These positions may change but it is important to have a starting place. It is vital that the spacing is correct for the actors and that the lighting designer has the specific correct marks when they are focussing. Guessing where a table was placed is not good practice and will cause problems during the tech.

Organizing Scene Changes and the Wings

Prior to the actors getting on stage, the SM will need to have thought about the scene changes. Talk to the director to find out how they want them to run. Involve the DSM as well. Find out what has been happening with the scene changes in rehearsals and, if you can, work through them together. Scene changes should be choreographed and detailed, just as a dance number would be. Plan who is moving what item of scenery or piece of furniture, whether any

> **TOP TIP**
>
> Don't forget to think about packing requirements. Collate the props together according to the side of stage they will be on as this will make unpacking easier, both in terms of time and organization. Have enough boxes or skips to pack into and don't forget to buy gaffa tape and bubble wrap. This is something else that can be overlooked and it is vital to protect the items from breakages. There is nothing worse than finding items broken when unpacking and having to replace them.

scenery needs to be flown and how many flymen you will need. Are there any quick changes and are the actors involved in the scene changes too? You will then be able to calculate how many people will be needed for the scene changes and formulate a working master cue sheet for everyone to follow.

Help the rest of the team organize the wings as this takes as much preparation as the scene changes. Space is usually at a premium backstage and you often need to find ingenious ways of solving storage problems. Set pieces or large items are often flown to save wing space and every area is utilized. Take into account the sightlines, any technical elements, such as any freestanding lighting in the wings, and quick change areas. Don't forget to leave fire exits and routes

The backstage area of a theatre that has been organized by the SM.

clear as everyone needs to move around backstage safely and with ease.

Scene changes and backstage settings should be planned in detail and as methodically as possible. Do not leave the planning until the last minute. Thinking ahead and solving problems before you get into the theatre will save you a lot of time and effort in the long term.

Helping with Prop Setting

As with the furniture and set, props will also need to have a home backstage and the SM will assist the ASM with this. The stage management team's job will be much easier if the prop tables are clearly marked. It is also a good idea to keep it as similar as possible to the setting in the rehearsal room, so that the actors know where to look for items.

Actors' Briefings

Most stage managers don't particularly enjoy this but the briefings are an important part of the job. Try to be as brief, concise and to the point as possible. The more direct you are, the more everyone will remember what was said and will pay attention. The main purpose is to ensure everyone knows what is happening in a particular rehearsal and, most importantly, any health and safety elements.

Make sure that, if the company is in the theatre for the first time, they are briefed on the emergency

THE MISER

Pre-Tech Briefing

Hello everyone and welcome.

I need to remind you of the general rules and information before we start.

- Please can you sign in and out whenever you leave or enter the building
- Please no smoking, drugs or alcohol in the space at any time. If you want to smoke, please do so outside and make sure your costume is covered. Some of the costumes are hires and we must take care of them.
- During lunch and dinner breaks, please don't wear your costumes while eating, you will be given 15 minutes to get out of and back in to your costumes on top of the hour break.
- Please don't bring food or drink in to the auditorium, you may bring a bottle of water in with you but please label it.
- Please leave your mobile phones in the dressing rooms.
- Please make either myself, Thomas or Ellie (SM team) aware if you need to leave the space
- Please be patient and try and keep the noise down as much as possible during the rehearsal.
- Please perform today at performance pace and pitch to aid the technical departments.
- Please stay hydrated and look after yourselves, it is a long and tiring day for everyone so please take care!

Emergency Procedure
- The code word for any emergency will be Mr Jet
- If there is an evacuation, please follow the instructions of the Stage Management team
- There are two fire escapes at Stage Level (point them out)
- The evacuation point is The Lamb pub

If you have a quick change, please flag it up. We will then run the sequence without the quick change, get the technical elements sorted then reset and run the sequence with the quick change.

Any Questions?

Trisha Jennings
SM The Miser
miser@email.co.uk
06543 332 554

An example of the pre-tech briefing that the stage manager gives before the technical rehearsal.

OPPOSITE: A stage manager giving a pre-tech briefing to the cast. DESIGNER: NICKY BUNCH

evacuation procedure and shown the fire exits, fire extinguishers and evacuation points. Inform them of any code words that are used in the event of an emergency. Code words are used regularly in the earshot of the public so no one panics. Make them aware of any obstructions, high-risk elements or hazards and then familiarize them with the back-stage areas and how they get to and from their dressing rooms.

Breaks

It is the stage manager's responsibility to ensure that the correct breaks are taken. Breaks are very important when working long hours and they are good for morale too. If breaks are not observed it can cost the production company money in over-time payments. This could run into hundreds of pounds on a large production, especially if you are working with musicians.

Contracts are all different, but here are some typical daily timings for breaks to follow:

- You can work a maximum of 5 hours per session, for example, 8.30–1.30.
- You can work three sessions per day.
- If you work over 3 hours you should give a 15-minute tea break within the session.
- After a session, you should give a 1-hour break.
- Once the cast are in costume this break becomes 1.5 hours, which allows the cast to have 15 minutes to get out of costume, an hour break and then 15 minutes to get back into costume.
- Everyone should get 11 hours between calls, so if you finish at 10pm, for example, you should not be called before 9am the next day.

A stage manager should be constantly keeping an eye on the time, both in terms of pushing sessions on and ensuring breaks are adhered to. A break should never be called without checking that the director is happy to have one. Forewarn your director 10 minutes beforehand that you need to call

a break. This means they can judge how long they have left and whether it is best to break earlier.

If you are in the middle of a technical sequence or sorting out a problem, you can often make the decision to take a break so that the actors aren't hanging around. For example, if the lighting designer is plotting a sequence and needs 15 minutes before they are ready to run it with cast members, this would be a good opportunity to call a tea break.

Contracts

There are many different contracts in theatre and, while you may not have an in-depth knowledge of each one, it is a good idea to have a working knowledge of them, especially the ones you are working under at the time and the guidelines you should follow. Know about the breaks, any over-time rules such as missed meal breaks or bank holiday rules, any extra payments such as understudy rules, and if the actors will get extra payments for helping with scene changes.

Actors and stage management are usually on an Equity contract, which differ according to the scale of theatre you are working in. There are West End contracts in association with SOLT or small-scale contacts in association with UK Theatre, to name just two. The technical departments will be employed under BECTU contracts and they will also be different depending on the type of production.

The Technical Rehearsal

The stage manager will run the technical rehearsal and is the driving force behind it. They are the voice of the rehearsal and will usually stand at the side of the stage communicating with the director, DSM, actors and technical teams. It is an intense rehearsal to run and the SM needs to have their eyes and ears everywhere. They need to watch the action, paying attention to the director in case they wish to stop, while making

A stage manager working onstage with the actors during a technical rehearsal. DESIGNER: NICKY BUNCH

sure the stage is set correctly, that the crew and technical personnel know what is coming up and what they need to do, and, most importantly, communicating well to everyone and ensuring that they are safe.

The SM needs to be loud and clear with their instructions, delegating effectively to the SM team and crew and making quick and decisive decisions. Try to think ahead. Be prepared for the sequences that are coming up and be positive, upbeat and polite. Using please and thank you in a tech is very important. Time is always short, so the SM must constantly be pushing everyone on, asking how they are doing, how much longer they need and prompting them to restart.

While the technical rehearsal is exhausting for the SM, it is also a rewarding session to work on as they are in control. The more you attack the role at this time, the greater the sense of achievement will be at the end.

Dress Rehearsals

Once the tech is over the SM will be working backstage, overseeing the crew and the ASMs. The SM will watch flying pieces in, help with scene changes and run the stage, ensuring that everyone is safe.

OPERAS

In opera there are two technical rehearsals. This is because the director's and the conductor's requirements are different and they are both equally important as far as the hierarchy of the production goes. The director focusses on the staging of the show and, as the only musician present is the pianist, this rehearsal is known as the 'stage and piano' rehearsal. The conductor will concentrate on the musical aspects of the production. This is known as the 'stage and orchestra' rehearsal as the full orchestra are present.

DURING THE RUN

The Stage

Once the show has opened the SM runs the stage. If there are problems during the show they will be the one that has to make the decisions. Show stops are the stage manager's responsibility. Any deviations from the planned show will be up to them to sort out. If a cast member is sick during a show, the SM will have to make the decision to get the understudy on. If a piece of scenery breaks mid-show, they will need to try to fix it and, if it can't be mended, then decide what to do, either continue the show without it or – the worst case scenario – stop the show. Nothing should happen on the stage without the SM knowing about it.

Set, Props and Furniture

Maintaining the show and all its elements is vital to the smooth running of the production. The more attention and time given to maintenance, the more you reduce the risk of things going wrong, which ultimately makes the job easier.

Rehearsals and Weekly Schedules

Just because the show is up and running doesn't mean rehearsals stop, and the SM is responsible for organizing the time onstage and ensuring the correct personnel are called for them.

Working in the theatre will be an in-house team of electricians and carpenters who need to know what is happening each day. The safety curtain will need to be taken out for a rehearsal, the working lights will need to be on and the crew may be required for a scene change. The best way to make sure this all happens is to issue a weekly schedule so all the departments in the theatre know what the plans are for the week. They can then arrange their own workloads around each other.

The SM also needs to attend understudy rehearsals, maybe setting up any keyboards and speakers for the MD onstage, making sure that the correct scene is set up for the rehearsal and facilitating anything that is required.

POST PRODUCTION

Clearing the Theatre

The stage manager will be helping the rest of the team with the get-out, packing props away, returning borrowed items and cleaning the theatre, making sure it is left in a good condition.

The SM needs to ensures all the information is in the book and that it is given to the producers, and that all the show paperwork is up to date. For example, check that the crew sheets are up to date, that any photos of the set are taken and lighting plans are included. Everything to do with the show is collated in the book and then handed to the producers.

Petty Cash and Budgets

Lastly, make sure that the petty cash and budget is finalized. Return any remaining petty cash to the PM and hand in any outstanding receipts.

TASK

Using the prop and furniture list that you made in the ASM chapter, try working out a provisional budget. The budget should always be based on research and should be an educated guess and not figures plucked out of the air. Once you have provisionally costed the items, why not see if you can reduce it further and see how little you could prop the scene for.

IN REHEARSALS

* CONTACTS THE DIRECTOR FOR REHEARSAL REQUIREMENTS

* CONTACT THE PM TO GET THE GROUND PLAN, SCRIPT AND ARRANGE REHEARSAL ROOM DETAILS

*LEADS THE MARK UP

* ATTENDS THE READ THROUGH, MODEL BOX SHOWING AND MEET AND GREET. TAKES NOTES

* COMPILES THE TECHNICAL CONTACT LIST

* ISSUES ALLERGY AND MEDICAL FORMS

* COMPILES AN INFORMATION PACK

* WRITES A PROVISIONAL PROP AND FURNITURE LIST AND HELPS THE ASM SOURCING

* LOOKS AFTER PETTY CASH AND MAINTAINS THE BUDGET

*KEEPS UP TO DATE WITH REHEARSAL NOTES AND ANY OTHER ISSUES THAT ARISE

* FOLLOWS UP ON REHEARSAL NOTES

* ATTENDS PRODUCTION MEETINGS

*COMPILES PERFORMANCE RISK ASSESSMENTS, FLAME, SMOKING AND WEAPON PLOTS

* WRITES THE COMMS AND CUE LIGHT LIST WITH THE DSM

* ARRANGES MEETINGS AND CALLS, EG FIGHT AND VOCAL CALLS.

* COMPILES PROGRAMME INFORMATION

* WRITES THE FLY PLOT, CREW CUES SHEETS AND MASTER CUE SHEETS FOR THE SCENE CHANGES

*ARRANGES TRANSPORT

* RELAYS INFORMATION

* WRITES A COMPANY SCHEDULE, THE DRESSSING ROOM LISTS AND SIGNING IN SHEETS

PRODUCTION PERIOD

* CLEARS THE REHEARSAL ROOM, PACKS THE PROPS AND FURNITURE

* TRANSFERS THE MARKS FROM THE REHEARSAL ROOM ONTO THE GROUNDPLAN AND THEN ONTO THE STAGE

* ORGANISES THE WINGS

* ORGANISES THE SCENE CHANGES

* BRIEFS THE ACTORS

* HELPS WITH PROP AND FURNITURE SETTING

* RUNS THE TECH

* ATTENDS TECHNICAL NOTES

* MEETS UP WITH THE TEAM AT LEAST ONCE A DAY

* LEADS THE SM TEAM

* OVERSEES THE WHOLE PRODUCTION

* LIASES WITH ALL THE OTHER DEPARTMENTS

* COLLATES THE TIMESHEETS

THE STAGE MANAGER

* HEALTH AND SAFETY

* KNOWS THE CONTRACTS

* ENSURES BREAKS ARE ADHERED TO

POST PRODUCTION

* LEADS THE SM TEAM GET OUT, CLEARNG THE THEATRE AND THE DRESSING ROOMS

* ENSURES THE PRODUCTION INFORMATION IS IN THE BOOK

* FINALISES THE PETTY CASH

THE RUN

* IN CHARGE OF THE STAGE

*ATTENDS, RUNS AND WORKS ON UNDERSTUDY CALLS.

* ORGANISES REHEARSALS

* MAINTAINS THE SET, PROPS AND FURNiTURE

The SM's job roles.

6
PROPPING

This chapter looks at sourcing props (propping) in more detail, covering how to prop and what things to bear in mind, as well as offering suggestions on where to look and how to get the best outcomes. Propping is vital to a play and the attention to detail is imperative. Like the actors, we want to take the audience into the world of the play, and getting the correct props helps to achieve this.

While all members of the team will be working with props in one capacity or another, it is the assistant stage manager who will take responsibility for the prop sourcing and looking after them during the run.

PROVISIONAL PROP AND FURNITURE LIST

Before the propping process can begin, you need to read the script thoroughly and make up

A variety of props that were sourced for a production of *Assassins*.

OPPOSITE: A prop table set up for a production of *Oliver* by Grange Park Opera. DESIGNER: RICHARD KENT

a provisional prop and furniture list. As previously mentioned, this information can be gleaned from either stage directions or from what is being said. It is really important to think about the items in detail and not just to rely on what is specifically mentioned. Not everything will be written down for you. There are scripts that list everything in the back, but if it's a piece of new writing you will probably have just the actor's lines and there will be no stage directions or anything else to help. For example, if your character is smoking, you will deduce that cigarettes are required, but what will the character light them with and how are they going to put it out? Make sure you consider the safety elements too.

Once you have a provisional list, start thinking about the detail of the items and questions to ask the designer. If a dining room table is scripted, what details will you need to know? To start with, the size will be important: how many people need to fit round it and what size is the set? This is important because there is no point in getting a table that is supposed to seat eight and then realizing that eight chairs won't go around it comfortably and no one can walk around it. After size, what shape is it? Oval, square, rectangular or circular? Then is made of wood, plastic or melamine? What colour is it? Does it have to match any other piece of furniture?

Finally, think about how the table is going to be used. You might think this is a strange question, but theatre can use everyday objects in strange ways. If the table is to be stood on it needs to be strong enough and it may need to be stabilized, especially if the stage is raked. If this was the case, the legs would have to be anti-raked – that is, the legs would have to be cut and angled

A simple set with a few well-chosen pieces of furniture for a production of *The Children's Hour*.
DESIGNER: RICHARD BULLWINKLE

so the table stands level on the stage and is safe. You may find that the table is used as a boat and ends up upside down with the cast sitting in it. In this case, the underside of the table will need to look good, be well made and be free of any splinters or rough edges. As you can see from this one item, the more time that is spent thinking about the items, the more specific you can be when sourcing them and the more successful you will be at it.

MODEL BOX MEETING

Viewing the model box will probably raise questions as well as answers. You will find out which time period you are working in and where the play is set. This will have an impact on the type of table you are sourcing. An English Victorian table will look very different to one from 1950s Russia.

Take copious notes during the model box showing as your designer and director will talk about the play and give lots of details and historical background. It is important to note the specifics of the furniture and set dressing. The designer will have spent time deciding what colour items are, so if they have designed flowery yellow curtains, that is

what they will want. Take photos. The designer will not mind as they are for reference and will help to find the right objects.

RESEARCH

Research is the next step and it is imperative not to skimp on this part. Become an expert in the era of the play. A lot of plays are based around specific times in history and the objects that will be needed will also be very specific. Remember the concept of the production, if there is one. Don't research a beautiful period armchair when the designer has specifically said all the furniture will be minimalistic and plastic.

TOP TIP

Base all research on pictorial evidence. While the written word is very useful because it is interesting and factual, the finer points can be demonstrated more effectively with pictures and photos. They may not be in colour but you can use the details that are shown and be really clear about the design of an item and the features you are looking for.

The internet has revolutionized both research and propping as you can find most things out by using a computer. A word of caution, however: you need to be sure that what you are reading is correct as there is a lot of misinformation on the internet and you shouldn't trust everything you read or see. Nonetheless it is an excellent resource and is probably the first place you will look when you start researching. Even if you don't find exactly what you need, you will probably come across pointers guiding you in the direction of further research.

Libraries are an excellent resource for research. Not only for the factual books that outline a period but also old newspapers and magazines, old antique books and other relevant documents. National libraries, like the British Library, are so comprehensive they are invaluable, while local libraries are particularly useful if you are trying to find out about a certain area.

Museums are also worth a visit, especially if there is a specific one that relates to your production. For example, if you were working on a production that was based on the London Underground you would visit the British Transport Museum, or if it was set during the First World War you might go to the Imperial War Museum. Talk to the staff as well. Most of them are knowledgeable in their field and are usually only too happy to help and advise.

You could go to an art gallery or historic house. Here you can see rooms and furniture either in situ or as the rooms were when the art was painted. You can get a real feel for a specific moment in

Museums and historical houses are good to visit for research purposes.

time. Once you have done some research, arrange to meet with the designer to discuss the prop and furniture list and clarify which items you definitely need and what you may not need.

SOURCING

There are four main avenues to explore when sourcing props and furniture: borrowing, buying, hiring and making. Whatever production you are working on, the main aim should be to spend as little money as possible. It can feel awkward at first, approaching people to give discounts or items for free, but once you have felt the excitement from your first success you will hopefully begin to enjoy it. It can almost become a game to see how well you can do.

Be fully prepared before you start looking. Make sure you know the dates of the production, when you need the item and what the item is going to be used for. Confirm with the stage manager how much has been budgeted for the item. Decide if the item can be borrowed and consequently returned without being damaged or if it must be bought as it will be used in such a way that returning it is impossible. Does the item need to be adapted or painted or are duplicates required, as the object gets broken every show?

It is important to find out if you can offer anything in return for any help or discounts. Offering discounted or complimentary tickets, or thanks or an advert in the programme, will help you in bartering the cost down or getting items for free.

When out propping, the watchword again is 'pictures'. Get visual images of everything that may be suitable for the show. Once again, this is where modern technology has transformed propping. There are very few of us who don't have a mobile phone with a camera. This means we can take a photo any time we find a prop, send the picture to the designer and director and get an immediate response as to whether to obtain it or not. On the rare occasions that you do not get a response, take a chance and get it anyway, but keep the receipt in case you need to return it.

When you are taking photos of props, remember that you need to show the size of the item. Photos can be misleading as they do not always show perspective. Take the two photos of the mug shown here. In the first photo there is no indication what size the mug is. However, once you place another mug into the picture you can see that it not the standard size.

The easiest way to show the size is by putting your hand into the shot, as the second photo shows. A hand is something that you will have immediate access to and it is a pretty good indication of the size of an object. If it's a larger item, stand next to it to show comparative size. Alternatively, put a tape measure against an item, which will give you the exact measurement to show the designer.

It is important that the designer and director can see the size of a prop. Use your hand or another item as a comparison.

Research where to find your item, who has the best price or if you can borrow it from anywhere. Obviously, the internet is a great resource, but again, be aware that not every item is as stated and always check the size of your items. An ASM bought the sextant shown here for a production and thought they had got a bargain. It was made of the right metal and it looked perfect. It was also a lot cheaper than anywhere else and had a quick delivery time. Of course the ASM bought it without delay. However, once the item arrived they realized that it was a model, produced for ornamental use and not, as was needed, a full-size working version. Such things will almost inevitably happen from time to time, but it's a great lesson to learn and to remember.

The various buying and selling websites on the internet are an excellent resource, but read the listings carefully to ensure you are buying exactly what is required. Watch the closing dates too. Buying an item immediately is better than bidding on it and waiting for the lot to end. You can acquire some bargains by bidding but just make absolutely certain that if you win the item you will receive it in time, and ensure that you have a back-up plan if you get outbid. There is nothing worse than pinning all your hopes on an item to find that the price goes too high and you haven't given yourself time to find something else.

A mug that has been sourced for a show.

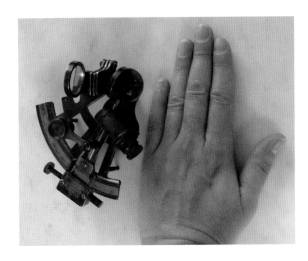

An item bought on the internet that turned out to be smaller than expected.

TOP TIP

When searching on the internet you should try putting the item into the search bar in a variety of different ways. You might have more luck putting 'wooden dining table' or 'circular dining table' into the search bar rather than 'Victorian dining table'. The more ways you input your search, the more options will open up.

The internet will also help you to find other places to try to source the props from. When you are propping try to imagine you are a detective and any leads you find will help you achieve your goal. You can find specialist shops that you may not have heard of or manufacturers or hire companies. Every avenue is open to you when propping and often the more 'alternative' solutions work out for the best.

Shops

Other than the internet, you can of course buy items from high street shops, but before doing that, it is worth calling their head offices to talk to their PR or marketing departments. Some of the larger companies may be willing to give discounts, especially if you are buying a number of items. Also, a lot of theatre companies are registered charities, which may help in gaining a favourable deal. It is also worth approaching managers of individual branches as they may be able to give you a discount, especially if they are local to the venue and they could get a complimentary ticket for the show.

LOCAL SHOPS

A smaller shop near the venue might not be your first port of call, but it should be. While their overheads are probably larger and their stock is limited you will find, more often that not, the staff at these shops are more personal, easier to talk to and keen to help, especially if they could get some free publicity in the programme. Local florists, for example, may let you have the flowers they are discarding for free.

ANTIQUE SHOPS AND AUCTIONS

You would be surprised at how successful buying in antique shops and auctions can be, despite the popularity of antique programmes on TV. The beauty of sourcing in this way is that items will be individual, often quirky and relatively inexpensive, depending on what you are looking for. Of course, if you are looking for a piece of Chippendale furniture you probably won't get it cheaply but you may find a bargain that could be Chippendale-like.

Antique shops will have all sorts of items for sale. You never know what you will find. For one production, my director requested an ashtray. He wanted it to be metal and, in some way, relating to the moon. Having looked in vain in shops and on the internet, I didn't think I'd find anything suitable but then decided to try my local antique shop. After some searching I found the exact thing I was looking for and after a bit of bargaining walked away with the perfect ashtray for £10.

Auctions can be cheaper still, and it's worth looking at a current sale catalogue to see if there is anything suitable. Go with a price in mind and don't get swept away by the thrill of the bidding.

Antique shops are a treasure trove for sourcing props.

You can find some bargains when propping in antique shops.

Don't forget to look in your local antique shop for props and furniture.

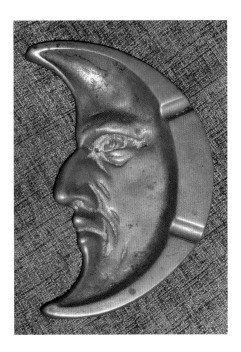

This ashtray was found for a production and was the perfect prop.

Reclamation Yards and House Clearance Shops

These places are worth making a trip to as you will find items such as old radiators and baths as well as garden items. While the house clearance items will probably not be of the highest quality, you can find cheap furniture that could be modified to suit your production.

TOP TIPS

When buying items, whether on the internet or on the phone, make sure you know if VAT is added or not and if there is a delivery charge. It may not be the bargain you think it is if you end up paying substantially more before it's actually yours. Also, do not get stung by paying more for the delivery than the item itself is worth, unless there really is no other option.

One of the golden rules when propping is to keep the receipts. If you don't, you may end up having to pay for the prop yourself.

Markets and Car Boot Sales

There are weekly markets everywhere in the UK and they are definitely worth a visit. You probably won't find the furniture you are looking for, but for inexpensive fabric, homewares and jewellery such as watches, they are definitely worth a look. Most of the items won't be of great quality but, with a bit of adapting, the ideal prop might be easy to obtain. A word of caution though – if you are buying fabric make sure its fireproofed before it goes onto the set.

Manufacturers

If you are buying items in bulk, why not find out who manufactures the item and approach them directly? They have less to lose in giving you a good deal than smaller concerns as they make the items. If the show is set in a pub, glasses will be required. Find a manufacturer who makes them, call and ask if they could sell them at a discounted rate. They may also have some seconds, imperfect glasses that they cannot sell but would be willing to donate or sell at a reduced cost. In this scenario, you could also approach local pubs – if a couple of them said yes, you could borrow all of the glasses for nothing and return them afterwards.

Specialist Societies and Organizations

If the production is based around a public organization or a specific genre, ask the people who work there for advice and try to borrow props from them. If the production is based in a hospital, it really is worth talking to the staff at your local NHS hospital to see if they have any old equipment they are getting rid of or ask if they know anyone who could help. Do talk to the right person though. A caretaker, however helpful, may not have the authority to help and, when propping, it is important to follow the rules and not do anything that could cause any complaints. Contact the Red Cross or St John

A production of *Guys and Dolls*, which is based around the Salvation Army. If a production references an organization, it is a good idea to ask their advice and see if they can help with any props. PHOTO: JOHN HAYNES. DESIGNER: PHILIP ENGLEHEART

Ambulance. While they may not have beds or ward furniture, they may have a stretcher they could lend you or other smaller pieces of equipment.

Prop and Furniture Hire Companies

These warehouses are usually full of every type of furniture and prop you could wish for. They will have multiple sofas in different colours, numerous tables with matching chairs and a multitude of telephones. The list is endless and they really should be somewhere you should explore. These companies usually charge by the week and will have a rolling cost whereby the cost goes down each week the item is hired. This can be the most expensive way of sourcing for a show but, if you do want a Chippendale chair, unless there is a large budget or a very friendly local antique shop who will lend you one, hiring it would be the way to go.

Other Theatres

The beauty of going to another theatre's store is that they will understand the uniqueness of the job and how hard it can be to prop for a specific item. They will recognize that budgets are often very limited. By developing a relationship with a local theatre, props can be shared and you can help each other out. A lot of stores have useful objects, especially the often-used items like glass, tableware, kitchenware and ornaments.

Drama Schools

Drama schools are worth a phone call too. Each one will have a prop store and you may find rehearsal props or some very varied items there. The stores at a drama school are quite limited

If you need a lot of identical items, a prop house is often your best bet.

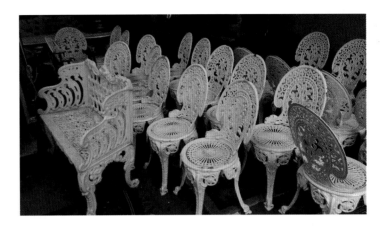

A prop store showing shelves of breakables, glasses and crockery.

The mirror was taken out of the stand for a production of *Bury Fair*. Sometimes items need to be adapted. DESIGNER: RUARI MURCHISON

as their purpose is to teach the students how to prop, so, unless an item was very expensive or hard to find, a lot of the contemporary everyday items aren't kept.

Makes

Making props is an excellent skill to master and it can allow you to be very creative. It may be that the only chairs that can be afforded are from a large company that sells them in bulk. But, with a bit of work, they could be adapted to suit another period. They could be painted a certain way, or some embellishments could be added to the back or seat. They may need to be strengthened, so add more struts, using wood glue and screws.

> ### Top Tips
>
> Do consider the amount of time it will take to make a prop compared to the cost of buying the item and whether you have the time to make it from scratch or if it's best to adapt an existing object. When making items, start with a rough prototype for the designer to see. It is much easier for them to see if something is going to work when they see it in 3D rather than just discussing it with a diagram. Don't overcomplicate prop makes – simplify wherever possible.

A box of cornflakes that was made for a production set in 1940s America.

Propping by Phone

More often than not, the first contact with someone will be on the phone and it is imperative to make a good first impression. Be enthusiastic and polite and be really clear about what you are asking for. Make sure to talk to the right person to start with and don't waste time pitching to the wrong person or the receptionist. The marketing and PR departments are a good place to start if contacting a large company. If there is no positive feedback or the other person isn't interested in helping it is important not to push the matter. Just be polite, thank them for their time and move on to the next source.

Think about what to say before starting the call. Begin with your name, the company you are working for and the title of the production. Ask about the item you are phoning for, what exactly is needed, how many are needed and what it will be used for.

Once you have gained the other person's interest, give more details, such as the date the item is needed for and what can be offered in return, for example complimentary tickets. Try to get a discount or ask to borrow the object by explaining you have a limited budget and don't forget to mention if the company is a registered charity. Have all the information that may needed to hand, in case more questions are asked. If successful, note down the contact details of the person you are dealing with. Follow up the conversation with an email and confirm everything in writing. If the item is being picked up, or being returned after the production, send an email or call the day before to confirm it's still a convenient time for them.

If the person cannot help, ask them if they know anyone who can. They may have a contact in the same line who may have exactly what you are looking for.

Enthusiasm is the key to propping, especially when it is on the phone. The person you are contacting will probably be as passionate about their field of knowledge as you are so use this to your advantage. By engaging with that person, asking for their advice and really showing an interest in what they are saying, they will feel more inclined to help you and it can be really fascinating hearing about something you know nothing about and learning from it.

That's the beauty of theatre: you never know what show you will work on next or what the subject matter will be, but whatever it is, you will need to become a mini-expert in it to achieve the best results. Enjoy the calls you make, put some energy into the conversation and have fun with it. Show your sense of humour and, where appropriate, flirt with and charm the other person. It can really help you achieve your goal.

Propping for a show can be really rewarding, especially if you work without blinkers and think around the prop or piece of furniture. Nowhere is out of bounds and you can ask anybody to help. After all, what's the worst that could happen? They say no. It can be easy to become disheartened if you are struggling to find an item. If this happens, you should briefly put that object on hold, go and find something else to tick off your list and revisit the tricky prop with renewed vigour later on. Always achieve something every day that will help you remain positive and do have faith that you will find the item or can come up with an alternative solution.

Finally, keep records of everything found, any contacts made throughout the propping process and anyone who was particularly helpful. The nature of propping means that you could be looking for the same item in five year's time and you will then be able to go straight back and see if you can get it from the same source.

SHOWING THE DIRECTOR AND DESIGNER

Once the item is acquired, make sure that the director and designer have seen it. While they have approved it from the photo they may change their mind when they see it in the flesh. Do this as soon as the item is received – there is nothing worse than thinking it's been approved then finding out, weeks later, that the director doesn't like it.

An umbrella and a plant pot that have been put together for rehearsals to take the place of a tree.

PROPS IN REHEARSALS

Early on, rehearsal props are provided for the actors to work with, but it is sometimes important to replace these with the actual items once they have been obtained. If a character has a set of luggage that they will be constantly opening, they need to have tried using it before the technical rehearsal. It must be an object they are familiar with so it is totally believable that the character owns it. If an actor knows how to use an object it will also cut down on the tech time.

Breakables and high-risk or expensive items should be kept for use in the theatre as you do not want them to break, but try to get the rehearsal prop to be as close to the actual one as possible and show your actors the actual item before they need to use it so they can be familiar with it.

> **TOP TIP**
>
> However well you prop and get exactly what the creative team want, there will always be props that are cut or changed. While this can be frustrating, and it's usually the prop you are most proud of, try not to take it personally and get disheartened. Changes are common in theatre as it's a constantly evolving environment.

BASIC PROPS

There are some props that will probably be required whether you are working on a classic play or a piece of new writing. These are items that are in everyday life though may have changed over the ages. If you follow the basics outlined here, you should be able to adapt them to suit whatever production you are working on.

Newspapers

Newspapers are used throughout the world and are printed daily. Obviously, the title of the newspaper is important and so is the subject matter – and for this, research is needed. In the UK, local libraries will hold some regional archives, while the British Library holds the national archives. Photocopies of the pages can be obtained for a cost and then you will be able to design and reproduce them for yourselves. There are some companies, such as John Frost Historical Newspapers, that also hold archives of newspapers and magazines and not just UK archives. For a cost, they will send the paper to a printer, such as Data Reprographics, to print the pages for you. This can be expensive, as you are paying to hire the paper and

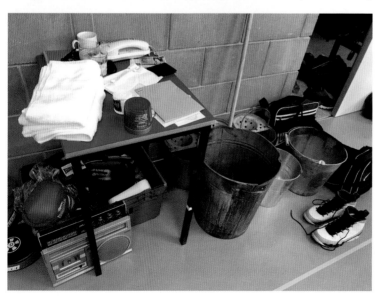

A selection of props set up in a rehearsal room.

A selection of period newspapers.

then paying to have it printed. The best way to get around this is to get only what you need printed and then use an existing newspaper to pad it out.

Think about the paper you are printing on: everyday supplies won't look right. Stationers do sell blank newspaper paper or, alternatively, you can buy flipchart paper and use that in a photocopier. This isn't as easy as it sounds, though, as most photocopiers do not like to print on this paper and it can be time-consuming.

In general, when making any kind of paper prop, be it a letter or a newspaper, you will need to do some research into size. Newspapers vary in size from broadsheet to tabloid, and you will find the dimensions have decreased over the years. Paper sizes too are metric, so for the right attention to detail, you will need to cut existing paper down to suit your era.

Colour is also important. Newspapers now include colour pages, photos and adverts and are also printed on white paper, whereas years ago it was only black and white print and the paper was cream-coloured. Often you will need to age paper so that it looks like an older document; this can be done with a light wash of cold tea. You should also pay attention to the font style and the size of the writing. In contrast to the paper size, writing has got bigger.

A selection of old money.

Money

Money is in constant use and will be required in most shows. However, it is imperative that you understand that copying money is illegal. If you are making banknotes these must not be identical to any current tender and you must clearly state on it that it is a copy and not legal tender. You cannot photocopy money as the silver line is recognised by the machine and will not allow it. You will have to make it up on a computer and then print it.

As with newspapers, think about the weight of the paper, and the colour and size of the note. Newer notes are more detailed to discourage forgery and have, as with newspapers, got smaller. Do think about wallets, too, in regard to the size.

Older wallets will need to be larger to accommodate larger notes. There are some companies that sell notes from different countries and eras so you could purchase one and use it as a reference.

Real coins can be used, though you may not get them all back! As an alternative, use souvenir coins that are often sold in petrol stations or cut your own metal discs and spray them the correct colour. Even metal washers can be used.

Cigarettes

Smoking has become unfashionable and, due to the law, it can be illegal to smoke during a production, although you may be able to obtain special

A scene showing an actor using food onstage. DESIGNER: RICHARD BULLWINKLE

permission from the local council. Nevertheless, cigarettes are still mentioned in a lot of plays and in certain periods it would be very hard to perform without reference to smoking at all. A 1920s play without smoking would be unusual as it was very fashionable to smoke in that era, so try to find a way round it.

Often herbal cigarettes are used but they smell unpleasant, contain tar and you still need to gain special permission to use them. Electronic cigarettes could be used and, although they do not burn down, if they are given a paint job on the outside they could be passable. At least they give off some vapour that looks like smoke. Again, check with your local council about any regulations. Another possibility is joke shop cigarettes and cigars. These are made from cardboard with some talc and cotton wool inside; they do look fake close up but with a bit of practice they can be made to look effective from a distance.

Think about how a cigarette is lit, with matches or lighters, what the packet looks like, whether the cigarette has a tip on it or whether it is hand rolled. All of these things have changed over time and it will add to the authenticity of the play if you do the research and get it right.

Finally, how is your actor going to put it out – in an ashtray onstage or in a sand bucket backstage?

If onstage, think about adding something to the ashtray so it can be fully extinguished. You can use a clear gel for this, a lubricant such as KY jelly or a non-flammable shower gel or hand wash. Water is possible, but it can be messy if it spills. Sand is also used but this obviously won't work in a clear glass ashtray.

Food

Food can be used onstage but think first and foremost about any allergies, dislikes or preferences that the cast may have. Also think about the smell, the cost and the preparation of any food. Strong-smelling foods such as fish and oranges are not widely used, as the odour can get into the costumes and the smell can linger onstage. Try not to give the actors anything too strong or salty, as they will still need to say their lines and this can be tricky if they have eaten the wrong thing.

Mashed potato is good to use if you need to substitute any food due to allergies as it can be dyed with food colouring and moulded to a shape. Polystyrene food can be made to replace any food that needs to be seen but not eaten.

When you are preparing food, you need to follow hygiene rules carefully. Wear food prep gloves, clean your hands thoroughly and keep food in the fridge, freezer or where the instructions dictate. Ensure food is cooked correctly and is neither too hot or cold. It is vital when using any crockery, glassware or bottles that they are sterilized and cleaned before the production and then after every show. Obviously use hot water and washing-up liquid in the first instance, but you must also regularly use baby bottle sterilizing tablets as well. This is an added precaution and will ensure your items are kept as clean as possible.

TOP TIP

The cast need to get used to eating while saying their lines so it is a good idea to practise with the food in the rehearsal room. You could hold a separate food rehearsal or bring in slices of bread, which, as well as being inexpensive, can stand in for any other item. If the actors need to eat as part of the action they will also need access to water onstage in case they need to drink. Try to hide it about the set for them.

A selection of alcoholic drinks made for the stage, without alcohol.

Drinks

As with food, drinks can be used, but obviously not alcohol. Pay particular attention to the colour of the drinks as it is something that everyone is familiar with seeing and you need it to look real. Check your drinks under the stage lighting and not just florescent strip light or daylight. Depending on the gel used in the lanterns, the drinks could look a very different colour onstage.

We use apple juice or white grape juice added to water for light drinks, such as white wine, while adding lemonade as well makes a convincing champagne. Cold tea or cola is used to colour water for brown spirits, such as whiskey or brandy, while red grape juice is the basis for red wine. Beer can be made by using lemonade and cola, but if you need to open the bottle onstage non-alcoholic beer can be used; this is more expensive than the previous option but it does look better. Cocktails need a bit more thought. Food colouring can be used, but do remember to let the wardrobe department know in case of spillages.

You still need to think about cast allergies and the taste of the drinks. However, while you wouldn't want to give a member of the acting company something disgusting to drink, the look is more important.

Pay attention to any bottles or cans and do thorough research into what was used at the time of the production. Ensure any labelling is correct. As far as sealing and opening bottles, you can buy corks, bottle tops and other miscellaneous items from wine or beer making companies and you can buy bottle-top fastening machines and corking implements.

Blood

Injuries, cuts and accidents are often portrayed in theatre and so blood is often needed. Sponges full of blood can be placed around the set and then squeezed onto an actor or syringes with pipes can be placed into costumes and operated by the cast member. Bags made of cling film with blood inside

Blood is often used on productions and it needs to look realistic. PHOTO: JOHN HAYNES. DESIGNER: LUCY OSBORNE

Rifles being used onstage during a production. DESIGNER: ADRIAN GEE

can be broken when needed; a condom filled with blood and strapped to the body can be pierced at the appropriate moment for a really effective big gush effect.

As far as the blood itself is concerned, there are some brilliant products on the market. Some are more washable than others, however, so make sure your costume department know you are using blood and have done a test to see it comes out of costumes all right. The blood made by Pigs Might Fly always washes out well.

Stage blood is basically a recipe of sugars and colouring, so if you can't afford to buy it you could always make your own. This can be done either with golden syrup or washing-up liquid and food colouring. Which one you use depends on whether it is going anywhere near anyone's eyes or mouth. Please be aware that food colouring will not wash out though.

Weapons

Armoury is something that is used a lot in theatre but is a really sensitive subject. Firing weapons live onstage is becoming trickier now as an armourer may have to be hired. Blank firers can be used, but the security and the safety of them must be vigorous and they must be cleaned after every performance. If you are planning on firing blanks onstage, it is advisable to attend a recognized course with a company such as RC Annie's, as it's not worth taking the risk of injuries or accidents. A lot of the time a recorded sound effect is used, which is the safest route by far. Obviously, if you are still using a non-firing weapon the security measures need to be followed too.

Other weapons, such as swords and knifes, are also used, but they must be blunted and kept locked away, as with any weapon.

Propping is an art form in its own right and you get the opportunity to be creative and to put your stamp on the production by the items you find. At times, it can be extremely challenging. Some requests can confound you and you worry about how you are ever going to achieve it, but with perseverance, a lot of thought and a bit of luck most things are possible. Think methodically about a prop: don't just go for the obvious route, as there may be an alternative solution that is better.

TASK

Choose a prop or item of furniture from your play and do some research on the period of the play and what the item would have looked like. Once you have done this try to source the item. Find a few places that could help and then find out how much it would cost.

The SM team performing a mark-up.

7
THE MARK-UP AND SCENE CHANGES

THE MARK-UP

The mark-up, also known as marking out, is an important part of the stage management team's job. It will help everyone in the rehearsal room plan the spacing of the show and visualize the playing space that they will have in the venue. The mark-up is a plan of the set that is taped onto the rehearsal room floor. This is made by placing lines indicating where the scenery is positioned as well as other design elements, such as entrances and exits, steps and windows. These marks are made by measuring the ground plan and transferring those measurements onto the floor with LX tape.

It is a good idea to do the mark-up as soon as possible so that the creative team and acting company can work with it. It is not unusual for the SM team to do the mark-up before rehearsals begin on the first day. The stage manager will obtain the ground plan from the production manager and, if possible, will do some preparation before commencing the mark-up. An experienced stage manager will probably not need to do this but it is prudent to be familiar with the ground plan so you can achieve a good result.

Before starting the mark-up, measure the rehearsal room dimensions to see if the set will fit in it. Take into account any obstructions in the room, such as pillars or entrances, as the mark-up will need to be positioned so there is as little disturbance as possible. The rehearsal room may be smaller than the stage area so you may need to omit some parts from the mark-up. Where possible include offstage masking or treads and try to leave enough space around the outside for the cast to walk round easily, as well as accommodating prop tables and furniture. This will prove beneficial as the cast will need to walk around without disturbing the action and the SM team will need to prepare for any scene change requirements.

Do check where the director would like to sit in the room. Make sure there is enough room for them to sit comfortably at a table downstage of the setting line while still being able to see the whole stage.

Before starting, the floor should be swept and be as clean as possible, otherwise your tape may not adhere to it properly. Set up a table with the ground plan and the other tools needed to complete the task. Check that you can use LX tape as some venues do not allow it, especially if it is a varnished wooden floor. If this is the case the best option is to buy some dance floor, lay that down and stick the LX tape onto that. Dance floor is a vinyl flooring that is sold on rolls and can be laid down on top of the existing floor.

Tools

The following are the tools you will need to carry out the mark-up:

- Ground plan of the set
- Scale ruler
- Pencil
- Rubber

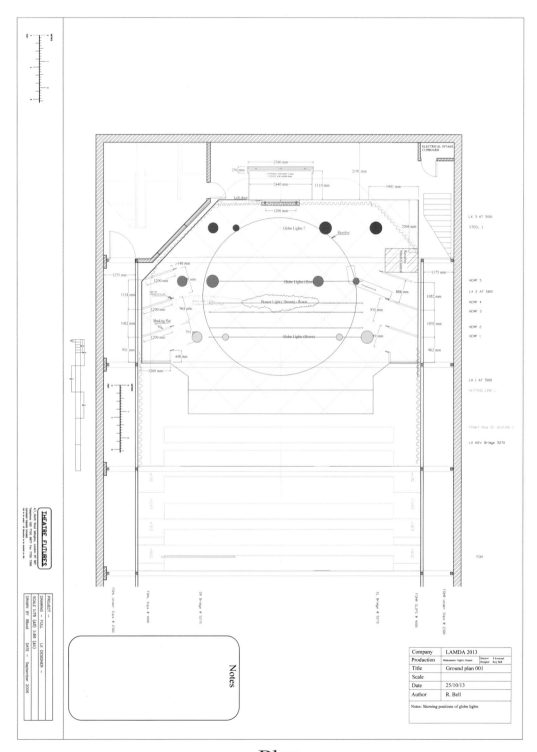

Plan

A ground plan of the set of *A Midsummer Night's Dream*. DESIGNER: ROY BELL

A typical rehearsal room.

LEFT: A desk set up ready for the SM team to do the mark-up.

BELOW: The tools needed for a mark-up: a chalk line, LX tape, a scale ruler and a cloth tape measure.

- PVC (LX) tape in various colours. A few rolls of each colour depending on the size of your mark-up
- Scissors
- Scalpel or Stanley knife
- Sticks of chalk
- Chalk line, often know as a snap line
- At least two cloth tapes
- Metal tape measure
- Marker pen to write on the tape

A scale ruler showing the scale typically used in the UK – 1:25.

A scale ruler typically has three sides and has different measurements written on it – 1:50, 1:25, 1:75 and so on. In UK theatre, the designer will usually have drawn the ground plan at 1:25, but do check on the plan as it should be written clearly. In large venues the scale used may be 1:50. In America, imperial measurements are still used, so you may find the scale is 1:24. The metric 1:25 scale means that the ground plan is 25 times smaller than the actual set. If you measure 1cm on the ground plan, this is equal to 25cm in real terms. If the theatre width measures 35cm on the ground plan, the actual width would be 8.75m. You do not need to have a scale ruler to correctly interpret a plan but it does make the job easier and quicker.

There are two different ways to execute a mark-up. The first method uses triangulation, working from two fixed points along the setting line and measuring from each point to create an arc. The second method uses the centre line and setting lines as the reference points, measuring along them to find a specific position.

Centre Line and Setting Line

A ground plan should show two lines – the centre line, often marked as CL, and the setting line. The centre line runs from US to DS down the centre of the stage that you are using, not the centre of your set. Venues usually have the centre line permanently marked as it is regularly used as a point of reference. The setting line is the line that links the two sides of the proscenium arch or downstage position and is usually upstage of the house tabs or safety curtain. The designer works from the setting line when planning the set.

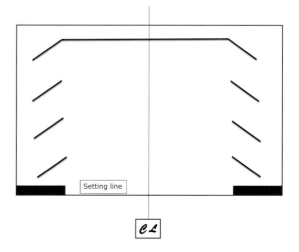

The setting and centre lines.

Mark your Setting Line

First place your setting line down. If your rehearsal room has a planked floor you could always follow the planks and use this as a starting point. If not, measure an equal distance from two points along the downstage wall and join them up using a chalk line, then tape the line in using LX tape.

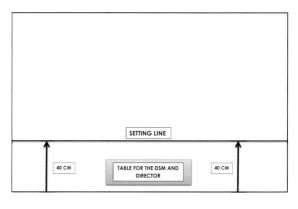

How to mark a setting line in a rehearsal room.

The SM team using a chalk line to mark the centre line.

BOTTOM: How to make sure the centre line is at right angles to the setting line.

Just because your rehearsal room floor is made up of planks of wood, never assume that the flooring is square, and resist the urge to follow the lines of the flooring for any straight lines other than the setting line.

Adding the Centre Line

The centre line must be at right angles to the setting line. First, find the centre point of the setting line by measuring the width of the line and dividing by two. Then mark 3m to the right and left of the centre point. Measure identical lengths from each 3m mark to create an arc. Repeat this step with a longer measurement so you have two arcs. Run your chalk line through each arc and the central point of the setting line, then tape the line in with LX tape.

The setting line and centre line are important details to mark permanently in the rehearsal room as they are a point of reference for your creative team and actors.

Triangulation Method

The centre line, setting line and both 3m marks should be drawn onto the plan and each point marked with a letter.

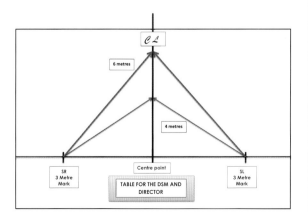

> ### TOP TIPS
>
> If you have some preparation time, you can put the measurements into a table to make it easier when you are in the rehearsal room. Each point that you need to show on the set should be marked with a letter so it is easy to refer to and you can see exactly where you are looking.
>
> Choose your LX tape colours before you begin the mark-up. It is common to use a different colour for each act and to use the same colour to mark any furniture or other items for the corresponding act. If possible, keep to the same colours throughout the process so that once you are in the theatre there is no confusion.

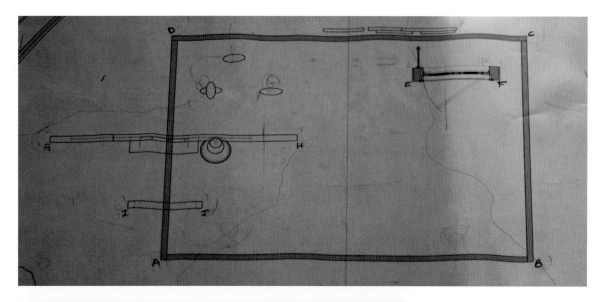

ABOVE: A ground plan showing the letters denoting the detailed points of the scenery that need to be measured and marked during a mark-up. DESIGNER: NANCY SURMAN

Triangulation from the centre point and the SL 3m mark.

To find the first point (A), measure the distance on the ground plan between A and the SR 3 metre mark, then measure between A and the SL 3 metre mark. Note down both measurements. Do this for every point of the set.

Now it's time to mark them in the rehearsal room. If possible, it is best to have three people on the floor, one at each 3m mark and the third holding the ends of the cloth tapes. The people at each 3m mark will hold the reel of the tape measure, reading the measurement, while the third person will make the arcs with the ends of the tape. Where the two arcs intersect is where the point

is and it is marked with the correct letter (A, for example). This is then repeated for every point.

Centre and Setting Line Method

As with triangulation, mark the centre line, setting line and number each point of the set on the ground plan. You do not need the 3m marks for this method.

On the ground plan, measure the distance from point A to the centre line, making sure your ruler is parallel with the setting line. This is the SL or SR measurement, depending on which side of the

How to measure from point A to the SR 3m mark on the ground plan when using the triangulation method.

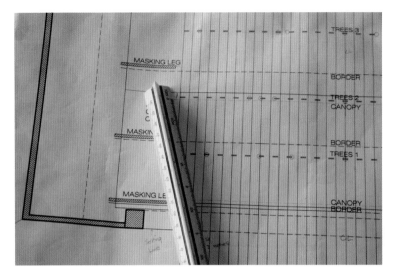

POINT	SR 3 METRE MARK	CS	SL 3 METRE MARK
A	1M 46 CM	80CM	
B	82CM	3M 24CM	
C		2M 12CM	1M 05CM
D		1M 42CM	1M 42CM
E	54CM	86CM	
F		1M 30CM	24CM
G	12 CM	67CM	

LEFT: How to record the measurements when using triangulation.

BELOW: An ASM marking the arc where the two tapes meet.

stage it is on. Then measure the distance from point A to the setting line, making sure the ruler is parallel with the centre line. This is your centre line measurement. Note the measurements down and continue this process for all the scenery points.

It is a good idea to lay a cloth tape down along the centre line. To mark the first point, A, we need to read the table for our centre line measurement, let's say it is 80cm. Work from DS to US and find 80 cm on the tape on the centre line, then place your second cloth tape on this point and lay it straight across to SR, parallel with the setting line. Let's say this measurement is 146cm. Find this point and mark it with your chalk, also writing an A next to it. You can always recheck this measurement by working from the setting line rather than the centre line.

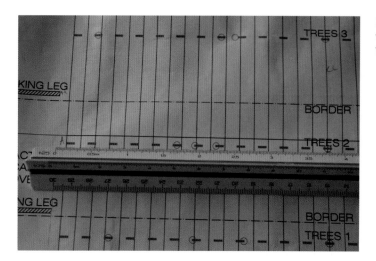

How to measure from Point A to the centre line when using the setting line and centre line as the reference points for the mark-up.

How to record the measurements when using the centre line and setting line.

POINT	SR	Centre line	SL
A	1M 46 CM	80CM	
B	82CM	3M 24CM	
C		2M 12CM	1M 05CM
D		1M 42CM	1M 42CM
E	54CM	86CM	
F		1M 30CM	24CM
G	12 CM	67CM	

ABOVE: When you are using the centre and setting line method, measure across from the centre line to find the mark.

When you are using the centre and setting line method, first find the measurement along the centre line.

The SM team using LX tape to mark a line on the rehearsal room floor.

BOTTOM: The way to mark a doorway on the rehearsal room floor.

Taping the Lines in

Once you have measured all your points, with whatever method you have chosen, you need to tape the set in, using different colours of LX tape. A wall or flat will be done in a solid line, windows or non-solid items can be shown in a broken line. The easiest way of doing this is to lay the whole line down and cut sections out of it. Treads are marked in with an arrow pointing up or down. Doors are shown with a gap, and it is really good to show which way they open.

Circles are quite easy to achieve. Find the central point of the circle on the ground plan and then mark it onto the floor. Measure the radius of the circle (half the diameter) and find the measurement on your cloth tape. Hold the cloth tape at this measurement on the centre point on the floor and rotate the end of your cloth tape around 360

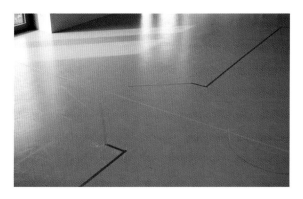

TOP TIPS

Try not to stretch the cloth tape, otherwise your readings will not be accurate. Also ensure that you know where the zero point is on the tape. Sometimes there is an extra metal loop that may add some dimensions and this will mean your mark-up will be incorrect.

LX tape also stretches if you pull it too hard and this is something to avoid, otherwise it could stretch back and come up off of the floor. Always let the tape relax before placing it onto your floor and walk along it to fix it in place. Use a pair of scissors or a knife to cut the tape as breaking it by hand will also stretch it and create an untidy end that will not last. Be careful about using a knife on a rehearsal room floor, though, as you do not want to damage the flooring.

degrees, marking this with chalk as you go. Finally, tape the line in. With a little bit of practice, taping in a circle isn't that difficult.

Furniture Marks

The DSM will mark the furniture in rehearsals so that it is positioned correctly every time and these same marks will be used once you are in the theatre. The marks are made by using two pieces of

A chair on the stage marked using LX tape stuck down in an L shape.

LX tape at right angles to each other to make an L shape, which is then placed on the upstage corners or legs of the furniture.

Try to avoid the stage being littered with numerous marks. Only mark what you really need to. For example, if there is a sofa, coffee table and rug, mark the sofa and use this as a reference point for the other items.

You can, of course, use either method to check that a mark is correct, though there are benefits to both ways and it's useful to know both.

SCENE CHANGES

A scene change is an art form in itself and takes a lot of planning and preparation to look smooth and to be timed to perfection. Most productions will have a scene change in them, whether it's seen by the audience or not. It may be an interval change that takes place behind the safety curtain or it could be a stylized scene change that is choreographed to suit the style of the production. Whatever form the scene change takes, it will be the stage manager who will organize it, working out the logistics, designing which personnel will do what job within it and choreographing it so it runs as smoothly as possible.

Once you have seen the model box, start thinking ahead to any scene change that may be needed. The director and designer will have discussed the scene changes in depth and may outline their ideas during the model box showing.

The stage littered with marks.

A scene change using crew and stage management in costume. DESIGNER: RUARI MURCHISON

Take note of everything they say, including the details of the set as well as furniture and props, as they may be awkward or heavy to move. Make a note of what set pieces need to be moved during the scene change and check on the ground plan the size of any entrances, as this will affect the dimensions of items that can go through them. This may have a knock-on effect to the ASM and their sourcing of the props and furniture. Obtain photographs of the model box showing the individual set plans. This is vital for reference and not just for when you are planning the scene change.

While the stage manager takes overall responsibility for planning a scene change, the director will have ideas too, so you must consult them. Some directors may want to use the actors rather than any crew and, while this is happening with more regularity nowadays, it doesn't mean that crew aren't needed. Technical aspects backstage will still need to be met. Scenery needs to be moved, both on the deck and any flying pieces, and the crew will need to collect items from the cast as they exit.

On larger productions, the master carpenter and production manager will assist the SM, as they will both be familiar with the set, having made it and put it up during the fit-up. They will know how many people it takes to safely carry an item and the best way to move it. The master carpenter will know which crew personnel he has hired and who is best suited to which job. The production manager also knows how many other personnel are employed, such as stage LX or dressers.

In Rehearsals

The SM team should get into rehearsals as often as possible so they are familiar with the show. They will see how the furniture is set up and how the cast are starting and ending any scenes. Take a note of props that are onstage at the start of a scene change and any items that need to be set for the next scene, and think ahead to any props that could be a problem. Anything that has liquid in, even something as simple as a glass of water, could be a hazard if spilled and could end up causing a show-stop.

The DSM should have a good understanding of what is required during scene changes so the SM and DSM should have a scene change planning meeting. This will help both parties, as the SM can choreograph the scene change and the DSM can start to put crew cues in the book. The more planning that is done, the smoother the technical rehearsal will be.

Scene Change Lists

Towards the end of the rehearsal period the DSM should compile various provisional lists to

Cast performing a scene change during a production. DESIGNER: RICHARD BULLWINKLE

distribute. Each department will then have a clear idea of cues that may be needed.

PROP AND FURNITURE SETTING LIST

This is a comprehensive list of where each item is set, from the top of the show and also from an interval. It will include information such as which character uses a prop, which page a book is opened at or how a tea service is laid out on a tray. The ASMs take charge of this list from this point and use it to set up for each show.

FLY PLOTS

This is a list of scenery that will be flown. It will itemize each piece in show order, listing the bar number it is on, which direction it is flying in and its speed. The SM, with the advice from the head flyman or master carpenter, will decide how many people are needed for each piece.

AUTOMATION PLOTS

This is a list of objects that are moved by automation and to which position on the stage and what speed. It is imperative to note if there is anyone on the automated pieces when they are moving.

QUICK CHANGE LISTS

These are itemized lists of any quick changes that the cast have, what costumes they will be wearing and a rough idea of how much time there is for the change. Entrances and exits are important to note. The SM will work out the best position for a quick-change area and arrange for flats to be erected and tables, mirrors and lighting to be set up.

LX AND SOUND CUE LIST

A list of LX and sound requirements is handy to refer to if you need to. It also helps the stage manager planning any scene changes as they will know

Camino Real

Q	Flown Piece	Direction	Speed	Flyman	Notes
	PROVISIONAL FLY PLOT				
Preset					
Tabs IN. CYC IN					
1	Tabs	OUT	Med	A	
2	Orange Parasol	IN	Slow	B	Flown on a line not a bar
3	Orange Parasol	OUT	Fast	B	Parasol will be removed from the line onstage
4	Radio Studio Flat	IN	Fast	A	
5	Radio Studio Flat	OUT	Fast	A	
6	Hotel interior flat	IN	Med	B	
7	Hotel interior flat	OUT	Med	B	Happens as neon sign flies in
7	Neon Sign	IN	Fast	A	Happens as hotel flat flies out
8	Tabs	IN	Fast	B	
	INTERVAL				
	Neon Sign	OUT			
	Night Flat	IN			
9	Restaurant flat	IN	Slow	A	
10	Restaurant Flat	OUT	Fast	A	
11	Fiesta banner	IN	Fast	B	
12	Tabs	IN	Fast	A	Curtain Call
13	Tabs	OUT	Fast	A	Curtain Call
14	Tabs	BOUNCE	Fast	A	Curtain Call
15	Tabs	IN	Fast	A	

F Grant
SM Camino Real
camino@email.co.uk 06878 545 131   V6 12/1/2017

A provisional fly plot showing the movement of the scenery.

The Countess Cathleen

Provisional Quick Change plot

Character	Act/ Sc	Page off	Pg on	Character	Page count	Time (approx)	Notes
Sheemus	1.1	23	24	Angelical Being	1	45 secs	Sheemus' clothes underneath
Countess	1.1	23	25	Angelical Being	2	1 minute 30 seconds	Countess clothes underneath
Oona	1.1	23	25	Angelical Being	2	1 minute 30 seconds	Oona clothes underneath
Aleel	1.1	23	25	Angelical Being	2	1 minute 30 seconds	Aleel clothes underneath
Aleel	1.1	27	29	First Merchant	2 pages	2 minute 30 seconds	
First Merchant	1.2	33	33	Aleel	Scene change	1 minute	
All Cast	1.4	46	47	Into Peasants	1 page 2 scene changes	2 minutes 45 seconds	

D DAVIS
SM THE COUNTESS CATHLEEN
cc@email.co.uk 06765 441 221
V1 25/3/2016

A quick-change list that the DSM compiles for the wardrobe department so they know the rough time of any costume changes.

what is happening technically too. It is especially important if there is a practical lamp or a practical radio onstage that needs to be struck or set.

HEADSET AND CUE LIGHT LIST

The sound department is responsible for setting up the prompt desk, headsets and cue lights and will ask the SM team for a list of where they would like them to be. It is a good idea for your LX board operator and sound operator to have spare headsets and cue lights in case pieces of equipment fails.

Backstage Working Lights

Let the LX department know what lighting – known as blues – will be needed backstage during the show so they can arrange this during the fit-up. Don't forget there needs to be light in the quick-change area and over the props tables. Extra lighting may also be useful on any treads or obstructions backstage.

Planning a Scene Change

Planning a scene change is done on paper rather than working with the actual set, props and furniture. It is a great idea to try to have some time with the SM team in the rehearsal room to work it through physically using the mark-up and rehearsal furniture. When planning the scene change on paper, use a shove drawing. A shove drawing is when you work with the ground plan and scaled cut-outs of your furniture and scenery. You can then work in stages and find the best order in which to move items. A diagram of each scene is really useful for the SM too. It will detail each set-up, where the scenery is, the positions of the furniture and any other important items.

It is always beneficial to keep the crew working in a specific wing and in pairs, so that they can work together to be responsible for one side of the stage. Divide the workload for each crew team and organize them so they enter and exit on the same side of the stage, hopefully avoiding any collisions with other crew members during busy periods. Crew members may have to do two jobs. For instance, a member of crew may be required to go to the fly floor for a busy flying sequence. Use letters or numbers for each member of crew rather than their names. Using crew A and crew B instead of Richard and Susie means that any documents created can be used wherever the show is playing. This is especially useful when you are touring or working on a long-running show, as there will be no need for paperwork amendments if the personnel changes.

Crew should be assigned to work with the scenery, moving furniture and larger items, whereas stage management will take care of the props and the detailed setting of the stage. If there are practical lights, such as a desk lamp, then a stage LX will be employed, and if a costume is required it will be the wardrobe department's responsibility. Each department is responsible for setting or striking items, but the stage management team should check the items are set correctly before continuing with the performance.

Determine how much time there is for the scene change. In a musical, there may be a certain amount of music or in a play the director will have chosen a piece of music. It is a good idea to talk to the lighting designer to find out how much light will be onstage, whether the change will be performed in a blackout or in a full lighting state so the audience can watch. This will influence how the change is undertaken and how to mark the scenery. If it's being performed in a blackout, glow tape may be used.

The aim with a scene change is to execute it smoothly in as few moves as possible. Try to ensure there is always someone onstage and the stage is never left empty. If nothing is happening onstage it may look like the change is complete or that there has been a mistake. By employing the

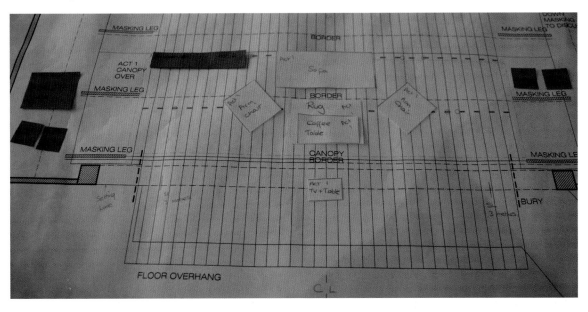

A shove drawing is helpful when planning the scene change.

A scene change taking place in low-level lighting. DESIGNER: ADRIAN GEE

The best way to carry two chairs safely.

ASM to strike and set props you should be able to ensure there is always something happening. Where possible no one should enter or exit empty-handed. Make every journey count. However, this isn't always feasible at the beginning or end of a scene change.

Think about how many people it takes to carry an item. There is nothing worse than seeing someone struggle with a chair that is too heavy for them. It could also cause an injury. On the other hand, you don't want to go to the other extreme and use two people to carry a table that could be easily managed by one.

Think about the items themselves. See if items can be taken off together rather than individually. Can the rug be put on the sofa and taken off together? Do not attempt to overload items and make them too heavy or awkward to carry. Make sure items are safely placed. Wherever possible, someone should have a grip on each item so it doesn't fall. Similar chairs can be put on top of each other and chairs can be placed on tables and carried off together.

Utilize everyone equally. Don't have one person doing everything and never have anyone standing around onstage just watching. The stage manager can perform cues but please bear in mind that they may have to deal with emergencies and problems that arise, so it is better that they do as little as possible and oversee the technical elements. As a stage manager, I always watch the flying pieces in and out so that I can ensure everyone's safety.

Try to clear the areas in front of the entrances and exits first so there is space to work, and do the reverse when setting items. Try to strike items

TOP TIPS

Resist the urge to leave items on tables and carry them off together, as items may slip off and break. It will take more time in the long run if you have to stop and pick something up or, worse, stop the show to clear up a mess. Get the ASM to clear the table of props first before the table is moved or stick items to the table (so long as nothing is hired).

Use containers to collect small props and awkward items. Hopefully this will keep breakables intact and nothing will get lost or damaged.

The best way to carry a table and chairs safely.

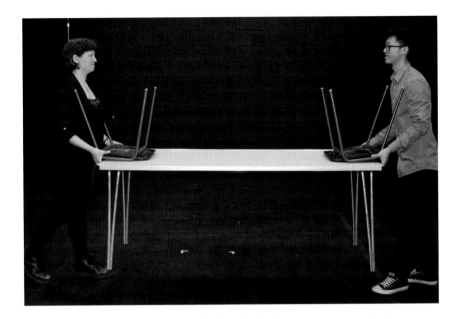

quickly that are in the same position or in the way of the next piece of scenery.

Touring Theatre

If you are touring a production there may not be time to go through your scene changes with the in-house crew, in which case cue sheets need to be clear and understandable. Take into account any changes that need to be made for different venues. In some theatres scenery may not be flown or wing space may be limited, so furniture may need to be stored differently.

Wing Space

The wings are as important as onstage when planning a scene change. It is like a jigsaw puzzle. The audience won't see them but you need to make sure that backstage is neat and tidy. Don't block the wings or entrances for the cast and adhere to any safety requirements. Make sure fire exits are clear at all times and that you know where the nearest fire equipment is. Don't block access to any fire extinguishers.

Furniture, props and scenery need to be placed in accessible places and close to their entrance position. Try not to do too much double handling. Think about the manoeuvrability of the furniture and scenery. Is there enough room to turn a table around or is it best to store the sofa on one end?

The wings showing how every inch of space is utilized. A quick-change area is set up on an unused piece of scenery. GRANGE PARK OPERA

Utilize all your space. Sometimes you may need to fly larger items in the wings to save space on the floor.

Documenting the Scene Change

Compose a master cue sheet, which will include everything that happens in order and what everyone is doing at any one time. Issue individual cue sheets; if you do not have time to do this, copy the master cue sheet and highlight the individual's tasks so they can see what they should do. The crew won't know the production or the set-up so diagrams are imperative, as are clear and concise directions on what they need to do. Include entrances and exits, descriptions of what they are moving and if they are striking an item with someone else. Make sure you specify the colour and position of any marks that they will be aiming for. They will need the cue

point. Is it on a cue light, a lighting change or an actor's line? The SM should try to keep a track of any changes, but this isn't always possible in the tech so everyone should make their own notes. Once the tech and dress rehearsals have taken place, collate the individual crew sheets so there is a definitive list of the cues and who does what.

Moving into the Theatre

Transfer any marks that were made in the rehearsal room onto the stage. To do this, measure the marks in the rehearsal room before taking the tape up, writing them down either in a table format or draw them onto the ground plan. You can then mark the furniture in the theatre by measuring the distances and placing tape in an L shape at the legs.

If you are lucky, there will be a dedicated scene-change rehearsal. This is used for the director, cast,

THE SEAGULL

MASTER CUE SHEET

Act One
Blue marks

Act Two
Yellow marks

WHO	CUE POINT	ENTER	ACTION	EXIT
SM	Cue light	USL	Strike 2 x lighting stands DSL	USL
SL ASM	Cue light	DSL	Place smoke machine from DSL into ammo box DSR Strike the box with the other ASM	USR
SR ASM	Cue light	DSR	Collect the loose props from CS and place into the ammo box DSR Strike the box with the other ASM	USR
Crew A & B	Cue light	USR	Strike curtain and rail	USR
SL ASM		USR	Take on blue bench and set CSL then strike the 2 benches USC	USL
SR ASM		USR	Take on garden table and chair and set them CS then strike Arkadina's chair USC	USL
Slider	Cue light		Close slider	

Act Two
Yellow Marks

Act Three
Green marks

WHO	CUE POINT	ENTER	ACTION	EXIT
SM	Once the radio table is set	USR	Take radio and set it on the USR table	USR
SL ASM	Cue light	DSR	Take lotto table and chair on and set DSR then set props from lotto table drawer.	DSR
SR ASM	Cue light	USR	Take radio table on and set USR then strike CS garden table and chair	DSR
Crew A	Cue light	DSL	Take on 2 dining chairs and place CS then exits	USL
Crew B	Cue light	USL	Take on foldable dining table and set CS then strike blue bench	USL
Crew A		USL	Take on 2 dining chairs and set CS then exits	DSR
Slider	Cue light		Opens slider	

Diana French Stage Manager
06567 774 654 seagull@email.co.uk   v4 26/5/2015

A master cue sheet is compiled by the SM to show what everyone is expected to do during a show.

A truck stored in the wings with the props and furniture set on it. GRANGE PARK OPERA. DESIGNER: RICHARD KENT

crew and stage management to practise the scene changes in working light without the other technical requirements. (Working lights are the everyday lights and not the production's lighting rig.) Distribute the crew sheets to everyone in advance so that they can look through them. Try to find time before the rehearsal to go through the plan with the crew. Walk through the set with them. Point out any marks and impart any information they will need. If there are any difficult changes it's worth walking those through with them without the acting company.

Scene Change Technique

As far as the techniques of undertaking a scene change are concerned there are some common rules you should try to follow.

Look for the marks from the wings before entering the stage, taking the shortest route and aim directly for them. Try to place the furniture confidently and correctly the first time, and don't shuffle furniture around.

A scene change should be executed with a sense of purpose at a brisk pace and in a calm and composed manner. No one should run, as it is dangerous. It also looks messy and uncontrolled and could look to the audience like a mistake has occurred.

If an object has been put in the wrong place, decide if you need to move it. If it is in completely the wrong place and will affect the action, reposition it. Walk on with confidence and the audience won't know it was an error. If it isn't drastically wrong, an actor could move it within the scene as this will be less disruptive. Whatever you decide, if an object is incorrectly set you must let the cast know. It might be an obvious mistake but it can throw an actor when they are in the moment and can be easily distracted.

Think around a prop and what additional equipment may be needed. A mop and bucket may be required if liquid is spilt, or if an ornament breaks there should be a dustpan and brush to hand.

The correct clothing is important and should be regarded as a uniform or costume. In theatre, blacks are worn backstage. This comprises a black long-sleeved top, trousers and soft-soled black shoes. If you are working on a production that has a lot of heavy scenery, you may be asked to wear shoes that have steel toe caps.

Costume may be worn for scene changes. Hopefully the costume will allow you the freedom of movement to do the job without being impeded.

Whatever is worn, try to be good-humoured about it and take the designers' requests seriously. Throw yourself into the ethos of the production as you have been asked to wear costume to blend into the show. Admittedly this can be a tall order. It is not natural for most stage management to feel comfortable on show, especially if you are asked to wear pink striped tights and a nightshirt, which has happened to me!

Scene changes always evolve during a production. During the technical rehearsal scene changes will be worked on and refined, but even once the show has opened they will never be set in stone. Things change, accidents happen, unforeseen events occur and timings vary. The SM should constantly strive to make the scene changes quicker, slicker and the best they can be. Scene changes are, after all, a thing of beauty and are an integral part of a show.

TASK

First, try to draw a simple scale ground plan for your play and practise measuring the marks using both mark-up methods. Then choose two scenes and design a set for each one, including any props and furniture, and have a go at planning a scene change.

The DSM's book.

8
THE BOOK

The deputy stage manager is responsible for compiling the book, also known as the bible, prompt script or prompt copy. It is a working document that is constantly updated and should be a comprehensive and exhaustive record of everything needed to produce the show.

Before starting rehearsals, the book will need to be prepared so it is ready to work with. The golden rule, when working on a book, is to always write in pencil. It is a working document, so the details will constantly change and evolve and you need to be able to keep them up to date. A

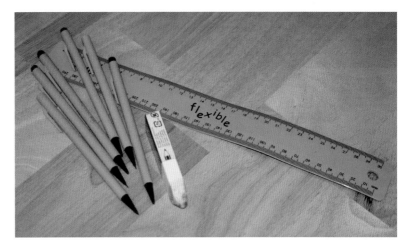

Pencils, rubber and a flexible ruler, the DSM's best friends.

A DSM's stationery kit.

Using index tabs on a book really helps the DSM be more organized.

rubber and ruler will also become constant companions.

PREPARING THE BOOK

First, obtain a copy of the script. It is important to use the same version as the director and cast as there will often be references to page numbers. The script may need to be formatted to a workable size. In the UK, we generally work with A4 pages. It is then printed out single-sided, leaving one side blank for use later on.

Next, prepare your blocking page. On a blank sheet of paper, draw three columns. The centre column should be around 5cm and the outside column should be of equal size to each other. In one column we write the cues, the middle column will be for any details about the cue and the final column is for the blocking. Whether you are right- or left-handed will determine which column is used for which, as your dominant hand affects how to lay out the pages in a file. If you are right-handed you lay the script on the left, if you are left-handed the script goes on the right. The column

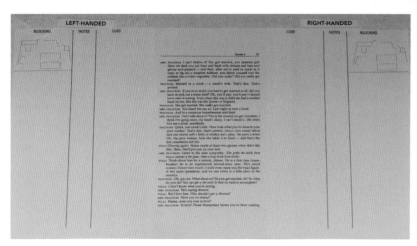

How you make up the book depends on whether you are right- or left-handed.

closest to the script is the cue column and the one furthest away is where the blocking is written.

Add a stage plan to the top of the blocking page. This is not to scale but will show where everything is positioned at the top of every page.

Once this is done, photocopy the sheet and insert one opposite each page of script. Finally place the script and the inserted pages in a lever-arch file. It is not uncommon, on larger productions, to use a separate file for each act as it does become bulky.

Read the script before you start rehearsals, making a note of any prop and furniture requirements, and any lighting, sound, costume and other technical elements that are mentioned. Ensure you are on top of the production before it starts and you understand, from day one, what everyone is talking about. A DSM should be fully prepared for every eventuality, especially when it comes to running rehearsals. Take special notice of any sound effects you will have to make, such as being a doorbell, telephone, or barking dog.

BLOCKING

The first element the DSM will write in the book is the blocking. Blocking is the actor's movements and the DSM notates the moves of each character and what they are doing. It is written in minute detail and, while this may seem extreme, it is crucial that every fact is recorded.

First, it will be used to rehearse any new cast members or understudies into a role, as each actor will follow the same track and do exactly the same moves as the original cast member did. This is so that the production can stay the same and technical elements don't have to change every time there is a new cast. The actor who is playing Marius in the London production of *Les Misérables* will undoubtedly be doing the same moves as Michael Ball did when he opened the show in 1985.

This may sound very restrictive for the actors but they make the role their own by their characterization and what they bring to the part.

The blocking is also invaluable in rehearsals in case the actors forget their moves. A scene may not have been rehearsed for a week or more and this can mean elements may be forgotten or written down wrong. Having the latest blocking documented, a DSM can help remind the actors what to do.

Scenery and furniture moves will also be recorded in the blocking. This will help the DSM set up each scene correctly in the rehearsal room. The lighting designer will also need to know the blocking for the lighting plot so that he can light the correct areas of the stage and focus any specials correctly. The DSM can ensure that the furniture is in the right position and will also direct the ASMs to stand in the correct places to walk the lights.

Blocking Notation

It would be very hard to write every move down in longhand. Even with only a few characters it can be tricky to get everything documented. To help with this a form of shorthand is used. Not every DSM uses the same shorthand and there are several variations, but the premise is always the same and you can usually still decipher and understand blocking if someone has written it another way. I still use what I was taught in training and it is primarily word based, but some variations use pictures instead. Not everything has a separate notation, otherwise the list would run to thousands, so it is only the usual moves and items. If you are working on a production that has a specific piece of furniture it is a good idea to make up a blocking symbol for the item to save time. As long as you have a blocking key, anyone can follow it. For example, if there was a grand piano on the set you might use its initials (GP) or if there was a fireplace, FP.

Before you start, you will also need to abbreviate your characters into shorthand, commonly using the character initials. If you have two characters with the same initials you would use the second

BLOCKING SHORTHAND	MEANING	ALTERNATIVES
SR	Stage Right	
SL	Stage Left	
US	Upstage	
USR	Upstage right	
USL	Upstage left	
USC	Upstage centre	
CS	Centre stage	
CSR	Centre right	
CSL	Centre left	
DS	Downstage	
DSR	Downstage right	
DSL	Downstage left	
DSC	Downstage centre	
PS	Prompt side	
OP	Opposite Prompt	
Off-St	Offstage	
On-St	Onstage	
X	Crosses	
NT	Enters	ENT
XT	Exits	EXT
↑	Stands	
↓	Sits	
⌊→	Kneels	
TBL	Table	▭
CH	Chair	⌐
⟲	Turns anti-clockwise	
⟳	Turns clockwise	
→	Moves	
◠•	Pause	
FOH	Front of House	
B/S	Backstage	
↔	Lying down	
STP	Stop	
+	Towards	
⌐⌐	Downstairs	
⌐⌐	Upstairs	

The blocking shorthand used by a DSM.

letter too, or possibly a surname. For example, all the following characters' names begin with the letter J, so you could either use their initials or maybe the first three letters of their Christian name:

Jake Thomas – Jak or JT
Janet Jones – Jan or JJ
Josh Roberts – Jos or JR
John Harvey – Joh or JH
Jennifer Goldsmith – Jen or JGo
Jerry Grey – Jer or JGr

Once each character has been given an abbreviation and you have a simple blocking notation you are able to begin writing the actors' moves in the book. Each move will form a sentence in shorthand and will start with the character's abbreviation and then a move.

So, if you wanted to write the move, John Harvey stands up, walks towards the centre stage table, you could annotate it as shown here.

A more complicated sequence would be if Jennifer Goldsmith moves towards Jake Thomas, then sits down on the stage left armchair, then stands and exits through the upstage left door.

The trick is to be as brief as possible while still including the detail. In the above description, you might not need to notate that Jennifer stands and then exits as she will need to stand to move to the exit. You can also include words, like 'then' in the example here.

We write it into the book by using numbers, placing a number on the script where the action takes place and the same number in the blocking column in line with the corresponding number. Where

A simple blocking sentence.

A more complicated blocking sentence.

possible the numbers need to be opposite each other. The number needs to be on a word that is spoken by a character and not a stage direction as you need to clearly define where any moves takes place. Stage directions are only one person's interpretation of what moves need to be made and they are not an instruction set in stone that is followed for every production. You cannot therefore rely on them for any precision as far as notating blocking.

Let's say that Josh Roberts is going to enter upstage centre when Jerry Grey says 'Janet'. The illustration overleaf shows what you would write.

On each new page start from number 1 and give each blocking move a separate number. Do not use continuous numbers from page to page as this could run into the millions; furthermore if you don't rehearse the play in sequence you won't actually know what number you have reached. When moves are changed or amended, add point numbers between the old moves, for example 1.1 or 1.2, or use the alphabet, for example 2a, 2b. As long as each move has an individual number on the page you will always be able to find the specific move relating to the numbers.

More than one character may move at the same time, in which case only use one number and place both moves under the same number.

Characters may also move as a reaction to another character move. Again, this would be placed under the same number but would have an additional linking word, such as 'then'.

The blocking can change constantly when you are in rehearsals and this can continue until opening night and beyond. A DSM needs to keep the book up to date and notating the blocking is a never-ending job. Each time the cast rehearse

TOP TIP

Not every DSM will understand your blocking so include a key with your book with the character abbreviations as well. It is a good idea to glue this to the inside left cover of your file. This is especially handy when you are using a lever-arch file, as you will be able to see it all the time whatever page you are working on.

① JR NT USC.

The curtain rises on a living room.

Janet Jones:	Goodbye Mr Grey.
Jerry Grey:	Good afternoon Janet.
Josh Roberts:	I'll put the light on.
Jake Thomas:	Yes, it is getting dark.
Jennifer Goldsmith:	I should be leaving.
Jake Thomas:	It's past my bedtime.

How to mark blocking in the book.

② JJ XT USC
JH ↓

How to notate two blocking moves that happen at the same time.

③ JGO ↓ SL CH
then
JGR ↑ →+ JGO

How to write a blocking move that follows on from another character's actions.

a scene follow the existing blocking and amend any moves. This may be as simple as moving a number in the script. Other moves may be cut or added, which is when additional numbers are required. It is a good idea to neaten the book on a daily basis, going through the scenes that have been worked on so it is clear and easy to read.

The plan of the set is a very useful diagram and will show clearly at the top of each page where each piece of furniture should be and where the individual characters are positioned. On each turn of the page the diagram should be updated to show this information.

The diagram is invaluable when trying to find an individual's last move, especially if they haven't moved for a while. Imagine one character is in bed for a long time. If the pictures weren't on each page, it would take time to read all the previous blocking moves to work out when they first got

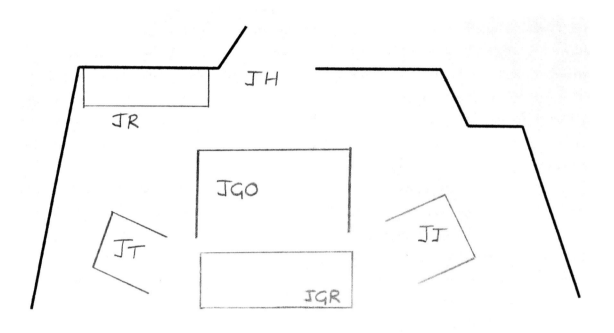

Set plans are useful in a book so you can see where furniture and characters are positioned.

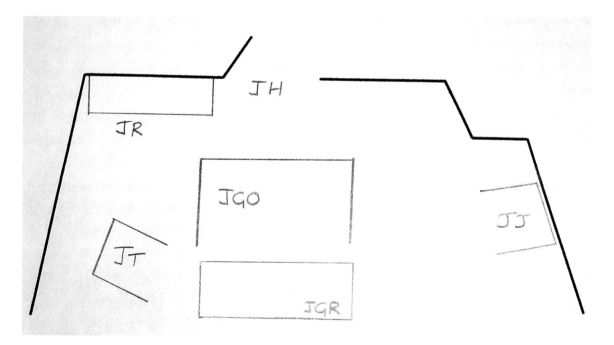

Using set plans on each page enables you to see what has changed from the previous page – compare the previous photo with this one.

TOP TIP

Ignore the stage directions. A director will want the production to be a new version and will not follow the moves created by someone else, unless it is vital to the piece. Some deputy stage managers highlight the stage directions to distinguish them from the characters' lines, but I think this is over-complicated and you would probably find your eyes drawn to the highlighted words.

into bed. By referring to the diagrams you can pinpoint the exact moment much more easily. The diagram is also very useful when you have to answer any questions about where furniture is positioned, when it was moved and who moved it.

CUEING

When a DSM cues the show, they are instructing the other departments when to start the specific cue and the exact time in which to do it. This is done by either saying the word 'go' or pressing the green cue light on the prompt desk, or both at the same time. This cue point needs to be notated

accurately in the book and it is written in the column closest to the script. This is so that cues can be read easily and followed during the pressure of a performance. Every detail that is specific to mechanics of calling the production is written in the cueing column, from the actual cues to any tannoy calls the DSM makes. This is for ease of use so that you only need follow the one column during a show.

Cues on a Word

First, the cue may be on a character's word. In this instance, the word is boxed in and a line is drawn across to the cueing column. The detail of the cue itself is written next to the line with the word GO.

In the example shown here, you would say 'LXQ 2 go', saying the word 'go' as the actor says the word 'grey'.

Cues Before or After a Word

The next way of cueing is if a cue is given before or after a word. On this occasion, an arrow is positioned next to the word indicating where to

Department	Abbreviation
Lighting Cue	LXQ
Sound Cue	SND Q
Upstage Left cue light	USL Q/L
Follow spot Cue	F/S Q
Fly Cue	FLY Q
Visual Cue	VISUAL or 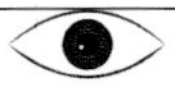
Musical Director	MD
Follow On	F/ON
Audio Visual Cue	AV Q
Revolve	REV Q
Automation	AUTO Q
STBY	STANDBY

Cueing abbreviations that the DSM uses when writing cues in the book.

Janet Jones: Goodbye Mr Grey. ———————— LXQ 2 GO

A cue called on a word.

Josh Roberts: I'll put the light on. ————— VISUAL AS JOSH SWITCHES LIGHT ON LXQ 4 GO

A visual cue.

say 'go' or press the corresponding button on the prompt desk. Some DSMs write a line upwards, but an arrow is very clear and easier to see than just a line. Be careful not to get confused: that the arrow is pointing upwards is not an indication that the cue is called on the line above.

In the example here, you would say 'LXQ 3 go', saying the word 'go' after the actor has said the word 'Janet'.

Visual Cues

If a cue does not relate to a word in the script, it can be called on a character's action or move. If the DSM is watching an actor and waiting for a move this is known as a visual cue. Actors do not always produce an identical performance as timings are often different on a show-by-show basis, but a DSM will know the rough time that an actor should do something. Instead of linking a cue to a word as in previous examples, a line is drawn across the script to indicate that the cue will take place at an approximate time but the actor needs to be watched. So, for example, if an actor needs to go to a light switch onstage and switch a light on, the timing will be very important and this will be a visual cue.

You would say 'LXQ4 go', saying the 'go' as the actor presses the light switch.

If the timing is crucial and you do not want a delay, you may decide to let the operator take the cue themselves as it will be more instantaneous. This is known as an operator visual, as the operator will watch the actor and is not cued by the DSM. It is written in the book in the same way as the visual above. However, there is no GO attached

Jerry Grey: Good afternoon Janet. ↑———— LXQ 3 GO

A cue called after a word.

to the cue and the cue is placed in brackets. This is so the DSM knows that it is happening but does not cue it.

A DSM may warn an operator that the cue point is coming up but will not say anything else at this point.

Follow-On Cues

Finally, cues often follow on from another cue point as a reaction to something else that is cued. This is known as a follow-on cue. When you are notating this, you will write the first cue in one of the previous ways and then indicate with an arrow down and the abbreviation F/ON. Both cues will have the word GO next to them.

When cueing this, leave no gap between the two cues, as they follow on from each other; so you will say, 'LXQ 5 go, SND 1 go'.

There are also operator follow-on cues that work in a similar way to the operator visual cues. An LX board, for example, is often programmed to have an automatic follow-on once the previous cue is completed. In this case, neither the DSM or operator needs to do anything, but it is important that the DSM has this recorded in the book in case it doesn't happen. As with the operator visual, the first cue is written and called as a regular cue and the follow-on cue is written

Josh Roberts: I'll put the light on. ————— VISUAL AS JOSH SWITCHES LIGHT ON LXQ 4 GO

An operator's visual cue.

Jake Thomas: Yes, it is getting dark. ———— LXQ 5 GO
↓
F/ON
SND Q1 GO

A follow-on cue that is called by the DSM.

Jennifer Goldsmith: I should be leaving. ———————— LXQ 6 GO
$$\left(\begin{array}{c} F/ON \\ \downarrow \\ LXQ 7 \end{array}\right)$$

A follow-on cue that is not called by the DSM.

Jake Thomas: It's past my bedtime. ———————— LXQ 8
SND Q 2   } GO
SL Q/L

How to write cues that are called at the same time.

with an arrow down and with the abbreviation F/ON. Again, there is a bracket around the cue, to indicate that the DSM doesn't need to do anything.

These examples only show you single-department cues. If there are various cues that are called at the same time, we do not write them individually with separate GOs, but link them together with a wiggly bracket and one GO. In this way, the cue point is the same for multiple departments. Often this is at the beginning or end of a scene or sequence.

By using these ways of marking cues in the book you can then write any sequence and make it clear for anyone else to pick up and cue from. The beginning and end of an act can be the most complicated to call as cues are often linked to each other in a chain reaction. The clearer but briefer you are the better, as you often don't have a lot of time to read any notes.

NOTES

The middle column is used for a description of what the cue does. The example here is for the cues shown above.

———— LXQ 8
SND Q 2   } GO
SL Q/L
| LX STATE UP
3 SECS
BIRDS UP
4 SECS
JANET JONES
ENTERS.

How to write what the cue does.

A book from a musical showing the cues, notes and blocking.

PLOT SESSIONS

Any lighting, sound or AV cues are initially written in the book during the various plot sessions. During rehearsals, pencil in any cues as the director mentions them, so that when it comes to plot sessions you have an idea of where they will be positioned. Remind the director of these if they don't mention them in the plot.

The plots are individual department sessions where the production is worked through slowly, building each cue with the director. Think ahead to the other plot session when writing cues in the book so you can layer the cues. If the LX plot is first, work out whether any other departments' cues are called at the same time. You often find that an LX cue will be called at the same time as a sound cue, especially at the beginning and end of an act, or that an LX cue is called as a reaction to a sound cue.

The first LX cue may be to bring the auditorium lights down, so ask the director if the front of house music continues or is cued to fade out with the LX cue. The director may then explain that the sound cue happens after the LX cue is complete, then the tabs are flown out once the music is out. You won't have all the numbers for the other departments' cues at this point, but you can start to shape the sequence of cues.

STANDBYS

Standbys are called in order to warn individuals that they have a cue coming up and they need to get

How to write the beginning sequence of a show.

STBY
LXQ 1-8
SND Q 1 & 2
FLY Q 1
SL Q/L

How to write standbys in the book.

ready to action it. Standbys are written in the cue column and are positioned half a page before the cue needs to be called; the exact timing is an approximation and is based on dialogue rather than music. The exact location of the standbys need to be judged accordingly to the individual department needs. An LX operator will not need much time to prepare as they will often just be pressing the GO button on an LX board. A flyman, however, may need longer to get ready. Ensure that the standbys aren't too long as that is where mistakes can occur. The LX operator will have their hand hovering over the button and can easily lose concentration, while the flymen won't thank you if they are holding the weight of the bar with the brake off for a long time.

Standbys are not linked to the script by lines like the GOs, as exact precision is not as vital. Standbys are also called in groups rather than individually. As you can see from the example shown here, you are asking the LX operator to standby for LXQs 1 to 8 because of the spacing of the cues that are about to be called. It is imperative to be able to get the GOs in the correct place and concentrate on their correct placing. By calling standbys in groups the focus is on the script and the action onstage rather than any standbys, which, when you are calling a show, are less important that the cue itself.

Place the standbys and calls in the book during the plot sessions. The creatives will take time to work out the sound levels or to build a lighting state, so you can make use of the time while they are working to get the book ready so you are fully prepared for the technical rehearsal.

CALLS

The DSM is the voice of the production, making announcements for those working backstage and

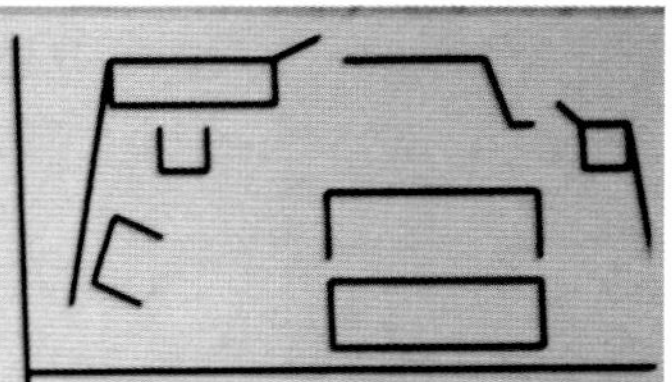

The curtain rises on a living room.

Janet Jones: Goodbye Mr Grey.

Jerry Grey: Good afternoon Janet.

Josh Roberts: I'll put the light on.

Jake Thomas: Yes, it is getting dark.

Jennifer Goldsmith: I should be leaving.

Jake Thomas: It's past my bedtime.

FOH CLEARANCE
5634
LXQ 1 - 8
SND Q 1 & 2
FLY Q 1
SL Q / L

LXQ 1 GO — FOH LIGHTS OUT 9 SECS

VISUAL
MS LXQ 1 COMPLETE
SND Q 1 GO — FOH FADE OUT 4 SECS

MS SND Q 1 COMPLETE
FLY Q 1 GO — Takes out SKID

LXQ 2 GO — LIGHTS BUILD 1 SEC   ① DR NT USC

LXQ 3 GO — WINDOW LIGHT UP 3 SECS   ② JT XT USC JTH ↓

VISUAL
MS JOSH SWITCHES LIGHT ON
LXQ 4 GO — LIGHT ON SNAP

LXQ 5 GO
F/ON
SND Q 1 GO — LIGHT BUILD 10 SECS / CAR HORN SNAP

LXQ 6 GO
F/ON
LXQ 7 — WINDOW LIGHT FADE 8 SECS / LX STATE FADE 2 SECS   ③ JGO ↓ SL CH then JGR ↑ → JGO

LXQ 8
SND Q 2 GO
SL Q/L — LX STATE UP 3 SECS / BIRDS UP 4 SECS / JANET JONES ENTER

CALL
MISS APPLE (GREG)
MISS ZERO (HARRIS)
MR ARTHUR (DENNIS)
MR 2ING (KING)

front of house as well as directing the audience. The purpose of the calls is to inform everyone what is taking place and what is happening next. By giving these calls the DSM will, hopefully, keep everything on schedule. Front of house and backstage calls will therefore need to be placed in the book ready for the technical rehearsal so that it can run smoothly too.

Backstage calls are made to let the cast know that they should make their way to the stage and their entrances are coming up. These calls are known as courtesy calls as they are just that – a courtesy for the cast. If a DSM is solving a problem and misses the call it is still the actors' job to get to the stage on time and, if a cast member misses their entrance, they cannot blame it on the lack of a call. In most theatres there is a show relay that plays a live feed of what is happening onstage to backstage. This is so everyone can hear the play and knows when to prepare for their cues or entrances.

Backstage calls are usually placed at least two pages before the cast member has an entrance. This will be dependent on how long their journey from the dressing room is and what is happening in the play before their entrance. The best way to judge this is to walk their journey yourself and time it, but you can't always do this, so an approximation is good enough.

Courtesy calls are put in the book, ladies first then men and alphabetically using surnames. Place the name of the understudy next to these in case you need them. If you are working on a busy production it is not always possible to call everyone individually so calls for specific scenes are made. The calls are then placed in a box in the cueing column.

So, for example, you might have:

<u>Call</u>
Miss Apple (Greg)
Miss Zero (Harris)
Mr Arthur (Dennis)
Mr Zing (King)

OPPOSITE: The elements mentioned in this chapter placed on a page.

LOOKING AFTER THE BOOK

The book should never be taken away from the rehearsal room or the theatre. It is vital to the running of the show and must never get lost, damaged or left at home by mistake. The DSM can be covered by someone else if they are ill or unable to attend the show or rehearsal but the book cannot be replaced. It is always a good idea to make a copy of the book once it is completed so that you have a back-up in case of accidents or unforeseen circumstances. The book belongs to the producers and is not the DSM's. When the show is finished, the book is handed over to the producer for their safe keeping.

Other calls are to inform both front of house and backstage about times. For example, front of house need to know when the interval is about to start, so the DSM should put a 5-minute call in the book. This is so the staff are ready at the bar or with the all-important interval ice creams. Backstage personnel will also need to know this so they are ready for any interval changes. This may be a scene change or a costume change with an actor. Before a show starts, calls are made so that everyone knows how long it is before the show so they are ready in time for curtain up.

When you are timing the run-throughs in the rehearsal you should indicate in the book every minute as it passes. In this way, you will have a good idea how long each page lasts in terms of time and you will be able to give accurate timings. A good DSM will always have their stopwatch to hand as they will be constantly timing sequences, the show and other aspects such as quick changes. Invest in a good one and ensure that you know how to silence it, as you don't want it bleeping at you every hour, especially during a quiet, emotional scene.

TASK

Why not try putting a book together for the script you have chosen? Have a go at putting some cues into your script and maybe write some blocking down.

A production of *Posh*. PHOTO: RICHARD HUBERT SMITH. DESIGNER: RUARI MURCHISON

9
HEALTH AND SAFETY

Health and safety is paramount and it is one of the biggest aspects of a stage manager's job. The well-being of everyone involved must be a priority. From the minute anyone steps into the rehearsal room until the end of the get-out, the stage management team must constantly review all aspects of the production, be vigilant and observant and adapt to any situation that arises. This not only includes protecting the company, creative teams and technical personnel, but the audience too.

According to the Institution of Occupational Safety and Health and their Managing Safely for Theatre and Production course, there are three main reasons why an organization needs to address health and safety: moral, legal and financial.

Moral Obligations Morally, any individual's well-being needs to be looked after. Staff and audience are essential to the production and their welfare must come first. Although accidents can happen at any time and can be extremely detrimental to an individual's life, the theatre company has an obligation to try to minimize the chances of an incident occurring.

Legal Obligations The Health and Safety Act of 1974 places a duty of care upon employers with regards to their staff and any other individuals that are affected by their work activities.

Financial Obligations Any incident may have financial implications, whether that is due to fines, covering staff absence or production downtime, so it is in the employer's interest to prevent them.

ACCIDENTS ARE RARE

This is a serious subject, but rest assured that accidents are a rare occurrence in theatre. This is because we do take everyone's welfare very seriously and all aspects of staging a production are taken into account and looked at in detail. High-risk elements are usually the safest as they are monitored very closely and will usually be subject to stringent health and safety checks. You are more likely to have an injury due to someone's carelessness, lack of concentration or an unforeseen incident than because of the technical elements of the show itself.

The stage manager is not the employer but may be personally liable for any accidents that occur as they are responsible for overseeing the rehearsal room and the stage. Health and safety needs to be taken seriously wherever you are working. Accidents can be reduced if attention is paid to any possible risks: whichever way you look at it, that can only be good for everyone.

RISK ASSESSMENTS

The best way to pre-empt any forthcoming issues is to write a risk assessment and to think fully about the problems that may occur. Risks could be directly show-related or things commonly faced in everyday life or simply when working within a theatre. The risk assessment should take into account any possible hazards, their consequences to someone's health and anything that can be done to try to reduce the risk of this actually happening and limit the impact if it does.

A production showing an actor working at height, which needs to be assessed carefully. PHOTO: RICHARD HUBERT SMITH. DESIGNER: JAMES TAYLOR

OPPOSITE: A template risk assessment form.

When completing a risk assessment, it is a good idea to follow this six-step approach. It may help to remember the acronym LIEERR.

L List work tasks Make a list of the work tasks. These could relate to an activity or equipment or a specific location.

I Identify the risks What are the hazards, who may be involved in any incident and how might they be harmed?

E Estimate the risk Work out the likelihood of things going wrong and how serious the incident could be. We use the formula Likelihood × Consequence = Risk to work this out.

E Evaluate the risk At this point decide whether you need to take further action to reduce the risk and how urgent this action is.

R Record your findings Formalize the findings and record them in a risk assessment. This is a

RISK ASSESSMENT

| Production: Name of the show | Assessment Stage: Rehearsal or performance | Assessor: The person writing the assessment |
| | Assessment Period: The date of rehearsal or performance | Assessment Date: The date it was written |

Work Activity	Hazard, hazardous event & expected consequence	People affected	Existing control measures	Assessment of Risk			Additional control measures required?
				Likelihood level X	Consequence level =	Risk level	
The event being assessed	The incident that may occur and the possible injuries or outcome.	Who may be affected by this risk	What procedures are in place to prevent accidents occurring	The possibility of the incident actually happening	How serious the resulting injury could be	The ultimate risk level.	Any further measures you need to put in place to avoid accidents and reduce the risk further

Likelihood:
1: Very unlikely   (1 in 1,000,000)
2: Unlikely   (1 in 100,000)
3: Fairly Likely   (1 in 10,000)
4: Likely   (1 in 1000)
5: Very likely   (1 in 100)

Consequence:
1: Insignificant – No injury
2: Minor – Minor injuries needing first aid
3: Moderate – Up to three days absence
4: Major - More than three days absence
5: Catastrophic - Death

Risk level (Likelihood x Consequence)
17-25: Unacceptable - Stop activity and make immediate improvements
10-16: Tolerable Look to improve within specified time scale
5-9 : Adequate Look to improve at next review
1-4 : Acceptable - No further action, but ensure controls are maintained

An actor being safely 'hanged' during a performance.
DESIGNER: NANCY SURMAN

legal requirement if any business comprises five or more people.

R Review your findings The final step is to review the risk assessments periodically, for example when there have been any changes to personnel, equipment or location. There may also be a specified time scale when the review needs to be undertaken.

The stage management team will produce three risk assessments: a rehearsal risk assessment, covering the rehearsal room and produced by the DSM; a production risk assessment; and performance risk assessment, written by the stage manager covering the stage and the theatre, taking into account the added element of an audience.

A risk assessment is written in table form and each specified hazard is given a numerical score that reflects the severity of the risk. This is the risk level (*see* below).

WORK ACTIVITY

The work activity is a description of the event that is being assessed. List activities that take place during the production from the minute anyone walks onto the stage until they leave. It is also worth taking into account any issues they may encounter on their way to the stage, such as the stairs from the dressing room. However, an accident there would fall under the jurisdiction of the theatre management, unless the actress caught her high-heeled shoe in the costume, in which case the production would be liable. Work activities could be a rehearsal of a fight sequence, the dance numbers that are taking place during a musical or an actor using a trapdoor.

HAZARD, HAZARDOUS EVENT AND EXPECTED CONSEQUENCE

This column relates to the incident that may occur and the possible injuries or outcome that may happen as a result of such an accident.

Hazard

The definition of a hazard is something that can potentially cause harm. So, in the above examples, the sword and the trapdoor are the obvious hazards. While there is no obvious external hazard in the dance number, it could be that the cast members may not warm up sufficiently or the stage floor is not being cleaned properly.

A trapdoor being used in a production, which could have safety implications. DESIGNER: DORA SCHWEITZER

Hazardous Event

The hazardous event is something that could happen that has the potential to cause harm. For example, the sword could accidentally come into contact with one of the actors or someone could fall through the trapdoor as it has been left open and unattended, or maybe a dancer pulls a muscle due to slipping on a piece of debris as the stage is dirty.

Consequence

The consequence is the result of the hazardous event. So, the actor who has been injured by the sword could sustain a serious cut or stab wound, the person who has fallen through the trapdoor may suffer from concussion and a broken leg or the dancer could tear a muscle.

PEOPLE AFFECTED

This column specifies which person or group of people could be affected by the risk that is being assessed. Thought must be given to everyone who may be affected. This includes anyone onstage and offstage as well as the audience.

In the fight sequence, you would obviously list the characters directly involved in the fight, but what about other actors that are onstage at the time? An actor might mistime a move and accidentally catch a chorus member with the sword. What about anyone in the wings or in the audience? What if the actor loses their grip on the sword and it ends up in the wings, injuring a crew member, or goes into the audience and hurts an audience member? You must try to think about every eventuality so that measures can be put in place to try to prevent this happening.

EXISTING CONTROL MEASURES

The existing control measures are procedures and practices that are already in place to prevent these accidents occurring.

There are a number of control measures in place for our fight sequence. The actors will have been choreographed by a fight director, who will have signed a document to say they are happy for the fight to be performed. The stage management team will have ensured that the swords used are fit for purpose, that they are blunted, the handles are secure and any extra dressing, such as leather binding, is fixed and safe. The stage management team will also do comprehensive visual inspections every day. The actors will be fully warmed up and do a fight call before each performance. Or, if in rehearsals, they will be asked to slowly mark the fight through before they can rehearse it at full speed. Shoes may also be required to have non-slip rubber soles on them.

A sword fight onstage needs to be risk assessed and choreographed by a fight director. DESIGNER: ADRIAN GEE

COSHH

The Control of Substances Hazardous to Health regulations must be followed. Any chemicals or other hazardous substances can be a risk to health. You must include details of their use in your risk assessments and ensure the substances are used correctly and stored in an appropriate place.

With regard to our trapdoor, there could be an arrangement of ropes and cones set around it if it is open at any time other than during the show. During the show a member of stage management could be in the trap to monitor safety and there may be a crash mat underneath to protect anyone if they do fall.

The dancers would have had a warm-up before the show and been provided with the right footwear to protect themselves from injury. The floor would have been cleaned and swept and treated to prevent slippages. The dancers would have been taught by a choreographer, who ensures everyone is safe. Any difficult or strenuous sequences will be rehearsed before each performance. The dancers would be expected to be honest about their physical condition and if they are feeling any injuries prior to the dance, they would be rested until completely fit and, on a big dance show, there may be a physiotherapist on hand to give assistance.

These are just some of the control measures that may be in place for the specific activities mentioned. There are other measures that should be in place all the time and can be listed on every activity. There should always be a trained first aider on site, for example, and stage management should be trained in basic first aid and have a first aid kit to hand. A member of stage management should always be watching the activity, whether it's the DSM in the rehearsal room or at the prompt desk, or the ASM or SM watching a high-risk activity from the wings. The sequence or activity should always be well rehearsed and the cast should be warmed up suitably for whatever activity they are expecting to do, both vocally and physically.

ASSESSMENT OF RISK

The next three columns deal with the assessment of risk and are written in a numerical format. Some use other number scales, but for this example we are going to use a scale that goes from 1 to 25.

Likelihood Level

This is the possibility of the incident occurring and how likely it will happen on a scale of 1 to 5, 1 being very unlikely and 5 being very likely. When trying to determine the likelihood use the following odds:

1: Very unlikely 1 in 1,000,000
2: Unlikely 1 in 100,000
3: Fairly likely 1 in 10,000
4: Likely 1 in 1,000
5: Very likely 1 in 100

Consequence Level

The consequence is how serious the resulting injuries of an incident or accident could be. Again, the scale we use is 1–5, 1 being insignificant (resulting in no injury), to 5, which is catastrophic and leads to death or a life-changing injury. The following guidelines will help you decide:

1: Insignificant No injury
2: Minor Minor injuries needing first aid
3: Moderate Up to three days' absence
4: Major More than three days' absence
5: Catastrophic Death or life-changing injury

The crew moving a flat safely.

Risk Level

Finally, by multiplying the likelihood and consequence level, we can record a score that is the ultimate risk level of the activity. This will be a number between 1 and 25, because 1 × 1 is the lowest possible score and 5 × 5 the highest possible. When looking at the final number in the risk level column, use the following table to determine the actual risk in real terms:

17–25 Unacceptable Stop the activity and make immediate improvements
10–16 Tolerable Look to improve the risk within a specified timescale
5–9 Adequate Look to improve risk at the next review
1–4 Acceptable No further action is required, but you must ensure control measures are maintained

As you can see from the table, only a score of 1–4 is acceptable. The risk between levels 5 and 16 should still be looked at in further detail with more procedures being put in place so that it can reach an acceptable level. If the activity you were assessing came out with a score of between 17 and 25 your producers and production manager would have serious concerns and would deem it far too risky to continue with this element of the production. You would then need to think about any control measures and try to put more measures in place to further reduce the risk.

Additional Control Measures Required

If your risk level is deemed too high, this final column is for any further control measures that you may need to have in place to reduce the risk even further.

Before anyone steps into the rehearsal room or onto the stage, the DSM and SM should write

a risk assessment. You won't always have had a chance to read the script or know the exact elements associated with the production, so list some standard risks that you will encounter and add to it as items come up. These generic items are things like fire or other security issues that will need an evacuation procedure in place, cables and trip hazards or lighting levels. Food and drink are also regular items to assess as the majority of the shows will have consumables. While you don't know exactly what food is being used, you can list the control measures undertaken such as checking with cast if they have allergies, storing and preparing food correctly and following cleanliness procedures. Think directly about the personnel. Both physical and vocal warm-ups are standard practice in theatre and are in place to protect the actors from any injuries.

Make sure you send all the risk assessments to the production manager, who will keep them on file and issue them to the relevant councils and theatres. Put them up in the rehearsal room and in the theatre so that everyone can read them. Ensure that the control measures outlined are followed exactly and that no one takes any short cuts; this is to protect everyone's well-being and to ensure that the activity is as safe as it can be. If you have stated that food preparation gloves will be worn when getting food ready, you must ensure this happens. If you don't, your risk assessment will count for nothing and you will be liable if someone falls ill.

RISK ASSESSMENT

Production: Beauty and The Beast	Assessment Stage: Performance Assessment Period: 12/01/2018-14/03/2018	Assessor: Sam Terrence Assessment Date: 12/12/2017

Work Activity	Hazard, hazardous event & expected consequence	People affected	Existing control measures	Assessment of Risk			Additional control measures required?
				Likelihood level X	Consequence level =	Risk level	
A fight sequence	The swords used could come into contact with someone causing cuts or wounds.	Cast Technical Teams Stage Management Audience Fight Director Creatives	• A Fight Director will choreograph the fight sequences. • The swords are blunted and checked by the SM team before every performance. • Appropriate shoes will be worn • A fight call will be undertaken each performance and the actors will warm-up before the fight call • A member of the SM team will watch the action.	3	2	6	
A dance number	Those dancing could pull or tear a muscle due to lack of warm-up or stage that has not been cleaned sufficiently.	Cast	• The dancers will warm-up before a performance. • Appropriate footwear will be worn. • The floor will be swept and cleaned before every performance • A choreographer will have taught the dance to the cast. • The cast members will be fit to perform.	4	3	12	
The use of a trap door	Danger of someone injuring themselves due to falling through the open trap door.	Cast Technical Teams Stage Management Creatives	• The trap door will never be left open and unattended. If it is open outside of a performance it will coned off. • A member of the SM team will watch the action when it is open during a performance • A crash mat is set below the trap door to break anyones fall.	2	4	8	

Likelihood:
1: Very unlikely   (1 in 1,000,000)
2: Unlikely   (1 in 100,000)
3: Fairly Likely   (1 in 10,000)
4: Likely   (1 in 1000)
5: Very likely   (1 in 100)

Consequence:
1: Insignificant – No injury
2: Minor – Minor injuries needing first aid
3: Moderate – Up to three days absence
4: Major - More than three days absence
5: Catastrophic - Death

Risk level (Likelihood x Consequence)
17-25: Unacceptable - Stop activity and make immediate improvements
10-16: Tolerable Look to improve within specified time scale
5-9 : Adequate Look to improve at next review
1-4 : Acceptable - No further action, but ensure controls are maintained

OPPOSITE: The risks that have been outlined in this chapter shown on a risk assessment.

RIGHT: The actors warming up onstage.
DESIGNER: NICKY BUNCH

BELOW: Personal protection equipment is an important health and safety requirement when technical departments are working onstage.

Using weapons onstage is becoming increasingly tricky due to the tighter safety regulations. DESIGNER: RICHARD BULLWINKLE

Never change anything without first assessing the new modification or activity and then amending your risk assessment. If you do and an incident occurs you will be liable for any injury and could be negligent.

There are other accompanying documents that you should attach to your risk assessment. These are for any high-risk items that need further explanation. What these are will obviously depend on the production and what activities are involved, but it is common to include more information on weapons, smoking, and naked flames.

FIGHTS AND WEAPONS

If there is any form of fight in the production, with or without weaponry, use a fight director or someone who has professional experience and who can ensure the safety and welfare of the company and crew. They should be engaged to work in rehearsals with the cast, to choreograph the fights and to work through the moves in a slow and detailed manner. Only then should the cast be able to work on the fight at the correct pace. This should always be watched by a third party who is not involved, such as the DSM or director.

Once in the theatre, the actors must not be allowed to conduct the fight sequence until the fight director has attended a session in the technical rehearsals. This is so that the fight can be worked through slowly to ensure everyone's safety. Once cast are in costume and with the correct set and lighting, the dynamics of the fight may be compromised and the fight director will be able to rectify any problems or issues. It may be that there is insufficient light for a sword fight to be performed

Stage Management Health and Safety Log

PRODUCTION... THE SEA .

Description of sequences

1	In Scene 5 Hatch slices Miss Rafi's arm with a pair of draper's shears.
2	Hatch stabs a "dead body" multiple times with a kitchen knife.
3	
4	

Actors or personnel involved

1	Mr Brown and Miss Dennis
2	Mr Brown and Mr Fox
3	
4	

Safety measure required:

1	The shears will be blunted
2	The knife will be retractable.
3	
4	

REHEARSALS — Log each time the sequence is rehearsed.

Date	Person Overseeing	Notes	Signed
25/11/2017	David Hamish	Seq 1 & 2 Choreographed.	David Hamish
27/11/2017	M Yang	Seq 2	Harry Yang
30/11/2017	M Yang	Seq 1 & 2	May Yang
1/12/2017	M Yang	Seq 1	May Yang
2/12/2017	M Yang	Seq 1 & 2	May Yang
4/12/2017	M Young	Seq 1 & 2	May Yang
5/12/2017	M Yang	Seq 1 & 2	May Yang
6/12/2017	M Yang	Seq 1 & 2 .	May Yang

Please note – the first rehearsal should be signed by the fight director or specialist

Theatre Rehearsal (To be signed by Fight Director or specialist)

I confirm I have rehearsed the described sequence in show conditions and authorise the action to take place in performance

FIGHT DIRECTOR, DAVID HAMISH   David Hamish   12/12/2017

Name/Job Title	Signature	Date

Performance Log

Date	Person Overseeing	Notes	Signed
15/12/2017	M. Young	Fight Call & Perf.	May Yang .
16/12/2017	A. Smith	Fight Call & Perf	A Smith
17/12/2017	M. Young	Fight Call & Perf .	May Yang
19/12/2017	A Smith	Fight Call & Perf	A Smith
20/12/2017	A Smith	Fight Call & Perf .	A Smith

Any accidents must be logged in the theatre's accident book.

Signed by DSM Mary Young .... Print Name MARY YOUNG .

Signed by SM A Smith .... Print Name A SMITH .

Date 20/12/2017

It is good practice to make a log of when fights are rehearsed and performed.

Actors performing a fight during a performance.

safely or maybe there is a light that shines too brightly into a performer's face. The fight director will also be able to see if the costume is too restrictive or the footwear needs changing.

It is a good idea to keep a comprehensive record of each time a fight is conducted, who was overseeing it and if there were any concerns or issues. It is also a good idea to get the fight director or professional to sign to say they are happy with the fight and that it is safe for the cast to perform it.

Fight Calls

A fight call should be carried out before each show to ensure that the actors are ready and

Fight calls are important.

happy to perform the fight that day. There are so many aspects that could alter the safety of a fight on any given day, such as an actor feeling unwell, wearing a new pair of show shoes, or even the stage not having been cleaned properly. It is imperative to rehearse each day in a controlled way.

Weapons

Weapons are used in performances on a regular basis and can come in all shapes and sizes. Obviously, weapons are a sensitive subject and no one must ever be allowed to walk around with a weapon, even if it is a replica or a fake, in case it is

TOP TIP

Don't forget that the DSM and SM are ultimately responsible for any accidents either in the rehearsal room or onstage. It is therefore in your own interest to get a professional to oversee any difficult elements. If your director wants to continue without a professional's advice, ask them to fill in the log to confirm that they will take responsibility and that if an incident occurs they will be liable.

Cleaning the weapons is important after they have been used.

mistaken for the real thing. It must be kept locked away at all times, unless in use during a performance or rehearsals, when it is strictly observed by a member of stage management at all times.

The guidelines in the UK are understandably becoming increasingly strict as far as the use of weaponry is concerned. If a weapon has to fire, an armourer may need to be employed. If you are using a blank firer, you may not need an armourer, but do ensure that you know how to fire it correctly and that you have taught your actors the appropriate procedures too. If you are in any doubt about the firing or the suitability of a weapon, consult a professional.

MAINTENANCE

It is vital that any weapon used is correctly maintained, that it is visually checked before each performance and that any working parts are oiled and tested too. It must be cleaned carefully after every use so that there is no danger of debris causing injuries.

Fight and Weapons Plot

You should document each fight on a fight plot and the weaponry on a weapons plot and attach these to the risk assessment. These are detailed lists outlining what needs to happen at any time.

The fight plot is a fight-by-fight plan of who is involved, what weaponry is used, if any, and the safety measures undertaken.

The weapons plot will document where the weapons are kept, who holds the keys to the

A close-up of the SM team cleaning weapons after a show.

HANDLING FIREARMS

Never point a weapon directly at someone's face, whether it is loaded or not. Always angle the gun away from the body. When firing, ensure that the weapon is at a safe distance from anybody else and, in particular, that no one is close to the barrel as the noise can damage an eardrum. Never rest a finger on the trigger. You could always use a sound effect of a gun firing or fire a weapon backstage rather than relying on the cast onstage. This solves the safety issue onstage and may also reduce any costs.

weapons cupboard, how they will be transported to the stage, how they are passed to and from the actors and other safety measures that are in place.

OPPOSITE: A fight plot documents the fights in a production.

Crime and Punishment

Fight Plot

When	Character	Description	Notes
1.3	• Katerina Ivanovna Marmeladova • Zosimov	Domestic fight. • Marmeladova frisks Zosimov then smacks his head against the floor. • Marmeladova picks Zosimov up by the hair and swings him in a circle	Zosimov will control the movements and will take it at his pace. He will have control of Mameladova's hand at all times.
1.5	• Amalia Lippeweschel • Raskolnikov	Axe Murder • Raskolnikov approaches Lippeweschel from behind and turns her around. • Raskolnikov hits Lippeweschel in the stomach with the axe. • Once Lippeweschel falls Raskolnikov hits her in the back with the axe.	The axe will be a prop axe made of foam. The actress will be wearing knee pads
1.5	• Raskolnikov • Razumikhin	Rugby Tackle • Raskolnikov falls over the back of the chaise. • Razumikhin grabs Raskolnikov • Raskolnikov escapes but Razumikhin rugby tackles Raskolnikov to the floor.	
1.13	• Katerina Ivanovna Marmeladova • Luzhin • Svidrigailov	Punch and lift • Marmeladova pushes Luzhin into the chair • Svidrigailov picks up Marmeladova • Marmeladova punches Svidrigailov	Luzhin will have feel the chair behind legs before being pushed. Marmeladova will not push with force. Marmeladova will not make contact with Svidrigailov at all.

Existing Safety Measures:

All fights will be signed off by a fight director before the actors enter the space and the fight director will hold a fight call during the technical rehearsal to sign off the fights in performance conditions.

A member of the SM team will be present for every fight to ensure that the proper safety requirements are being met.

There will be a fight call before every performance,

During performances, a member of the SM team will watch every fight from offstage, to ensure that any injuries can be dealt with as soon as the actor(s) come offstage.

The SM team are first aid trained and a first aid box will be back stage for every performance and on stage rehearsal

Debbie Julian
DSM Crime and Punishment
CP@email.co.uk 06950 866 663

V1 24/02/2017

MACBETH

WEAPONS PLOT

Perf Dates: 25-18th June 2017

The firearms are stored in a locked weapons case in the weapons cabinet in the technical office. The SM will ensure the weapons are cleaned and checked before the show.. Only the PM will have keys to the office. A member of Stage Managemenet will watch the weapons onstage at all times.

Time	Action
The Five	The SM borrows the keys from the PM, unlocks the weapon cabinet and take the case to the SL wing.
Beginners	The SM unlocks the case and hand Mr Grove the Bruni 96 and Mr Summers the 1911. They enter USC.
Act 1 Scene 2	The SM collects Bruli 96 from Mr Summers and 1911 from Mr Grove USC and locks the weapons in the case.
Act 1 Scene 5	The SM unlocks case and hands the Range Revolver and knife to Mr Last who enters SR.
Act 1 Scene 6	The SM collects Range Revolver and knife from Mr Last SL and locks the weapons in case.
Act 1 Scene 7	The SM hands Master Bennett the AK47 who enters SL.
Act 2 Scene 1	The SM collects AK47 from Master Bennett SL and locks it in weapons case.
Act 2 Scene 2	The SM hands the ASM 2 x daggers covered in blood SL. The ASM hands them to Miss Fisher SR.
Act 2 Scene 3	The ASM collects the daggers from Miss Fisher, Front of House, then returns to the SL wing and hands them to the SM. The SM locks the daggers in the weapons case.
Act 2 Scene 3	The SM hands the Bruni 96 to Mr Johns who enters USC.
Act 2 Scene 4	The SM collects Bruni 96 from Mr Moody SL and locks the weapon in the case.
Act 3 Scene 2	The SM hands Miss Russell the AK47 who enters USC
Act 3 Scene 2	The SM collects the AK47 from Miss Russell and locks it in the weapons case.
INTERVAL	

Grant Russell. SM. Macbeth
Macbeth@ email.co.uk   06762 554 443

V3 18/6/2017

ABOVE: A weapons plot outlines which weapons are used during a show.

Naked flames being used during a production.
DESIGNER: RICHARD BULLWINKLE

Lit candles being used during a show.

NAKED FLAMES

Any form of naked flame in a performance will need to be carefully assessed and fully thought through in terms of safety. If you are using a candle, you will need to specify who lights it and what it is lit with, the duration that it is lit for and how it is extinguished. You will also need to think about the surface that it is on and other safety precautions that need to be in place.

You will need to fill in a flame plot and attach it to the risk assessment. Similar to the weapons plot, it is a comprehensive list of all the times flames are used in the production and the exact details.

Sand is often used whenever fire is present as it will ensure that flame goes out on contact with it. Often it is kept in a sand bucket in the wings or you could have it in the vessel that the candle is placed on.

Any material, wood, scenery or props must be fireproofed whether using naked flame in the production or not. Some of these items may be

JULIUS CAESAR

Flame plot

Scene/ Page no.	Item	Location item is Ignited	Action	Location item is Extinguish	How item is disposed or stored
Scene 14 Pg. 30-35	4 Flambeauxs	The ASM's will light the flambeaux's in the FOH foyer and hand them to the actors. One of the ASM's will open and close the auditorium door for the actors to enter and watch them until they reach the stage.	The actors will appear from the FOH foyer and move to the stage via the 3 different audience aisles. While onstage the actors will be positioned up stage away from the audience.	The actors will extinguish the flambeaux's onstage by letting go of the "safety bar", which releases the spring and allows the metal casing to shut. The casing surrounds the flame and cuts off the oxygen, which extinguishes the flame.	Two of the ASM's will be waiting by the upstage centre door to collect the flambeauxs and place them in 2 two large buckets for extra safety. The flambeaux are stored in a lockable metal container in the SM office
Scene 16-17 Pg. 41-44	Candle in candleholder	The candle will be lit in the wing space stage right by the Stage Manager.	The actor carries a tray with the candle on from the upstage centre entrance and places the candle on the steps downstage of the gold circular platform.	The candle is blown out on stage from it's orginal position on the steps.	A member of the acting company brings the candle offstage where a member of stage management will collect it.

Existing control measures

The candle will be lit by a long taper and the flambeaux by a long-nose lighter.
The ASM's will ensure they carry a fire extinguishers FOH when they are preparing the flambeaux. The SM will also have an extinguisher backstage.
The actors will be given a health and safety talk. They will also be given clear instructions on how to use the flambeaux's and how to extinguish them safely.
The SM team will inspect the flambeauxs before each performance and also ensure the candle has a long wick and is not too short.
A member of Stage Mnaagement will watch the lit items at all times.
The flambeaux, candles and lighting equipment will be kept in a lockable metal container when not in use.

Ellie Baker
Stage Manager – 'Julius Caesar'
baker@email.co.uk   0625 5306709

V1 03/04/2017

A flame plot shows the details of any naked flames that are used during a production.

FIRE AND EMERGENCY PROCEDURE

Never use the words "FIRE" or "BOMB" as this may cause panic amongst the public.

In the event of an emergency use the following code words:

MR JET = FIRE

A FRIEND OF MR JET = ANY OTHER SITUATION

(E.g. Mr Jet is in the building)

---

1) As soon as any emergency is discovered, inform the Front of House Manager.

2) The FOH Manager is responsible for phoning the fire brigade, and must decide whether it is necessary to evacuate the building.

3) If the decision is taken to evacuate the building, the FOH Manager will allocate ushers to man the exits and then make an announcement to the audience.

4) The SM will warn the backstage areas of the decision to evacuate the building

---

ASSEMBLY POINT

The Dukes Head Pub car park

---

5) Do not stop to collect any belongings

6) Once the evacuation is complete, if possible, a full search of the building will be made.

7) The FIRE OFFICER will stay at the Assembly point until:

   a) Confirmation has been received that all the allocated search areas are clear.
   b) The Fire Brigade has arrived.

A fire and evacuation procedure for a theatre.

pre-treated in their manufacture or they may need to be treated with a flame-retardant liquid. There are various proprietary brands available for this, such as Flamebar or Flamecheck, to name two. These are sold in different types depending on what item you are fireproofing, for example straw or paper or cloth. The liquid is sprayed onto the item and left to dry. This must be done regularly.

Ensure that you know where the fire extinguishers are and that you are aware of the fire procedures for the theatre you are working in. Make sure you know where the meeting point is and that all the information has been passed onto the cast and crew. Each company or building will have their own code words for emergencies that are used in earshot of an audience to avoid panic. You will often find that fire is given a man's name, such as 'Mr Sands' or 'Mr Jet'. Any other possible incidents, such as a bomb or other such related occurrence, could be another man's name – 'Mr Black' – or could be coded as 'a friend of Mr Sands' or 'a friend of Mr Jet'.

SMOKING

Smoking is another high-risk item that is often required during performance, though it is, quite rightly, becoming harder to include due to the health risks.

An actor smoking onstage during a show. DESIGNER: RICHARD BULLWINKLE

At the time of writing, it is illegal to smoke inside any building in the UK. However, depending on the individual theatre or the council who oversees it, you may be able to obtain permission to smoke during a performance in England. The director or producer would have to justify the reason that there was a specific need to smoke and outline, in the script, where it takes place and who smokes. The council would have the final say as to whether they would allow it or not. If permission is granted, you can only smoke during performances and not rehearsals, including technical and dress rehearsals.

It is advisable for the stage manager to have a private discussion with the actor concerned to see if they are happy to smoke as they may feel they have been coerced into saying yes. Think about replacing tobacco cigarettes with herbal varieties or using e-cigarettes or an e-pipe. Cigars should be avoided wherever possible as they smell very strong and the smoke is denser.

Obviously, the health issues must take precedence over everything else when you are thinking about the risk implications of smoking, but don't overlook the safety aspects and the fact that cigarettes are a lit item and could therefore cause a fire. Think about how and where they will be lit and extinguished and use a substance to ensure they have been put out correctly. You could use either sand or water, but we often use a lubricant jelly or a hand soap or shower gel as these are more controllable and don't spill over. Whatever you use, ensure that it is not flammable itself.

As with the other high-risk items, attach a smoking plot to the risk assessment. Again, it is a detailed description of who smokes what and when, how the cigarette is lit and extinguished and the duration of the smoking.

The items outlined above are the most common risks that need to be considered when compiling your risk assessment, but there may need to be further documents depending on the show. I have

Twelfth Night

| Production: Twelfth Night |
| Date 12/08/2017 V1 |

Stage management will always watch during these scenes and have a fire bucket/extinguisher to hand.
All receptacles will have clear, non-flammable gel in them.
Herbal cigarettes will be used where possible.

Page	Character	Substance	Amount	How and where it is lit	How and where it is extinguished
8	Sir Toby Belch	Cigarette	1 whole	Sir Toby Belch, Lighter DSL	Either in an empty beer can or in a container on the reverse of mast
8	Sir Toby Belch Sir Andrew Maria	Cigarette	1 whole	Sir Toby Belch lights it in Sir Andrew's mouth using a lighter SL then Maria takes it off Sir Andrew	In the wings, SR
10	Sir Toby Belch	Cigarette	1 whole	Lighter USC	Either in an empty beer can or in a container on the reverse of mast
17-18	Sir Toby Belch	Cigarette	1 whole	As Sir Toby Belch enters from SR using a lighter	In the wings, SL
32	Sir Toby Belch	Cigarette	1 whole	Sir Toby Belch DSL using a lighter	Either in an empty beer can or in a container on the reverse of mast
64	Sir Toby Belch Maria Fabian	Cigarette	3 whole	Sir Toby Belch + Fabian lit USR with lighter.	Empty beer can USL

Steve Simons Twelfth Night SM
Twelfth@email.co.uk 06889 125 677

A smoking plot details who smokes, when and for how long.

worked on a show where the actors had to smash the set each night. This included smashing a TV as well as bottles and glass. This was rehearsed very well and, where possible, plastic and Perspex was used, but even though it was controlled there was always a risk that something could go wrong, so a smash plot was written. Similarly, when working with animals it is always a good idea to add a detailed description – for example, a dog plot was written for a production of *Of Mice and Men*.

MEDICAL FORMS

It is imperative that everyone fills in medical forms. This is so the stage management team can ensure no one is given anything that they may be allergic to or that can risk their health. Also, if an accident does happen, the stage management team may need to inform a medical professional about any health issues that an individual has.

The welfare of everyone is vital to the smooth running of the production, and stage management always need to keep a close eye on anything that changes as well as the day-to-day running of the show. If you follow the guidelines that you have written in the risk assessments and use your common sense, you should have no issues and a happy and healthy personnel.

TASK

Have a look at your script and see what activities you think may be a hazard and what control measures you would need to put in place. Use the blank risk assessment in this chapter and have a go at filling it in.

10
RUNNING A SHOW

Once all the preparation for the production has been completed, the fun task of running the show can begin. The whole team will be tasked with ensuring that the show remains faithful to the first night performance and retains the vision that the creatives had.

OPPOSITE: Grange Park Opera's performance of *Oliver* taking place.
DESIGNER: RICHARD KENT

ASSISTANT STAGE MANAGER

The assistant stage manager will run the wings, making sure that all the props and furniture are set correctly, helping with scene and quick changes and doing anything that may be required.

Prop Tables

A well laid-out prop table is a joy to see and makes everyone's life easy, including the stage management team's. Try to replicate the setting that was used in the rehearsal room. Tables should be placed in the same area in the wings so that props and furniture can be found easily be the actors. Each item should have its place and should be permanently marked. We do this by placing lines

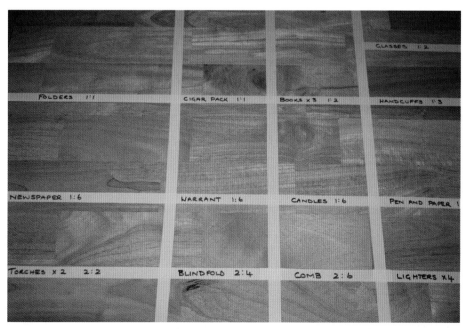

A prop table marked up ready for the props.

of LX tape on the table marking the object's area and then writing what the item is on the LX tape. If the item is too big to be on a table, it will be positioned in the wing and marked out in a similar way. This means that when we are setting up we can always see what is missing. If an item starts onstage it should still have a home backstage so it doesn't get lost.

Personal Props

Personal props are items that the actors should have on their person at all times during a performance. They are usually small props that are 'personal' to their character, such as a pair of glasses, jewellery or maybe a wallet or handbag. The stage management team should collect them at the end of each show and hand them out after the half-hour call for the next performance. They should be taken to the actors in their dressing room or handed to them as they arrive onstage. Include these props on the setting list so nothing is missed and everything is checked and working correctly.

Setting Lists

To help set up the props and furniture identically for every rehearsal or show, produce a setting list. This

An actor wearing glasses, which are personal props. DESIGNER: RICHARD BULLWINKLE

is a comprehensive list of each item that is needed with explanatory detail as required – for example how much liquid is in the teapot or how the desk drawer is set. It can throw an actor if something is not as it usually is and it is stage management's job to assist them with their performance.

The DSM will have supplied a prop and furniture setting list that is generated during rehearsals. This should be comprehensive and detailed, listing each prop and where it starts at the top of the show. All members of the team should already have a good idea of the set-up but it is best to work from the same initial document and adapt it as the production week progresses.

The ASM will take charge of the list from the scene change rehearsal onwards, keeping it updated at all times and constantly referring to it when setting up. Once the production period is over and the production is finely tuned, the list can be typed up and issued to the DSM and SM.

The setting list should be methodical, working from one side of the stage to the other and it should include detailed photos and diagrams. Anyone should be able to pick up the list and set the show up. Include everything, from the onstage setting to the wings and backstage areas. It is important to be very precise when writing a setting list as the specific setting is imperative for your actors.

Let's go back to the desk drawer mentioned earlier. If your setting list showed that the drawer has a notepad, pen, book of stamps and a wallet in it you would assume you had set it correctly if all the items are inside. But this assumption would be wrong as the actual placement of the items is crucial for the actor using them. If they are left-handed, they might want the pen to be set to the left of the notepad whereas if they are right-handed it might be the other way round. If the wallet wasn't needed until the final scene the actor may want it set behind the rest of the items, or if it is used first it would be at the front of the drawer. When you are writing a shout check (*see* below), you should list the items accompanying it with a photo or diagram.

Shout Check

While using a setting list is vital, even more imperative is a shout check. This is when two of the stage management team take a tour of the set and backstage areas to check the items are set correctly. The aim of this list is to enable the team to set the stage identically and accurately for each performance. It is primarily the ASM's job, but if there is only one ASM, the SM or DSM will need to help.

The shout check should be performed before every rehearsal and performance and even each act if there is a big interval reset. It is usually carried out just before the house is open, often during the actors' warm-ups.

When undertaking a shout check, one person reads from the setting list while the other checks the items are present and set correctly. They then confirm this verbally, hence 'shout' check. It is important that the items are inspected visually to see that they are on their marks and set correctly but also checked physically too, ensuring each object is functioning and working as it should be. The best way to do this is to handle the props – try the lighter, for example, to test it is working and write with the pen to check it does have ink. If you have a table with a drawer, open the drawer to check that it is operational and then check the right items are in it.

TOP TIP

It is very easy to become blasé about shout checks, especially when you are working on a long-running production, and you may feel that doing one is not necessary because you know the show so well you do not need to double-check everything. In fact, this is the very time that a shout check is vital; as you get into the routine of running a show, one day can roll into another and items can be easily forgotten. Furthermore, if something is misplaced or goes wrong, you can with confidence say to your actors that it was all set correctly.

 CHILDREN'S HOUR SETTING LIST

ACT 1 – Preset on stage (blue marks)

USR

Cross backed wooden chair - SR of double door Desk with • Wooden box USR (make sure there's room for the lid to be open entirely). • Inside the box a small blue & white tin box with at least 3 X biscuits • Typewriter centre • Library lamp, DSR • Blotter DS of typewriter • Martha's fountain pen between blotter and typewriter –check working US desk drawer • Small tray with a key • 4 notebooks Notice board on hook above desk. with notices and pins Arm wooden chair -SL of desk	

Window seat

1 x red cover book DSR	

DSR

Small desk In drawer • Scotch tape • Karen's fountain pen – check working 2 chairs SR and US of desk	

Centre Stage

Sofa • 2 cushions on SR side white and orange • 2 cushions on SL side white patterned and black pattern	
Side table -SR of sofa Sewing basket SL set with: • red band on top • flowers, • a needle with thread in a pin cushion, • 4 thread spools, • a pocket of pins, • a tape measure, • a pair of small scissors • Burgundy hat on top of sewing basket • 3 books USR • 2 x red covers • 1 x blue cover	

Terry Clark ASM The Children's Hour
hour@email.co.uk 06543 432 321   V 6 9/1/2107

ABOVE AND OPPOSITE: A setting list for a production. The ASM will use this to set the stage and to perform a shout check.

Sofa table - US to sofa Wooden tray, SR set with: • a jug of water, half full, • 4 tumblers • a handkerchief covering them • White towel under it • 3x books SL • 1 x red cover • 1x burgundy cover • 1 x green cover	

DSL

Bench Chair US of bench set with • Evelyn's satchel with apple and comb inside	

USL

Square table set with; • Tall lamp USR • Telephone DSL • China kitten centre • Chair, DS side to table • Tin bin with a piece of serge in, US of table	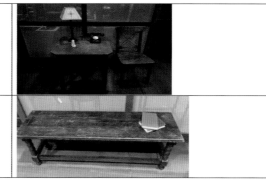
Bench • 2 x books red-cover SL of bench	

USC (US of flat).

SR of door Coat stand • Jacket and a hat hanged SR side Small table SL of table	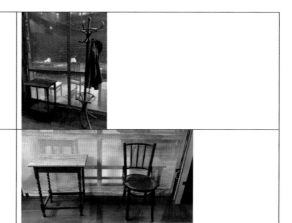
SL of door Chair Small table SL of chair	

Terry Clark ASM The Children's Hour
hour@email.co.uk 06543 432 321   V 6 9/1/2107

A prop table set up for a show.
GRANGE PARK OPERA. DESIGNER:
RICHARD KENT

Setting up for the show in terms of the scene changes and wings is very important, and the more thought and preparation put into it, the easier the process will be. It also makes it more straightforward when things change or items are requested at different times as you know where everything is meant to be and where you can find it.

Book Cover

As an ASM you may get the opportunity to be book cover and call (cue) the show. It is the individual's responsibility to learn the show and to keep up to date with any changes that occur. It is rare for a rehearsal to be held for a new DSM or ASM to learn the book and usually you will have the daunting, yet exhilarating, experience of calling your first show in front of a paying audience.

The best way to learn the show is to shadow the current DSM in the corner and watch them cue the show. Then work through the book at the prompt desk with an audio recording of the show. While you will not get to cue the visual cues, you will get to dry call the show and feel the timings. Then sit with the DSM and call some sequences during the performances and gradually take on more and more until you can call the show on your own.

Once the book is learnt, try to call it regularly so you can keep up to date with the show. Often, in larger productions, the ASM/book cover will get the opportunity to regularly swap roles with the DSM each week so this can happen.

DEPUTY STAGE MANAGER

The DSM runs the show from the prompt desk and is responsible for the timekeeping and cueing the production. This is known as calling a show. In the event and conference side of the profession, you will hear the job referred to as a show-caller.

Prompt Desk

The prompt desk is made up of cue lights, headsets, monitors, microphones and speakers and has everything a DSM needs to run the show. This will include calling the cues to tannoy calls, front of house and backstage.

Always check the prompt desk before every session and in plenty of time so that it can be fixed if there is a problem. This should be before each dress, performance and understudy call. Check that all the cue lights are working, the comms system is on and functioning and the clock is showing the correct time. If there is anything wrong talk to the sound department as they are responsible for the prompt desk, the cue lights and comms system.

Monitors

It is imperative that the DSM can see the stage at all times and, as the prompt desk is usually situated on the SL side of the stage, a DSM will often get a restricted view. Monitors are provided so the DSM can clearly see the stage and, depending on the production, there will be a number of camera angles available. A DSM will always need to see the production from the auditorium to

The prompt desk is where the DSM sits and works during a performance.

see the whole stage. They may also have a view from above so they can see from US to DS. This will help when scenery is flying or moving so they get a clear perspective as it is not always easy to judge if someone is too close to a piece of scenery from just the front view. There may also be an infrared camera, which is essential when you have cast onstage during a blackout and scenery is moving at the same time. If you are working on a production with an orchestra it will be crucial for the DSM to be able to see the musical director or conductor. This is because many cues will be taken off their directions, such as the start or end of a musical piece or cue points given to the actors.

Show Relay Speaker

There may be a speaker, which will enable the DSM to hear the show better. This is especially useful during a quiet scene when there is a cue point on an actor's line and they can't be heard clearly.

Show relays are a live audio feed that is sent to speakers backstage, in the dressing rooms and front of house offices. It is so that everyone knows what is happening onstage and can be on time to fulfil their jobs, whether actors' entrances or scene changes. Do be aware that the show relay will probably not be switched off before and after the show and in the interval, so you can be heard at all times.

Microphones

The DSM is the voice of the production and will be the timekeeper too. The DSM makes front of house and backstage calls before, during and after the performance.

Clock

Always check that the clock on the prompt desk is showing the correct time. The DSM will refer to it to perform any pre-show announcements backstage and front of house and to ensure the show goes up at the right time. They will also use it to time the duration of the production.

BACKSTAGE AND FRONT OF HOUSE CALLS

PRE_SHOW CALLS

TIME		NOTES	CALL	SPEECH
		BACKSTAGE	Vocal and Physical warm-up	
1.25	6.55	BACKSTAGE 35 minutes before curtain up	Half-an-hour call	Good afternoon/evening Ladies and Gentlemen of the "insert show's name" company, this is your half an hour call. You have half an hour, 30 minutes please. Thank you."
		FOH When the SM has opened the house to the audience		Good afternoon/evening Ladies and Gentlemen and welcome to the "insert name" Theatre. The auditorium is now open for this afternoon's/evening's performance of "insert show name". May we remind you that the use of cameras or recording equipment is strictly prohibited and please turn off all mobile phones. Drinks may be brought into the auditorium in a plastic cup and you can now order your interval drinks at the bar. Thank You
1.30	7.10	BACKSTAGE 20 minutes before curtain up	Quarter of an hour call	Ladies and Gentlemen of the "insert show's name" company, this is your quarter of an hour call. You have quarter of an hour, 15 minutes please. Thank you"
1.40	7.20	BACKSTAGE 10 minutes before curtain up	Five minute call	Ladies and Gentlemen of the "insert show's name" company this is your 5 minute call. You have 5 minutes. Thank you"
1.55	7.25	BACKSTAGE 5 minutes before curtain up	Beginners call	Ladies and Gentlemen of the "insert show's name" company this is your Act One Beginners Call. Your call please: Miss Andrews, Miss Wilson, Mr Arnold, Mr Yates Mr "insert Conductor or MD's surname" And Ladies and Gentlemen of the Orchestra. Standby please, Stage Management, LX, Sound, Crew, Flys, Wigs and Wardrobe. This is your Act One Beginners call. Your call please: (Repeat as above)
1.55	7.25	FOH	3 bar bells	Ladies and Gentlemen, would you kindly take your seats. This evening's performance will begin in 3 minutes. This evening's performance will begin in 3 minutes. Thank you.
1.57	7.27	FOH	2 bar bells	Ladies and Gentlemen, would you kindly take your seats. This evening's performance will begin in 2 minutes. This evening's performance will begin in 2 minutes. Thank you.
1.58	7.28	FOH	1 bar bell	Ladies and Gentlemen, would you kindly take your seats. This evening's performance will begin in 1 minute. This evening's performance will begin in 1 minute. Thank you.
1.59	7.29	FOH	1 long bar bell	Ladies and Gentlemen, would you kindly take your seats. This evening's performance is about to begin. This evening's performance is about to begin. Thank you.
2.00	7.30	FOH & BACKSTAGE	CURTAIN UP	Lights up on Act One

ABOVE AND OPPOSITE: Backstage and front of house calls: what to say and when.

BACKSTAGE AND FRONT OF HOUSE CALLS

		FOH & BACKSTAGE 5 Minutes before the interval	1 bar bell	Standby for Lights down on Act One, standby for lights down on Act One. Thank You
		INTERVAL		
		BACKSTAGE 10 minutes before the show resumes	Five minute call	Ladies and Gentlemen this is your 5 minute call. You have 5 minutes please. Thank you
		BACKSTAGE 5 minutes before the show resumes	Beginners call	Ladies and Gentlemen of the "insert show's name" company this is your Act Two Beginners Call. Your call please: Miss Andrews, Miss Wilson, Mr Arnold, Mr Yates Mr "insert Conductor or MD's surname" And Ladies and Gentlemen of the Orchestra. Standby please, Stage Management, LX, Sound, Crew, Flys, Wigs and Wardrobe. This is your Act Two Beginners call. Your call please: (Repeat as above)
		FOH 5 minutes before the show resumes	3 bar bells	Ladies and Gentlemen, would you kindly take your seats. This evening's performance will continue in 3 minutes. This evening's performance will continue in 3 minutes. Thank you.
		FOH 3 minutes before the show resumes	2 bar bells	Ladies and Gentlemen, would you kindly take your seats. This evening's performance will continue in 2 minutes. This evening's performance will continue in 2 minutes. Thank you.
		FOH 2 minutes before the show resumes	1 bar bell	Ladies and Gentlemen, would you kindly take your seats. This evening's performance will continue in 1 minute. This evening's performance will continue in 1 minute. Thank you.
		FOH 1 minute before the show resumes	1 long bar bell	Ladies and Gentlemen, would you kindly take your seats. This evening's performance is about to continue. This evening's performance is about to continue. Thank you.
		FOH & BACKSTAGE 5 Minutes before the end of the show	1 bar bell	Standby for Lights down on Act Two, standby for lights down on Act Two. Thank You
		END OF THE SHOW		
		BACKSTAGE		Thank you very much Ladies and Gentlemen. The times for this evenings performance are; Act One "insert time" Act Two "insert time" Making a total of "insert running time – including interval) Your call for tomorrow's show is "insert time" Thank You

Backstage Calls

Before the performance, the DSM calls the actors to the stage for warm-ups and announces pre-show time checks so that everyone is ready to start the show 5 minutes before the advertised start time. Hopefully this means that once front of house clearance is received, the performance can start. During the show the DSM puts courtesy calls out backstage. After the show an announcement is made thanking everyone, telling them the times of the show and what their call time is tomorrow.

Front of House Calls

The DSM will make a series of announcements to front of house. Before the show, it will be to inform the audience that they can take their seats, how long they have before the show starts and where they can order interval drinks and to request they turn off mobile phones and not use cameras.

Headsets

Known as cans or comms, the prompt desk is equipped with a pair of headsets so the DSM can talk to the operators and give them their cues verbally. There are usually two separate rings so that the departments don't hear what the other one is

Stage management wearing costume and cans. DESIGNER: RUARI MURCHISON

saying and they can talk independently of the others. However, it's good practice always to have both rings on as you should never need to have a private conversation with an individual that the others can't hear, and what you are saying might be relevant to another department even if you don't think it is.

Cue Lights

Cue lights are another way for the DSM to cue the show. They work on a traffic light system, where red is the standby and green is go. There is often a yellow bank of cue lights, which are there so the greens can be pre-set in case you run out of fingers to operate the buttons. Each set of red, yellow and green cue lights will be marked up to show where they are connected to, for example, the LX operator, or the flys or the DSR door. Cue lights are then placed around the set linked to the desk so that the DSM can cue anyone they cannot speak to, such as the actors for their entrances or

CANS ETIQUETTE

There are various rules of etiquette that should be followed when you are on cans. There should be no talking about anything other than the show. I'm not saying chatting doesn't happen, because it does, but it is best practice not to and it should *never* occur between the standby and the GO of a cue. You should never shout on cans and if you are talking or relaying information to someone not on a headset, please switch the microphone off. Do not chew when your mic is live and do your upmost not to swear.

The cue lights that the DSM uses to cue the show.

crew for any scene changes. It is also customary for the LX and sound operators, as well as the fly-man, to have cue lights as well as headsets. This is so they can see and hear their cues at the same time. You may find that sound will only use cue lights during the show as they need to listen to the show. It is also best for the fly floor to only have one set of cans to avoid any confusion.

Cueing the Show

Using the book, the DSM will cue the show using a combination of cue lights and headsets. First, give the operators standbys, either verbally on headsets or by pressing the departments' corresponding red standby button. The standbys will be acknowledged by the individual departments to say they have heard or seen it. The standby lights will flash until the operator has engaged the button from their end.

For example, if the book says:

STBY
LXQ1–5
SND Q1–4
DSR Q/L

You would say and do this:

DSM: 'Standby LXQ 1 to 5' and then press the LX standby button so it flashes.
LX Operator: 'LX standing by' and then press the standby button so it stops flashing.

DSM: 'Thank you. Standby sound Q 1 to 4' and press the sound standby button so it flashes.
Sound operator: 'Sound standing by' and then press the standby button so it stops flashing.
DSM: 'Thank you' and then presses the DSR cue light. The actor whose cue it is DSR will then press the standby button to stop it flashing.
The DSM should wait for each department to acknowledge their standbys so they know who has answered it. It is too easy to miss a response if the operators reply at the same time and talk over each other. It is also important if you are touring as you probably won't recognize the individual's voices and you won't know who is who.
To execute the GOs, you must either follow the script or watch the action for the cue point. Let's say the following cues are on the word 'Hello'. When you say the single GO, you must say it at the same time as the actor says 'Hello'.
In the example shown here, you would execute it like this:

DSM: 'LXQ1 and SNDQ1 ... go', while pressing the green LX, SND and DSR cue lights at the same time.

Cues that are called with a single GO.

TOP TIP

It is imperative that the SM teams use pleas-antries such as please and thank you. For a DSM it is important to acknowledge the op-erators' standbys on cans so they know they have been heard. As a stage manager and, to some extent, an assistant stage manager, the role involves delegation and a simple please and thank you helps you gain respect and shows you value the other person and are not just bossing them around.

A larger prompt desk that is found on a large-scale production.

A DSM will get into a rhythm when cueing and the operators will soon recognize how an indi-vidual DSM cues a show. The aim, when cueing and saying a GO, is to leave a beat between the cue name (such as LXQ1) and the GO. If you do not leave a gap it may panic the operator, while a long gap will keep the operator on tenterhooks and could easily cause errors by the operator ex-ecuting the cue early. And let's not forget the poor flyman who is holding a rope with a weighty flying piece.

Pay attention to how you are saying GO. First, you should never say the word GO un-less you are calling a cue. If you do need to say it, always spell it out, so G. O., so no one can mistake it for a cue. When saying GO as part of the cue, be clear about how you say it. Don't make it so quick that the operator misses it, but also don't extend the word, like you are saying it in slow motion, or the operator won't know where exactly to operate the cue – on the G or the O.

When you are using the cue lights for a depart-ment that is not on a headset you do not need to verbalize the cue as they can't hear you. Also leave the green GO light on for a good length of time. If they blink or turn away they may miss seeing it if you make it too short and they will not execute the cue. Try to resist resting your fingers on the cue lights unless you are about to press the button. This can lead to mistakes caused by inadvertently pressing the wrong button at the wrong time, which could have disastrous conse-quences.

When you call the first show you will be as ap-prehensive and nervous as the actors are, but it is important to remain as calm as possible. The beauty of the DSM role is that everything is written down in the book so you do not have to memorize anything. Read what is written and, if things don't go to plan, adapt and respond quickly. The more you call a show, the more relaxed you will become and, eventually, you will be able to 'feel a show'. This means you can be empathetic to the timings of the actors and the audience's responses and slightly change the cueing accordingly. A good DSM will also adapt their cueing to the individual operators to ensure that the cues are executed on time.

As a DSM, there will be times when you need to make split decisions for the sake of the show.

NERVES

Nerves can be healthy when you are work-ing on live productions. Whether you are an actor onstage, a DSM on the book or a fly-man, everyone will feel nervous at some point. Nerves help to produce the adrenalin that will help keep you sharp and alert and ready for anything, and they show you care about what you are doing.

A DSM cueing a show.

For instance, when an actor misses a line or a chunk of script that includes a cue, it is the DSM's responsibility to sort out the problem. If the cue is a slow lighting fade and there is still time to call it then give the cue late. If it is an immediate change, a snap cue, or a distinct effect, then you need to decide if you can leave it and move on to the next cue, or whether you need to find another appropriate point in the script to execute the cue.

Show Reports

The DSM collates all the information to go into the show report. It includes the exact timings of the show, who was operating on the performance and what, if anything, went wrong or was out of the ordinary. It should be a complete record of the individual show. It is good practice to include the reason for the error and a resolution. Each observation should, like the rehearsal notes, be numbered for easy reference.

For example, if an actor has tripped up, you would write:

1. Mr Smith fell over in Act 1 Scene 2 due to the sole of his shoe becoming loose. Wardrobe will have his shoes re-soled.

The resolution is important so that the producers know that the other departments are aware of the problem and they are dealing with it. It is also good to see who is working on a production in case a particular error occurs only when a certain operator is on the show. The weather should also be noted, as this may affect audience numbers.

The show report will often be typed up by the stage manager, who will then send it to the technical personnel on the show so any issues can be resolved. The SM will also forward it to the company manager, who will fill in the financial details, such as tickets sales and advance bookings. The completed show report will then be sent to the producers. Professionally we will send the completed report on the same night, after the curtain is down, but the deadline is usually by 10am the next day.

MOTHER COURAGE AND HER CHILDREN

SHOW REPORT

Date: 2nd June 2017
Venue: The Crescent Theatre
Performance number: 67

Show Time: 19:30
House Number: 82
Weather: Windy and Sunny

	TIME UP	TIME DOWN	PLAYING TIME
Act One **Part 1-7**	19.30	20.43	1 hr 13 mins
Interval	20.43	21.04	18 mins
Act Two **Part 7-Part 12**	21.04	22.18	1 hr 14 mins
TOTAL PLAYING TIME			2 hr 27mins
TOTAL RUNNING TIME			2hr 45mins

Observations

1. The canvas covering the cart has started to rip by the right-hand wheel. The ASM will try to repair it.

2. Miss Dickenson's shoes need new soles as the rubber has become worn and she is slipping on the stage. Wardrobe are aware and will replace the soles for the next show.

3. LXQ 25 and Sound Q 13 were late due to DSM error.

4. Mr Jensen dropped his basket during part 5 and the wood fell over the stage. He quickly put it back in the basket but there was a lot of debris left which would have caught in the cart wheels. The ASM went onstage with a broom and cleared up it up during the scene change.

SM	Peter Inscoe	LX Op	Simon Dodd
DSM	Bella Reardon	Sound Op	Mary Last
ASM	Harry Faith	Flys	Colin Toms
ASM	Kathy Ford		

A show report is issued after each performance.

STAGE MANAGER

The SM will oversee the production as a whole and will be in charge of running the stage. Nothing should happen without their say so or knowledge and, if anything goes wrong, it is their call what to do and how to resolve the situation.

The stage manager will have their own cues to do but these should be limited, so that if there is a problem they can easily deal with it while the show continues. It is a good idea for the SM to give the DSM clearance when it is safe for scenic items to move and to then watch these elements from the wings. This is especially important when set pieces are flying in and out. Any high-risk items should also be watched by the SM, such as naked flames or fight sequences; if weapons are used, the handling of these often falls to the SM.

The stage manager should also keep abreast of the safety elements backstage and onstage. As you know, health and safety is paramount and this needs to be upmost in the SM's mind at all times. Obstructions backstage should be marked using gaffa or hazard tape and should be lit wherever possible. The edges of treads and low-hanging lanterns are always a hazard, especially when anyone is in a rush or not paying attention.

Show Stops

When a production is running smoothly and without a hitch, the stage manager should be able to go about their tasks calmly and with the minimum of fuss and drama. It is when things are going wrong, however, that the SM will come into their own and prove how competent they are. It depends what the issue is as to whether there is a quick-fix solution or whether the show will have to be stopped to resolve it. A show stop must be the last resort, but it is often the only solution to the problem.

It is a good idea to think about any possible scenarios that could occur before they actually

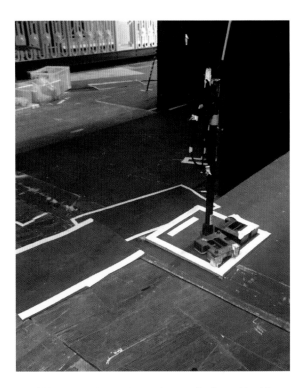

The SM must mark any obstructions on the floor with white gaffa tape. GRANGE PARK OPERA

Scaffolding bars are marked so that they can be seen clearly. GRANGE PARK OPERA

Treads and handrails are marked with hazard tape for safety.
GRANGE PARK OPERA

happen. Always try to have a plan B. For example, if the show includes a revolve, what happens if it were to break down? Could you do the show without it moving and have a pre-planned set of scene changes that could take place instead? If you are working on a show with automation, would you be able to continue if the mechanics stop responding? Is there any way the crew could move the set into place?

There also needs to be a show stop procedure in place. What will the DSM do, how will the actors know and how will you inform the audience about what is happening? Where possible, you want to get on with fixing the problem without the audience knowing.

One way of stopping a show is to bring in the house tabs and make an announcement to the audience. By doing this the problem can be worked on behind the curtain. This isn't always possible as your cast may be directly under the tabs. The way to stop a show at this point is for someone to walk onto stage, stop the cast and inform the audience what is happening in person. Then, once the cast are clear, you can bring the tabs in.

Either way the announcement needs to be brief but informative, always keeping the audience informed of what is happening – for example, 'Ladies and gentlemen, we are experiencing technical difficulties. Please remain in your seats while we try to resolve them. We hope to continue as soon as possible.'

Once you have decided to perform a show stop, the DSM must let everyone know what is happening. Usually this is done with a tannoy call backstage or a phone call to front of house. The DSM needs to ensure that the operators know there is going to be a show stop, so that the LX state can be changed, sound is stopped and the conductor or MD knows to stop playing.

The stage manager must then work out what to do and how best to deal with the problem.

If it is a problem with one of the actors, for example if they are sick or had an injury, your first priority is to call a first aider and get the actor cared for. Next, if there is an understudy you need to get them ready as quickly as possible. Inform the understudy that they are 'on' and then wardrobe and wigs so they can be in the correct attire. The sound department will need to be told if mics are involved.

If it's a set issue, you would need to call the master carpenter to the stage to see if they could resolve the issue or to see if there is a way round the problem. If the solution was to work without the set you would need to let the cast know of any changes and the LX operator may need to adapt the lighting.

Whatever you do, communication is key. While it is on a need-to-know basis, everyone must be told why the show is stopping, what the problem is, how you are going to resolve it and, very importantly, what each department must do to facilitate

A performance of *On the Razzle*. PHOTO: JOHN HAYNES. DESIGNER: NORMAN COATES

SUPERSTITIONS

Theatre people can be superstitious and, whether or not you are yourself, it is important to recognize that others can be. There are some superstitions that are well known, while others are not so familiar.

Macbeth
Saying the word Macbeth backstage is supposedly cursed and a lot of people say 'the Scottish play' instead. If someone does say Macbeth they will be asked to leave the room, turn around three times, spit, swear and then knock and be asked back in. The origins of these rules are widely attributed but most are associated with the witches, their lines and possible curses.

Whistling
Before the invention of communication systems, sailors were hired to fly the scenery and they were cued by whistles. I have seen this in practice recently in a French theatre so beware, if you whistle watch for something landing on your head!

Good Luck
It is bad luck to wish someone good luck so instead 'break a leg' is used. Possible origins for this could be that the ancient Greeks stamped their feet instead of applauding and also legs are used to mask the wings and therefore when an actor enters the stage they break the leg of the masking.

Real Flowers
It is said that if you receive flowers before the curtain call it causes a lacklustre performance as the actors have not performed and do not deserve to receive them yet. There is also a superstition that you should give flowers from a graveyard on the last night to symbolize the death of a show and putting it to rest. This is not necessarily a good idea!

No Peacock Feathers, Mirrors, Real Money and Jewellery
These items are supposed to cause forgotten lines, broken set and disasters. The peacock feather has an 'evil eye', mirrors are bad luck as they affect the lighting and it wasn't good practice to use items that could be stolen.

A Ghost Light
It is said that leaving a single light on upstage when the theatre is empty will ward off any ghosts.

Other superstitions include never having three lit candles onstage, not wearing green or blue onstage and that having a bad dress rehearsal means a good opening night.

HER NAKED SKIN

ACT ONE

1   Check SR Beginners and hand out props
    Emily W Davison - Hat, Sash, bag with purse. Place banner in her inside right coat pocket
    Seely
    2nd Suffragette – Toffee hammer
    Charlie Power
    Herbert Asquith – pocket watch
    Lady Celia Cain - bag with gavel and coins inside

2   Go USC and hand Charlie Power drinks tray with 4 tumblers and 2 decanters.
    Wait for Emily Davison to exit, collect her hat, bag, gloves, banner and sash and check she is OK after her fall.
    Place props on SR prop table.

3   Collect flower basket from Flower Seller USR and return to prop table
    Collect tray from Charlie Power and reset with 2 wine glasses, 2 ● decanters, ■
    2 tumblers ○ and gin bottle. ◻

4   Go DSR and hand Dr Parker the force-feeding funnel, tube and cleaning cloth after the force-feeding scene
    wait DSR and collect force feeding funnel, tubing, 2 jugs, cleaning cloth and white sheet from Dr Parker and
    put them on DSR table.

5   Collect the Speaker's Jacket and tie from the SR quick change area and go USC. Help the speaker with his
    quick change, then take cloak, bow tie and glasses and hang them up in the quick change area.

6   Go DSR and check Eve Douglas has her hat and prison book, then hand Emily Davison her sash.

7   Collect Dr Klein's pen and glasses from the SR Prop table and set them into his coat in the quick change area.

8   During the 1st parlour scene go USC, page the curtain for Nurse Parker to enter with the tray and then take it
    from her on her exit and return it to the SR prop table.

INTERVAL CHANGE

1) Go on stage and remove the 2x beer bottles and 1 bed sheet

2) Place the boxes along the US edge. - see the diagram for the order.

Claire Unwin ASM Her Naked Skin
skin@email.co.uk 07879 909 989   V5 23/2/2016

HER NAKED SKIN

3   Wet the Rag in the Basin, Take the playing cards out of their packaging and go to the dressing room 2 and collect the toffee hammers and Mrs Briggs key.

ACT TWO

1   Check SR beginners and hand out props
Young Suffragette – banner
Florence Boorman
2nd Suffragette – banner
Mary Nicholson
William Cain – written statement (folded in ½)

2   After the club scene go DSR and help Dr Vale out of his doctor's coat and hand him his notebook and pencil. Take the coat to the SR quick change area.

3   Go SL and collect the drinks tray from the SL prop table. Go to the kitchen and wash the glassware and return it to the SR prop table. Collect Mrs Majors hat and gloves and go to USC.

4   After parliament scene hand Mrs Majors her hat and glove as she exits USC and collect the metal tray with tea things from Miss Brint. Take the tray to SL prop table

5   Collect the Ritz bedding from the SL prop table and go USC. As Lady Celia Cain exits after 2nd Parlour scene hand her the bedding and collect her coat and hat. Take the coat and hat to the SR quick change area.

6   Help Emily wilding with her quick change. Skirt over her head and do up her shoes.

7   Go to SR prop table and re-set the props. During final scene go DSR and ensure the cast are all there for the curtain call.

End of show.

Take all the washing u to the kitchen
Sterilise the force feeding tubing and funnel.

Claire Unwin ASM Her Naked Skin
skin@email.co.uk 07879 909 989

V5 23/2/2016

An ASM cue sheet listing the cues that must be followed during a performance.

any changes. Once the problem has a resolution, you need to make sure everyone knows what has changed, if anything, and exactly where you are restarting the show from.

You cannot always foresee problems and have a plan in place, and it is in those instances that the SM needs to think clearly and remain calm. There will always be a chain of events to think through so that the show can continue as quickly as possible; or, if the show is unable to continue, that decision needs to be made as promptly as possible so front of house can deal with reissuing tickets for another performance or reimbursing the audience.

DURING THE RUN

Cue Sheets

The ASM and SM will need to record the tasks they are doing on a production and will need to compile cue sheets. These needs to be detailed and easy to follow, so that anyone would be able to pick them up and work on the show. You need to include what the cue point is, whether it's a music cue or a word cue, where in the theatre it happens – backstage, on-stage or front of house – and what the cue involves, such as paging a curtain or handing an actor a prop.

Often on long-running shows the SM team will rotate the job roles to keep them fresh. For example, ASMs may swap roles so they are working a different wing or an ASM may swap with the DSM to cue the book. You may also have deps employed to cover illness and holidays. This is when a freelance person knows several of the show plots and can come in at short notice and help cover the team.

It is not just the stage management team that will need to write cue sheets. Anyone who is working on the show and who has cues will need to have a record of exactly what they do. The stage management team will collate all the cue sheets so that they can be used by anyone at any time.

Understudy Calls

Once the show is up and running, there may be regular rehearsals for the understudies to be put through their paces. This can be as intensive as the first rehearsal period as they will be working through the show scene by scene. Eventually they will need to have time with all the technical elements in place so they can run the show.

The stage management team will set up in preparation for the rehearsals. You may be setting up a keyboard for a music rehearsal or moving scenery and setting furniture and props for a staging rehearsal. As a DSM you might, in the absence of an assistant director, be teaching the actors the blocking.

These understudy calls will continue regularly over the production's lifetime as the understudies need to keep practising so that they remember what to do in case they need to go on and perform in front of an audience.

Most of the time understudies will actually get an opportunity to go on during a public performance.

If, however, you are working on a short run and the understudies have not been on, there may be an understudy performance in front of an invited audience. This is so the understudies can invite friends and family as well as agents and casting directors. This gives them the opportunity to perform the piece and show off their skills.

If you are working with children, you will find you will have constant rehearsals. Depending on the production, you will probably have a few teams of children who play performances on a rota. This is because children are not allowed, legally, to work the long hours that theatre demands. They are also only allowed to be contracted for a certain period and cannot work for years at a time. This means constant recasting and rehearsals for new children.

Also, depending on the contracts, there may be regular cast change rehearsals. Often long-running shows will employ actors on a year's contract. This means that you will be holding auditions and recasting every year. This doesn't apply to your lead

The SM team maintaining the props.

performers, however, who are often on shorter contracts.

Maintenance

Maintenance of the set, props and furniture and the look of the show is important, and it is quite usual on productions to have a regular maintenance afternoon. This could involve making more paper props or doing general maintenance, for example cleaning and dusting the set or mending items that have broken – in fact, anything that your show requires. It is vitally important that the SM team keep up the show and take care of all the elements so that it looks as good as it did when it first opened, and so there are no issues or problems during a performance caused by neglect.

Discipline

Finally, once the show is open and the creative team have left, it is up to the stage management team to maintain the discipline and ensure the smooth running of the production. The team becomes the eyes and ears of the management and will continue to set the standards for timekeeping, safety and order. Everyone will need to

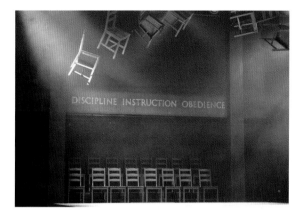

A set that could have been made especially for the SM department. DESIGNER: PHILIP ENGLEHEART

be motivated to turn up on time, keep quiet in the wings and stay focussed on the job in hand. On a long-running show, everyone settles into the rhythm and routine of the performance and is comfortable with what they are doing. This can sometimes mean that people go onto automatic pilot and don't pay as much attention as they did in the beginning. This is often when silly mistakes occur or problems arise. It is important that the stage management team do their best to minimize any risks or issues by maintaining the discipline.

Sometimes it may feel that you have to be a nag, always telling others what to do and how to behave, but it is an important part of the job and one that you must not be scared to do. When you take on this aspect of the role you will gain the respect of others by doing the job and not shying away from it. If you can do it with good humour and humility, everyone will respect the fact that you are just doing your job.

REPAIRS AND SPARES

You should always have a kit of useful items backstage so you can mend anything that breaks or needs work. The kit should comprise the basics, such as glue, scissors, LX tape, sticky tape, string, gaffa tape and so on as well as show-specific items, such as candles and spare lighters, if they are used in the production. Spare props are also imperative. For example, have multiple copies of paperwork, such as letters or newspapers, to hand as well as spare rings, glasses or umbrellas. Items can and do break during shows and the SM team needs to be able to replace or temporarily fix items quickly.

TASK

Use the book you compiled in an earlier chapter and have a go at calling the cues you have plotted. If you record yourself speaking the lines you can play it back and try to cue the sequence. You could also write a cue sheet or setting list, making sure it is detailed and easy to follow.

11
MOVING BEYOND THEATRE

And finally…

The skills that are learnt and utilized in stage management are not just useful in the theatre but are highly transferable to other jobs and mediums. Management skills are always desirable in whichever career is chosen and the people skills that are so important in stage management are invaluable throughout life.

I have been lucky in my career and I have been able to use my skills working within events, television and film as well as teaching. While each new experience has required me to learn a new vocabulary of terms and a different way of working, I have always relied on my stage management skills to see me through.

TELEVISION AND FILM

Floor Manager

Floor managers are usually found on programmes or events that are live or recorded as live. It could be a studio-based show or on an outside broadcast. Floor managers are used to assist and support the presenters and are a link between the director and producer, who are usually based in the gallery. This is where the creative team sit watching the action, and the different cameras output, choosing which pictures to use.

The floor manager is responsible for ensuring that the presenter and any guests are comfortable and at ease. They will relay timings to them, counting down the time to broadcast and any

changes or alterations that may be taking place. The presenter, while being able to hear the director in their earpiece, will rely on the FM and it is a very important relationship. The presenter must have confidence in the floor manager and in their abilities to cope with last-minute changes. The FM will also count down the remaining time of a live link or interview while the presenter is talking. This is done with a series of hand gestures. Like the DSM's blocking notation, the hand gestures are fairly universal so that any presenter can understand.

Floor managers are also used to relay information from the event itself. The creative team will be removed from the event that is taking place, so will rely on the details that the floor manager passes on. During a live concert, for example, the floor manager will need to let the creative team know if there is a delay in an artist making it to the stage so they can get the presenter to 'fill' until the artist appears.

Assistant Director

You tend to find an assistant director works in recorded drama or film. They are not tasked with directing in the theatre sense, but will be the director's assistant, running the shoot and helping them achieve the shots that they want. There are three roles as an assistant director, 1st AD, 2nd AD and 3rd AD.

The 3rd AD is the junior member of the team who works on the shoot, assisting the 1st AD in organizing the cast, ensuring everyone knows what is happening and that they are ready for the scene.

They will also direct any background artists or extras, making sure that the scene looks realistic.

The 2nd AD looks after the scheduling of the artists. Working away from the shoot, they will prepare for the next day's scenes, planning which artists will be needed and sending call sheets out. They will arrange cars for the cast and look after any problems that may occur off-set.

The 1st AD runs the shoot. They will be the voice on the studio floor, letting everyone know what scene is being shot and when the recording is about to start. They will make sure that the make-up, costume and props departments have made any 'checks' before starting and will call 'action'. They will also be the person to shout 'cut' when the director has finished shooting the scene and 'it's a wrap' when the final scene has been shot.

Stage Manager

Stage managers are employed in TV but the job is not the same as it is in theatre. As you have seen from the other roles, the running of the shoots and the liaison between artist and creative falls to other positions. As an SM, you will be in charge of any

The studio floor on a BBC TV shoot. BBC TV. DESIGNER: DINAH ENGLAND

crew that are employed on a programme and you will be responsible for ensuring the set changes happen smoothly and that the props are correct and ready for the next sequence.

Runners

Working as a runner involves being asked to do numerous tasks. Runners are responsible for escorting cast, presenters and guests to the set and looking after them and getting them anything they need. They will look after the production team, making beverages and collecting their meals if they are working over their break times. They will ensure updated schedules are distributed, as well as any script changes and other important paperwork. They will also work on the shoot itself, often giving cues to actors and generally supporting the ADs and FMs.

Props

In TV and film there will be a separate prop and art department. They will be responsible for the set dressing and achieving the look of the show and ensuring the actors have the items they need for a scene.

Script Supervisors and Vision Mixers

These people work in the gallery with the director and call and cut the camera shots for the output. The script supervisor will note timings and will keep an eye on continuity.

In theatre we have the three main job roles and the work is shared between them. In TV and film there are more people to do the same job. It was a big learning curve for me when I started work on *EastEnders*. As a member of a theatre stage management team I am used to helping in whatever way I can as well as ensuring props and furniture are set in the correct places. However, in TV you are not expected to help with those elements. I will never forget my first Queen Vic scene when I took a newspaper from the prop crate to hand to an extra and was told that if I wanted any props for the scene I had to ask the prop team to do it.

EVENTS

Working in events, you could be employed as a show-caller. This is a similar role to the DSM and you cue the show. It is quick and fast-paced and is often a short few-days contract. You will not get the rehearsal period as you would in theatre. You could be hired on a product launch, such as for a new car, or you could be cueing for a conference, with a keynote speaker. Live events, such as music festivals or concerts also require show-callers. They will co-ordinate the artists and relay the information to various departments, making sure sound and lighting know what is happening at all times.

Stage managers are also employed on events. They are responsible for ensuring the stage is set correctly and working closely with the crew. For example, on a live music event they will lead the crew to strike a band's equipment and set up the next band's equipment.

ASSOCIATIONS

There are various associations that look after stage management teams.

Stage Management Association

This association is run by stage managers and offers advice, support and guidance to those in the profession. They raise stage management issues within the industry and negotiate with companies, organizations and professional bodies to resolve problems and to ensure stage management teams are treated fairly. They run various courses, such as cueing to music and weapons workshops, helping the members to keep their skills fresh and updated. The free list is an invaluable tool in finding the next job. It is compiled monthly and is a list of members who are available for work. The list is sent out to theatres and production companies and is available to anyone who contacts the association looking for stage management staff. The SMA also produces a magazine called *Cue Line*, which has articles and advice written by the members.

A rehearsal of the BBC's *Proms at the Royal Albert Hall*. BBC TV

Equity

Equity is a trade union for performers and creative practitioners. They negotiate the contracts across the theatre industry for actors and performers, stage management and creatives. They will give advice to members, look after your welfare and answer any questions you may have contractually. If you ever are involved in disputes or contractual problems they can step in and help you find a resolution between you and your employer. As a member, you will also be covered by their public liability insurance and by their accident and backstage insurance.

LOOKING FOR WORK AND KEEPING UP TO DATE

The Stage

The Stage is a newspaper that is published once a week and focuses on the theatre industry as a whole. It has news, reviews and jobs pages. Its website is excellent and the jobs are updated daily on this.

Mandy.com

Formerly stagejobspro, this is a website that advertises jobs and allows employers to search for staff. It has definitely become an important resource for everyone working in the theatre industry.

Contacts

This book is produced by *The Spotlight* and it is an essential book to have. It isn't just for stage management but is a one-stop book for stage, film, television and radio. *Contacts* includes listings for theatre companies, producers and theatres, as well as TV companies and other related organizations. There is a section on properties and trades, which lists prop companies as well as makers and specialists. Digs guides are included, as are rehearsal rooms.

Institution of Occupational Safety and Health

The IOSH is the world's biggest health and safety membership organization. They issue codes of conduct and set the standards for health and safety. They also run training courses and events. It is important that you keep up to date with current standards.

Apps

The internet has revolutionized our career, and now apps have also been introduced to help with shows. Show Box and Show Stopwatch are just two that will help calculate the timings of a show. Anything that helps you calculate interval timings, especially when you are working on an opera season with a 90 minute interval, is a useful aid.

Many of you will be reading this book with a view to making a career in stage management. Hopefully this book has shown you how much fun the job is and encouraged you to take the next step. If you are part of an amateur group, you will be able to put some of this knowledge into practice. The roles outlined in this book are not always present in amateur theatre but the basic stage management skills should be of some use to you.

You can now appreciate what a stage management team does and the work that goes on behind the scenes of a production. However, please don't forget that you can never know everything. Stage management is a constant learning curve, but so long as you do your best, look after everyone and use your common sense, you won't go far wrong. Lastly, remember to have fun – after all, that is what theatre is all about.

GLOSSARY

See also the list of abbreviations at the front of this book.

Act The division of a play. A play is usually split into acts and then the acts are divided into scenes

Acting area The performance space

Actual Items that are actually going to be used for the production as opposed to rehearsal props

Ad lib When the actors have to improvise owing to an unexpected event

Advances Money that has been taken for future ticket bookings

Allergy form A form that the company fill in detailing any allergies and health details that the SM team should know about

Alternative theatre Theatre productions or companies that produce unconventional shows that often push boundaries and explore cultural and personal differences between individuals

Amateur A member of a company who is not paid, non-professional

Angel Someone who invests money in a production

Anti-raked An item adjusted to compensate for the rake (incline) on a slope to make it stable, for example a chair so that someone can sit on it safely

Apron The extension of the stage downstage in front of the proscenium arch or iron line

Audition Trying out for a part

Auditorium Where the audience sit to watch a performance

Auditorium left and right A sound and lighting term used to describe the stage from the operators' perspective in the auditorium rather than the actors' perspective onstage.

Automation Scenery that is moved by mechanical and electronic means and not by the crew

Backers Another term for angels, people who invest money in a production

Backstage The area behind the performance space that is usually unseen by the audience

Bar Metal pole suspended in a theatre from which lights, speakers and scenery are hung

Bar bells Bells that are rung front of house to inform the audience and FOH staff that the performance is about to begin or resume at the end of the interval; operated by the DSM

Bastard prompt When the prompt corner is situated on stage right as opposed to the usual position stage left

BECTU The union that oversees technicians

Beginners The actors who are in the opening of a play. Also, the beginners call that the DSM makes to call the company and all departments to the stage to start the show

Bible Another term for the prompt copy or book; the DSM's script

Biographies The creative team and actors' précis of their careers, which is often used in a programme and on theatre and production company's websites

Black box A flexible studio space, usually with black walls, curtains or scenery

Blackout When all the stage lights are turned off, usually at the beginning and end of acts and scenes

Blacks The clothing that those working backstage wear and also the plain black curtains that are used at the side of the stage to mask the wings

Blocking The moves that the actors make, noted by the DSM

Blues Blue low-level lights that are on backstage during the show

Book Another name for the prompt copy, prompt script or bible

Book cover Someone who covers the book and calls the show when the DSM is unable to, usually an ASM

Box The control room from which the LX operator operates the lighting board during a show. The sound operator and DSM sometimes work from there too

Box set Set made up to give the appearance of a room, with the fourth wall being imagined.

Briefings Usually given by the SM, briefings are made to the cast before the technical and dress rehearsals

Call There are various calls in theatre. There are calls that the actors and technical teams attend, such as rehearsal calls and show calls. The time everyone is due to arrive is known as their call time. The DSM issues rehearsal calls and also gives courtesy, front of house and backstage calls from the prompt desk during the show. The actors also take a bow at the end of a performance, which is a curtain call

Cans The headsets that the technical teams wear during a show to communicate with each other

Cast The acting company

Casuals Staff hired on a show-by-show basis. These include crew, dressers and follow-spot operators

Centre line Line running from upstage to downstage that divides the stage in half

Centre stage The centre point of the stage area

Chaperone An adult hired to look after the children on a production

Chorus A group of cast members who perform together and appear in the dance numbers, crowd scenes and other scenes of a show to support the leading artists; also a group of singers who perform together

Clearance FOH clearance is when the audience are seated and the show can start; also, the removal of a flying piece of scenery

Commercial theatre Theatre that is run purely for profit; usually large-scale productions with well-known actors

Comms Another term for cans or headsets that the technical teams wear during a show to communicate with each other

Community theatre Theatre aimed at a particular community or that works with members of a community to put on a production

Comp Complimentary ticket. These are issued by the producers to important guests and VIPs. The company and crew may be given comps for their friends and family. They are also offered to people who lend props to the SM team

Company The cast

Company schedule The schedule of events during the production period that the cast need to be present for. It is a scaled-down version of the production schedule, showing only what the cast need to know

Consequence Relating to risk assessments, the possible result of an incident

Contact sheet List of personnel involved in a production and their contact details. There are two – one with the cast's details and one for the technical teams

Control measure A procedure that is put in place to reduce the risk of an accident happening

Corpse A performer laughing onstage when they are not meant to

COSHH Control of substances hazardous to health

Courtesy call A call that is made over the tannoy to let the cast know that they need to make their way to the stage

Creatives The team that creates the show and puts it together – the director, designer, MD, choreographer, sound and lighting designer

Crew Members of the technical team who are employed by the construction department to move the scenery

Crossfade A lighting or sound term describing when one lighting state or piece of music fades whilst the next one builds

Crossover The area that enables you to cross from one side of the stage to another

Cue An action during a show that makes a change technically, for example a lighting cue, a sound cue or a cue to change the scenery. It is also a line or action that is made by a performer that indicates something else should occur, such as another actor's entrance or a cue point

Cue lights A series of lights that are operated by the DSM to cue an action, for example an actor's entrance or a sound cue

Cue sheet A list of cues that need to be conducted during a show; it could be a crew cue sheet or the ASM's cue sheet

Cue-to-cue During a technical rehearsal, moving from one cue to the next, missing out the action in between to save time.

Cyclorama A cloth that is upstage of the set, which is used as a backdrop for the set

Dance captain A member of the company who will lead the warm-up and look after the dance aspects of a production in the absence of the choreographer

Dance floor A roll of flooring that is made especially for dancing on, often used on rehearsal room floors to create the mark-up

Dark When a theatre is empty and no show is currently performing in it

Dark time When the lighting department are onstage working and they need to have a dark stage to see the individual lanterns or states

Dead This refers to flying the bars for scenery and lighting. There will be an in-dead, which is a position on the ropes that shows when the bar is at its correct height onstage; and an out-dead, when it is out of view of the audience

Digs The temporary accommodation that you stay in when you are touring on a theatre production

Dock door A large door in the wings that is used to bring the scenery onto the stage from outside

Downstage The area of the stage closest to the audience

Dress Dress rehearsal

Dressing room The room that the cast use to get changed and wait during the production

Dry tech A technical run onstage without the actors

Elevation A side view of the stage or set

End-on staging – A stage where the audience are at one end and the playing area is at the other

Ensemble The actors who are not leads and support the big scenes, similar to the chorus

Entrance When an actor enters the stage

Equity The trade union for actors, stage management and many of the creative personnel within theatre

Exit When an actor leaves the stage

Extras Characters who support the lead actors, usually on a film or TV shoot, also known as supporting artists

Fade A lighting or sound level that decreases

Fittings When the actors try on their costumes with the designer and wardrobe department and any alterations are planned

Fit-up When the set is first constructed and set up in the theatre

Flat A piece of scenery that is made of a frame covered in canvas or wood

Flys The department that is responsible for operating the scenery that is moved up and down

Fly floor Where the flyman works and operates the ropes to move the scenery

Focus Where the lights are pointing

Follow-on A cue that follows on from another one

Follow-spot A light that is used by an operator to follow a character onstage

Fourth wall The imaginary wall of a set downstage between the actors and the audience

Fringe A small-scale theatre or production that usually works with a small budget and often with new writing

Full house A full audience

Gaffa tape Heavy-duty tape

Gallery An area used by the creative team in TV and film

Get-in Moving the scenery, props, furniture and technical equipment into the theatre

Get-offs Another name for treads or steps. Used backstage for the company to access high areas of the set

Get-out When a production is taken down and moved out of a theatre

Glow tape Tape that glows in the dark

GO The word used by the DSM to execute a cue

God mic Microphone used by the director during a tech so that everyone can hear their instructions

Going dark A shouted warning the lights are being turned off, used at the end of the day or during a plot or tech

Green room The room that the company and crew use backstage during breaks

Grid A wooden or metal structure above the stage from which the bars are suspended

Ground plan A scaled plan of the stage and the scenery

Half-an-hour call The call the DSM makes 35 minutes before the show

Hard masking Masking at the side of the performing area that is made up of a solid flat

Hazard Something that could potentially cause harm

Hazardous event An event that could cause injury

Heads A warning that something is falling or being brought in from above

Headshots Professional pictures of the actors' and creatives' faces, used in the programme

High-viz Florescent vest worn for safety

House The audience numbers as well as the auditorium; for example used when opening the 'house' for the audience to enter and asking FOH how many were in the 'house' for a show

House lights The lights in the auditorium

Information pack Helpful information about the venue and local area prepared by the SM and kept in the rehearsal room and at the theatre

In-house Staff employed by the theatre

Iron The safety curtain positioned downstage, which is made of metal to prevent fire spreading between the auditorium and the stage

Lanterns The stage lights

Leg The scenery that is used to mask the wings, made of cloth

Lighting board The technical equipment that the lighting department use to operate the lights

Lighting state The lights that are set for each scene

LX tape PVC tape that is used on cables and for the mark-up in the rehearsal room

Makes Props that are made

Manual handling Using the body to handle and move loads

Mark A sequence that is worked through slowly; for example, the actors will mark a fight

Mark-up/mark-out A plan of the set put down onto the rehearsal room with LX tape

Masking Scenery that is placed to stop the audience seeing backstage

Meet and greet The first day when cast, creatives and stage management meet and introduce themselves and their job roles

Model box A scale model of the theatre and the set

Notation The shorthand used by the DSM to note down the blocking

Notes Rehearsal notes that are issued by the DSM on a daily basis, and the comments and changes that are made after a dress rehearsal or show by the creative team

Off When an actor misses their entrance

Offstage (right and left) The areas at the side of the performing area unseen by the audience

On When someone is entering the stage, or when someone is instructed to perform (for example, the understudy is on)

Paging Holding a curtain or door open for someone to pass

Paint call When the scenic painter is onstage painting the set

Period The year and time that the show is set in

Personals Props that are specific to a character, such as glasses or a watch

Plot A lighting or sound plot is when the designers and director plan what is happening during a show and set it in place. The DSM writes the information and cues in the book during a plot. Other plots, such as a fight or weapons plot, are lists of what happens and when it takes place

Practicals Props that needs to work, for example a practical table lamp or a practical radio

Pre-set The items that are set and ready before the show. This could be the props and set dressing or the sound and lighting state

Pre-show The time before the show, usually from the half-an-hour call onwards

Press night When the press are invited to review the show

Preview When a production is first shown to an audience but it has not officially opened. Tickets are usually at a reduced price

Producing house A theatre that puts on its own productions.

Production desk The desk in the auditorium at which the creative team work during the production process

Production meetings Regular meetings with the technical and creative teams to discuss issues that have arisen about the show

Production period The time in the theatre when rehearsals have moved into the theatre and before the show opens

Production schedule The schedule that the PM produces showing the sequence of events in the theatre and what is planned to happen when

Profit-share Usually in fringe. This is when there is no pay unless the show goes into profit and then the profit will be shared

Promenade A type of staging where the audience move from area to area to view the performance rather than staying in one place

Prompt copy The script that the DSM works from

Prompt corner The area in the wings where the DSM sits and cues the show

Prompt desk The desk where the DSM sits and calls the show. It includes cue lights, monitors, speakers and a microphone to make the calls

Prompting Reminding an actor of their lines

Propping Finding the props, furniture and set dressing for a production, usually by the ASM

Props The items that are used by the actors during a production

Prop table A table that is set up in the wings that has the props set out on it

Proscenium arch The frame between the auditorium and the stage

Push and pull When the actors move the scenery and furniture

Quarter-of-an-hour call The call the DSM makes 20 minutes before the show starts

Quick change A costume change that has to happen quickly

Quiet time When the sound department works time onstage with no other noise so they can listen to their cues and work

Rake An incline onstage

Read-through The first time the cast read the script out loud together

Receiving house A theatre that is hired by producers to perform a show

Rehearsal The time when the production is worked on, with either the cast or technical teams

Repertory A theatre style that produces a series of productions

Repetiteur A pianist that plays for a rehearsal

Reports Documents that the DSM produces that list what happened during a dress rehearsal or performance.

Returns Items borrowed or hired for a show that have to be taken back

Revolve A piece of flooring that rotates, usually used to change the scenery

Rider The technical list of the production's requirements or a theatre's technical equipment list and details. A high-profile artist will also issue a rider, which includes what they must be provided with

Rig A lighting or sound rig is the equipment needed for a production and the action of arranging it in the correct place

Risk assessment A document that highlights the hazards that may be involved in a production and the measures that will be taken to reduce the risks

Rostra or rostrum Raised piece of scenery

Run A rehearsal or performance of the show or a scene

Runners Carpet that is placed in the wings to reduce the footsteps backstage, or an entry-level member of staff in TV and film

Safety curtain The metal curtain between the stage and auditorium used to prevent fire spreading from front of house to backstage, also referred to as the iron

Scale The ground plan, model box and working drawings that are made to scale, usually 1:25 in the UK

Scene A section of the act or play

Scene change When the scenery is changed between each scene or act

Scenery Items that make up the set

Scene synopsis A précis of each scene – what happens in it, who is in it, where it happens and when it takes place

Scenic breakdown List of which characters appear on each page of the script

Script The written document that the playwright produces

Set The scenery

Set dressing The items on the set, such as curtains, rugs and ornaments

Setting line Line downstage that links two fixed points, such as the two ends of the proscenium arch; used by the designer to position their set and to work from

Setting list List of where the props, furniture and set dressing is placed

Shout check Undertaken by two members of the SM team who check that items are set in the right place before a performance

Shove drawing A useful tool when planning a scene change using the ground plan and scaled pieces of paper to represent furniture

Show-caller Similar to the DSM, the staff who call the cues on an event

Show relay A live relay of the show that is transmitted backstage so that the company and crew know what is happening onstage

Show report A document that outlines the timings of a performance, the errors that occurred and who worked on the show

Show stop When a show has to be stopped unexpectedly

Sightlines Imaginary lines that show how much of the stage and the wings can be seen from the extreme points in the auditorium

Signing-in sheets A register that is filled in when people enter and exit the theatre

Sitzprobe The first time a cast sing with an orchestra or band

Snd Sound

Soft masking Usually made of cloth, the scenery that is rigged to mask the wings from the audience

Sound balance When the sound department listens to the cue and ensure that the speakers are in the correct positions and working as they should be

Source Where the props and furniture are found and from where they are borrowed, bought or hired

Special A light that is focussed onto a specific area

Spike A mark on the stage to show where an item is set

Stage directions Outlined in the script, they are the character's movements and detailed information that the playwright has written that need to happen during the play

Stage door The entrance to the theatre backstage

Standby The DSM prepares the operators for a cue by asking them to standby or activating the standby cue light

State A lighting term used to describe the individual cues

Strike To clear items from the stage

Studio A flexible theatre space

Tabs The theatre's curtains, positioned just upstage of the proscenium arch

Takings The money that is taken for tickets

Tech The technical rehearsal

Theatre in education (TIE) Theatre that is produced to take into schools to educate and amuse the pupils

Theatre in the round A stage that has the audience positioned all around it

Thrust stage A stage with the audience on three sides

Timesheet A record of the hours worked

Touring house A theatre that is hired by touring productions

Track An actor's role and their blocking. Also, a curtain or tab track, which is used to rig a curtain from

Trap A hole in the stage floor used for entrances and exits

Traverse staging Where the audience are seated on two sides of the stage

Treads Stairs or steps

Triangulation One of the methods used to achieve an accurate mark-up

Trip hazard Something that could cause someone to trip

Truck A moveable platform on which scenery is built

Understudy An actor that covers another actor's role in case they are unable to perform

Upstage The area onstage that is furthest from the audience

Visual A cue that is taken from something that is done rather than a word from the script.

Walking the lights When someone moves about the stage so the lighting designer and director can see that they are lit correctly

Warm-up Vocal or physical exercises to prepare the actors for the show

White card model The first draft of a set design

Whities Petty cash vouchers

Wings The sides of the stage

Working drawings Drawings produced by the designer for the technical teams to work from

LIST OF SUPPLIERS

Brodie and Middleton
Theatrical supplies, art and scenic supplies
brodie.net
Tel 0207 836 3289

Data Reprographics
Printed items
datarepro.co.uk
Tel 01784 243996

Film Medical
Medical props
Filmmedical.co.uk
Tel 0208 961 3222

Flints
Specialist theatrical paint and hardware
flints.co.uk
Tel 0207 703 9786

History in the Making
Weaponry, prop and costume hire and armourer
History-making.com
Tel 023 9225 3175 or 023 9226 5743

John Frost Newspapers
johnfrostnewspapers.co.uk
Tel 01797 361952

Keeley Hire
Props and furniture
keeleyhire.co.uk
Tel 01992 464040 or 01992 444584

The National Theatre Prop Hire
nationaltheatre.org.uk
Tel 0207 820 1358

Newman Prop Hire
Furniture and lighting
www.newmanprophire.co.uk
Tel 0208 743 0741

Pigs Might Fly
Stage blood
pigsmightfly.co.uk
Tel 01722 340927

Rc-Annie Ltd
Weaponry, fight direction and courses
rc-annie.com
Tel 0207 820 3933

Russell Beck Studios
Prop makers
russellbeckstudio.co.uk
Tel 0203 241 0000

Superhire Group
Includes Super Hire, Old Times and Modern Props Ltd
Prophireuk.com
Tel 0208 453 3900

FURTHER READING

van Beek, Marco, *A Practical Guide to Health and Safety in the Entertainment Industry*

Bond, Daniel, *Stage Management: A Gentle Art*

Davies, Gill, *Stage Source Book: Props*

Fraser, Neil, *Theatre History Explained*

Govier, Jacquie, *Create your Own Stage Props*

Griffiths, Trevor R., *Stagecraft: The Complete Guide to Theatrical Practice*

Hartnoll, Phyllis, *The Theatre: A Concise History*

Harvey, Jackie with Kelleher, Tim, *Stage Managing Chaos*

Kershman, Andrew Richard, *The London Market Guide*

Menear, Pauline, *Stage Management and Theatre Administration*

Millers Antique books for research on antiques

Opie, Robert, various titles for research on branding

Pallin, Gail, *Stage Management: The Essential Handbook*

Thorne, Gary, *Stage Design: A Practical Guide*

Time Out for London's best shops

Wilson, Andy, *Making Stage Props: A Practical Guide*

Winslow, Colin, *Handbook of Set Design*

INDEX